Masters of Contemporary Glass: Selections from the Glick Collection

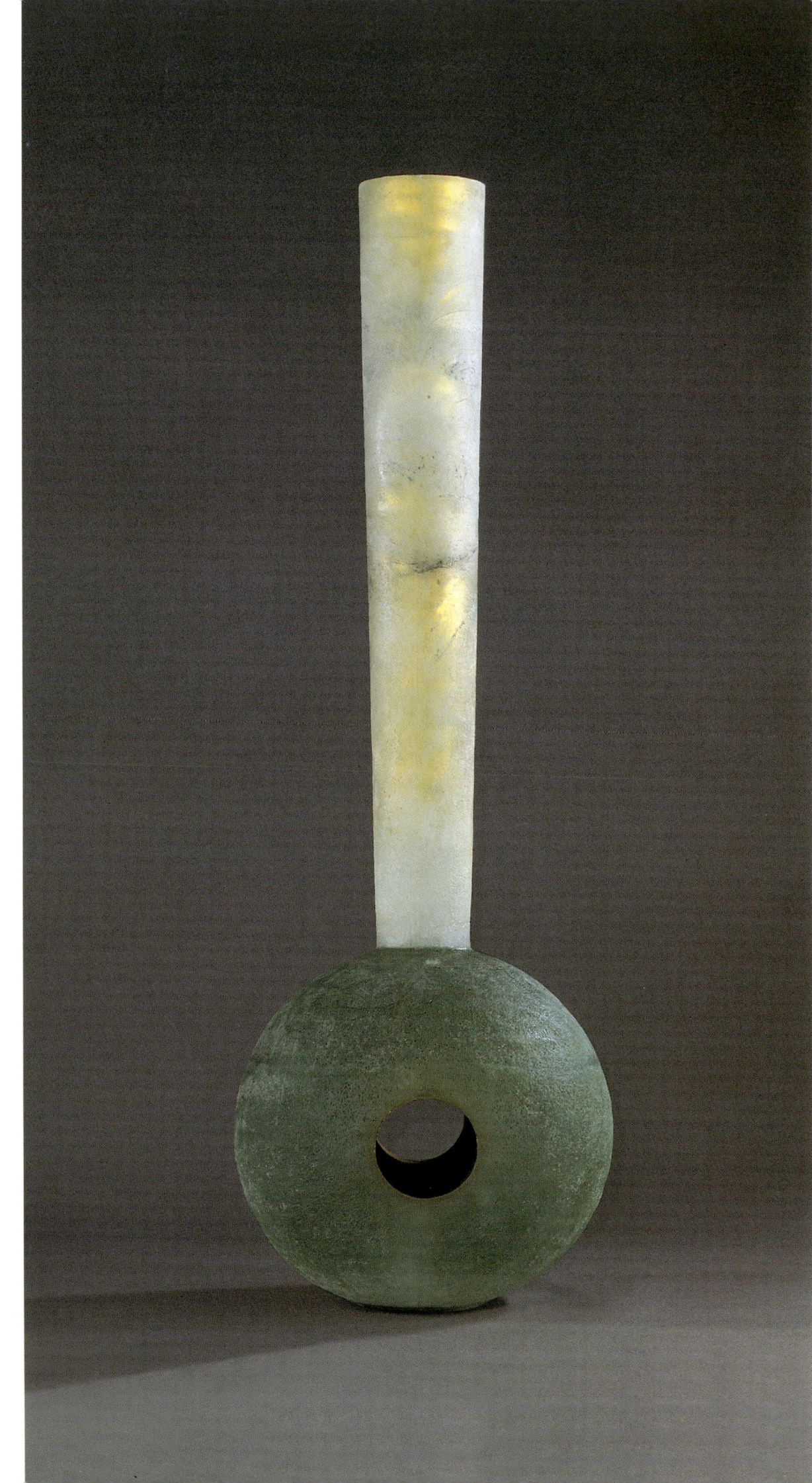

MASTERS OF CONTEMPORARY GLASS

SELECTIONS FROM THE GLICK COLLECTION

Martha Drexler Lynn

with contributions by Barry Shifman

Indianapolis Museum of Art in cooperation with Indiana University Press

Masters of Contemporary Glass: Selections from the Glick Collection has been published in conjunction with the exhibition of the same name, organized by and on view at the Indianapolis Museum of Art, September 4 through November 19, 1997.

©1997 Indianapolis Museum of Art
1200 West 38th Street
Indianapolis, Indiana 46208-4196

All rights reserved. No part of this book may be reproduced, except for that permitted under the U.S. copyright law, without the express written consent of the publisher.

Distributed by Indiana University Press
601 North Morton Street
Bloomington, Indiana 47404-3797

Library of Congress Cataloging-in-Publication Data
Lynn, Martha Drexler.
  Masters of contemporary glass : selections from the Glick collection / Martha Drexler Lynn ; with contributions by Barry Shifman.
    p. cm.
    Includes bibliographical references.
    ISBN 0-936260-65-3 (pbk.)
    1. Art glass—History—20th century—Catalogs.
2. Glick, Eugene—Art collections—Catalogs. 3.Glick, Marilyn—Art collections—Catalogs. 4. Glass art—Private collections—United States—Catalogs. I. Shifman, Barry. II. Title.
NK5110.L93 1997
748'.09'045074—dc21   96-51643
                                CIP

Clothbound edition ISBN 0-253-33338-5

COVER

Marvin Lipofsky
Assisted by Gianni Toso
Serie Fratelli Toso — Split Piece, 1977–78 (detail)
cat. 26

FRONTISPIECE

Howard Ben Tré
Second Vase, 1989
cat. 2

24,739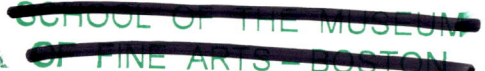

CONTENTS

Foreword — 6
Bret Waller

Acknowledgments — 8
Barry Shifman and Martha Drexler Lynn

Introduction — 11
Barry Shifman

The Studio-Glass Movement in America and Beyond — 15
Martha Drexler Lynn

Glossary — 148
Martha Drexler Lynn

Catalogue of the Exhibition — 151

FOREWORD

The Indianapolis Museum of Art is a collection of collections. Throughout its 113-year history the museum has been given shape and substance through gifts of art from private donors. In addition to the many individual works gratefully received by the museum, there have been, at intervals, gifts of entire collections that have changed the whole character and direction of the institution. The names of their donors are writ large in the institution's history. To that list must now be added the names of Marilyn and Gene Glick, whose superb collection of contemporary glass, now promised to the museum, is celebrated in this catalogue and the exhibition it accompanies.

Watching a collection grow is a bit like observing the birth of a volcanic island. Periods of great eruptive activity are followed by intervals of slow accretion, suddenly shattered by the emergence of some spectacular, but hitherto unexpected, atoll. Underlying it all, of course, is the unseen engine of creation, the white-hot magma of passion that fuels the collector's need not merely to own beautiful things, but to shape with them a meaningful assemblage, a collection. So it has been, and continues to be, with the Glicks' great adventure, an adventure in which, through this exhibition and catalogue, all of us can participate vicariously.

Elsewhere in this book Barry Shifman, curator of decorative arts at the Indianapolis Museum of Art, outlines the story of the Glick collection's formation, of Marilyn Glick's unquenchable enthusiasm and Gene Glick's supportive pride in her accomplishment. For the better part of the past decade, Barry Shifman has had the privilege of working closely with Marilyn Glick, of sharing her interest in contemporary studio glass, and participating in the evaluation of works considered for addition to the collection. The selection of works for inclusion in the present exhibition was made by Barry Shifman in consultation with Mrs. Glick and with assistance from Martha Drexler Lynn. I want to take this opportunity to thank Mr. Shifman for bringing the exhibition and catalogue into being with his inimitable combination of passion, persistence, and precision.

In 1989 Marilyn and Gene Glick began seriously to consider making a gift of the collection to the Indianapolis Museum of Art. To the delight of the museum and its many friends, that decision was confirmed and publicly announced in 1991, at the time of the opening of the Caroline Marmon Fesler Gallery, the museum's first exhibition area permanently dedicated to the decorative arts. Here, for the first time, contemporary glass could be regularly seen in the context of other decorative arts forms of the nineteenth and twentieth centuries. Since then, Marilyn Glick, in close consultation with the curator, has refined and shaped a collection that, in a museum context, will enable viewers to see and appreciate the history of the studio-glass movement. To that end Mrs. Glick has added numerous important works from the early years of the movement. She also has acquired works that exemplify the full range of contemporary glassmaking techniques, from *pâte de verre* to sand-casting. And she has collected certain important artists in depth, thus giving the collection a unique and personal shape and coherence. With this gift the Indianapolis Museum of Art will become one of the select group of American museums with collections that must be seen by anyone interested in contemporary studio glass.

This year marks the fiftieth anniversary of Marilyn and Gene Glick's marriage as well as the fiftieth anniversary of the founding of the Gene B. Glick Company. All of us at the Indianapolis Museum of Art are grateful to Marilyn and Gene Glick for their commitment of the Glick collection to the museum, and we join with all their family and friends in extending congratulations on this double fiftieth anniversary.

Bret Waller
Director

ACKNOWLEDGMENTS

Masters of Contemporary Glass: Selections from the Glick Collection would not have been possible without the constant support and encouragement of Marilyn and Eugene Glick, in addition to their generous promised gift to the Indianapolis Museum of Art that is the occasion for this exhibition and book. From the outset they have been helpful, responsive, and wonderful patrons of art. Over the past seven years during which we have worked together, I have additionally valued the special friendship that has developed between myself and Mrs. Glick. This project is the result of the Glicks' vision, dreams, and commitment to the studio-glass movement. Their pledged gift to the Indianapolis Museum of Art will make the museum's collection of contemporary studio glass one of the largest such holdings on view in the United States. We are most grateful for the Glicks' patronage.

This publication, which presents not only documentation for selections from the Glick collection, but an extensive discussion of the origins and development of the studio-glass movement as a whole with thorough biographies of the artists represented, is the excellent work of Martha Drexler Lynn. She also assisted in the selection of objects for the exhibition and this catalogue. Her expertise, cooperation, and good will have been a real contribution to the entire project. Thanks also go to Susanne Frantz, curator of twentieth-century glass, The Corning Museum of Glass, New York, who served as a reader for the manuscript and gave wise counsel. Terry Ann R. Neff of t.a. neff associates, inc., Tucson, Arizona, edited the catalogue with sensitivity and insight, and her wise counsel and experience have been greatly appreciated. The beautiful design was achieved with great patience and attention to detail by Elizabeth Finger, Belmont, California.

The valuable assistance provided by numerous members of the Indianapolis Museum staff is most appreciated. Hadley Fruits, assistant photographer, with the guidance of John A. Geiser, the museum's photographer, spent many months producing the splendid photographs for the catalogue. Ruth Roberts, photographer's assistant, also deserves my appreciation. Anna Bennett, curatorial administrative assistant, helped in the preparation of the manuscript for the book and for the installation of the exhibition. My thanks also to Jane Graham, publications manager, for her assistance during the production of the book. My gratitude also to the registration department, and especially to Vanessa Burkhart, registrar, and Sherry Peglow, assistant registrar. I also appreciate the help provided by Jesse Speight, supervisor of storage and packing. I am grateful to the exhibits department, particularly to Sherman O'Hara, chief designer, and Andrew Michael Bir, who provided the mounts for a number of objects. Virginia Hamm, manager of educational services, along with Susan Longhenry, director of education, contributed much needed direction regarding programming and gallery labels.

I would especially like to thank Director Bret Waller and Chief Curator Ellen Lee for their continual support for this project. In 1991 they both agreed to display late nineteenth- and twentieth-century decorative arts in the Caroline Marmon Fesler Gallery. In this first gallery in the Indianapolis Museum of Art dedicated to the permanent display of decorative arts, one can see superb pieces of contemporary glass that have already been given to the museum by Marilyn and Eugene Glick. *Masters of Contemporary Glass: Selections from the Glick Collection* contains many more splendid examples.

Barry Shifman
Curator of Decorative Arts

I wish to thank Barry Shifman, curator of decorative arts at the Indianapolis Museum of Art, for his collaborative help and constant generosity; Susanne Frantz, curator of twentieth-century glass at The Corning Museum of Glass, New York, for her insights and deep factual knowledge; Dr. Lynn Matteson of the University of Southern California, Los Angeles, for his faith in my abilities; the Getty Research Library in Santa Monica, California, for allowing me a readership to complete my research; Jo Lauria, assistant curator, decorative arts department, Los Angeles County Museum of Art, for access to their files; Terry Ann R. Neff of t.a. neff associates, inc., Tucson, Arizona, for her intelligent editing; and Robert N. Danziger for his unflagging support and encouragement.

Martha Drexler Lynn

František Vízner
Czechoslovakian, b. 1936

Untitled, c. 1993
Cast glass, cut and polished
3¾ x 11¼ dia. inches (9.5 x 28.6 cm)
cat. 66

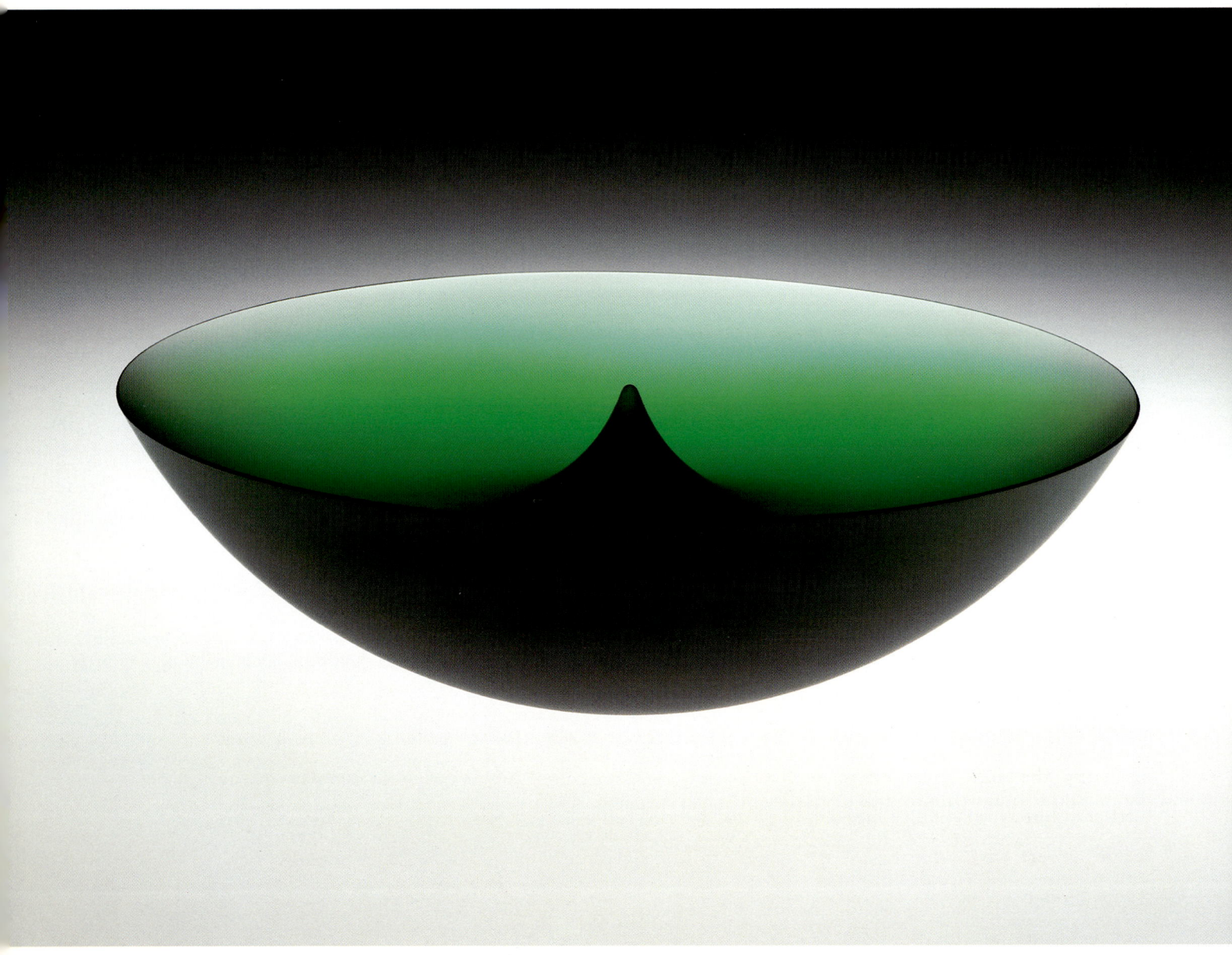

Barry Shifman

INTRODUCTION

Over seven years have passed since I first met Marilyn Glick and her husband, Eugene Glick, an Indianapolis-based builder. Mrs. Glick had contacted the museum about a possible donation, and I went for the first time to see their collection of contemporary studio glass. Although at that time I did not know very much about contemporary glass, I was excited by the collection, which contained examples by many of today's major artists working in glass.

Marilyn Glick's involvement with glass began two-and-a-half decades ago. She grew up in the Detroit area and always loved art—a pleasure she nurtured and informed over the years in art-appreciation classes. During the 1960s and 1970s, she bought contemporary art for her husband's office and for their home. In 1972 Mrs. Glick, with her friend Lucretia Osterman, visited The Toledo Museum of Art in Ohio, where she was impressed by its renowned glass collection. Upon hearing about a talented glass artist who lived nearby, Marilyn Glick hoped to visit this artist on a future trip. In the meantime she continued to concentrate on contemporary art.

It was ten years later before Mrs. Glick returned to Toledo, this time to see an El Greco exhibition. She traveled to Detroit, where she spent the night with her childhood friend Dorothy Gerson, an early collector of studio-glass art. That evening she learned a lot about the glass movement and especially enjoyed viewing the Gerson collection and hearing about artists Harvey Littleton and Dale Chihuly in particular. The two friends drove to Toledo to see the exhibition and once again enjoyed the glass collection.

The next week the Glicks were in Palm Beach, Florida. Mrs. Glick made a point of visiting the Holsten Gallery to see the Harvey Littleton show. She was drawn to a mobile arc by Littleton, but as was her habit, she set out to research the work before purchasing it. She first contacted Robert Yassin, then the director of the Indianapolis Museum of Art, for advice about the studio-glass movement. A telephone call to Penelope Hunter-Stiebel, then a curator at New York's Metropolitan Museum of Art who had written the Littleton gallery brochure, yielded information about the movement and also cited Dominick Labino. She also told Marilyn Glick of two major dealers in contemporary glass: Heller Gallery, New York, and Habatat Gallery, in the Detroit area. Mrs. Glick immediately contacted Michael Heller of Heller Gallery and Tom Boone of Habatat, who provided information about Littleton's work. Finally, she spoke at length with the artist himself, before making this prophetic first purchase of contemporary glass (see fig. 1).

When Mrs. Osterman returned from Europe, Marilyn Glick contacted her to find out the name of the artist they had hoped to visit ten years earlier. She was delighted to learn that the artist was Dominick Labino. Her pursuit of studio glass began in just a few days. Mrs. Glick and Mrs. Osterman drove to the Labino home and studio, where Mrs. Glick purchased an untitled work from the "Emergence" series (cat. 22). Marilyn Glick's commitment now became strong: within less than a month, she had acquired ten pieces of glass, including Dale Chihuly's untitled work from the "Macchia" series (cat. 7). She admits that the die was cast: "I had become a hopeless addict, hooked on contemporary studio-glass art."

As a collector, Mrs. Glick began spontaneously, attracted to what she loved, rather than following any particular program or plan. Initially, "the collection just unexpectedly grew like Topsy." Yet even in these early years, when the Glicks collected glass for their own pleasure and to adorn their living space, there was a distinct and marked air of generosity that would prove prophetic:

> *Collecting glass has enriched our lives in so many ways. We are grateful for all we have learned about art, about glass, and the materials and techniques artists use in making glass. We have met so many wonderful people. And through glass we have developed many new and special friends. We love having people come to our home to see the glass. Collectors, artists, students, teachers, museum staff and trustees come individually and by the busload. I love to tell people about the glass and the artists. There are so many stories to tell about our acquisition experiences. It's great fun!*

With the decision in 1989 to consider making a gift of the glass collection to the Indianapolis Museum of Art, Marilyn Glick's collecting process underwent a subtle change: I have had the pleasure of working closely with Mrs. Glick on all ongoing dialogue and a fruitful and happy collaboration has ensued between collector/patron and museum. No longer were acquisitions made without regard to the shape of the collection as a whole. With the museum in mind, Mrs. Glick has tried to create a representative selection of the major artists working in glass today, with special emphasis on American studio-glass artists, but including European artists as well. Moreover, certain artists, such as Dale Chihuly, Richard Marquis, Klaus Moje, Joel Philips Myers, and Toots

FIG. 1

Harvey Littleton
American, b. 1922

Mobile Yellow Parabolic Arc, 1981
Pulled and cased glass, with glass base
13 x 14 x 3½ inches
(33 x 35.6 x 9 cm)
BASE: 2 x 6¾ x 4¼ inches
(5 x 16 x 11 cm)
Collection of Marilyn and Eugene Glick

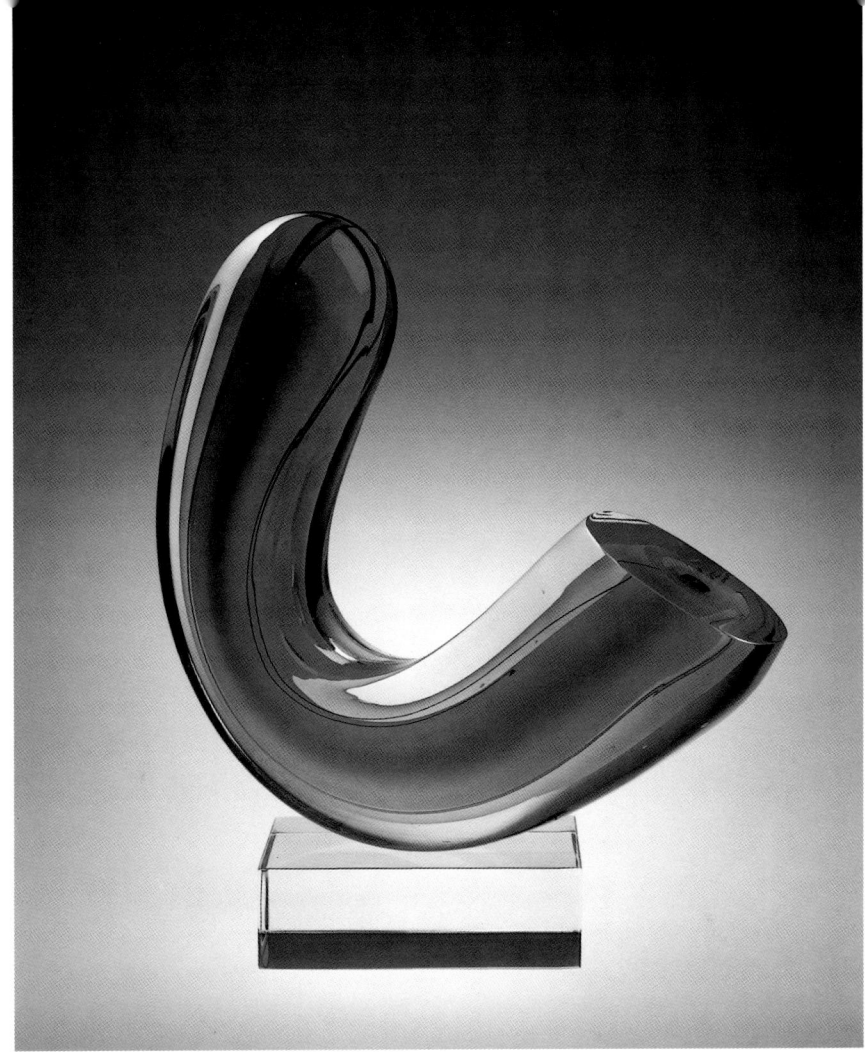

Zynsky, have been developed in greater depth. In order to provide a more complete historical overview of the studio-glass movement, an effort has been made to track down objects from the 1970s to complement the large group from the 1980s and 1990s. And finally, Marilyn Glick has also tried to acquire examples that demonstrate the variety of glass-forming techniques, such as blown glass, glass with enamel painting, and *pâte de verre*.

The Indianapolis Museum of Art is extremely pleased to be the future repository of the Glick collection. This important promised gift to the institution is a great addition to our collection and a tribute to the generous spirit that has marked the Glicks' collecting from the beginning. The museum already had on view examples of European and American glass from about 1850. Numerous gifts of contemporary glass from Marilyn and Eugene Glick presented to the museum starting in 1989 have added objects by David Huchthausen, Erwin Eisch, Howard Ben Tré, and others. Further splendid examples from the studio-glass movement will continue to be added. When the gift is complete, most of the movement's key artists, with works in various techniques, will be represented. The mission of the Indianapolis Museum of Art is to collect and preserve the world's great art. In the spirit of that mission, the valuable and thoughtful gift of Marilyn and Eugene Glick is greatly appreciated.

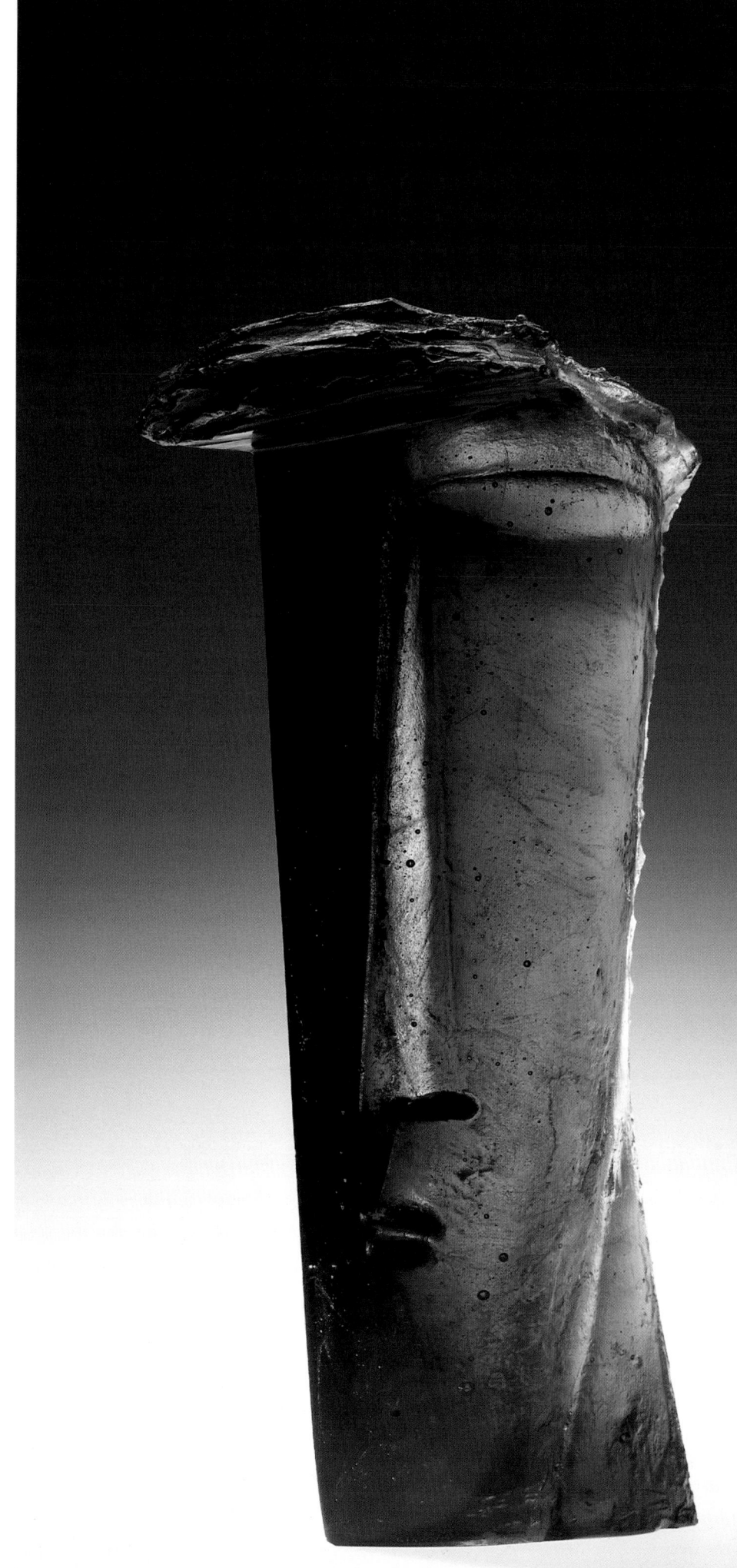

Stanislav Libenský
Czechoslovakian, b. 1921

Jaroslava Brychtová
Czechoslovakian, b. 1924

Head I, c. 1957–58
Mold-formed glass, cut and polished
$14^{1}/_{2} \times 6^{5}/_{8} \times 4$ inches
(36.8 × 16 × 10.2 cm)
cat. 23

THE STUDIO-GLASS MOVEMENT IN AMERICA AND BEYOND

Martha Drexler Lynn

Glass is a seductive medium and, ironically, it is its very seductiveness that tends to obscure the art made with it. Its sparkle may be mistaken for content and its beauty taken for artistic merit. Blessed with transparency and a captivating shine, glass can easily counterfeit precious gems—a property glassmakers have capitalized on since Egyptian times. Glass also has a simulacrum relating to its physical appearance. During the early Christian era, glass, when activated by sunlight, became a metaphor for God's own brilliance. This notion of conveying spirituality through the medium of glass is a leitmotif still evident today in the work of contemporary glass artists.

The Glick collection of contemporary glass spans five decades of international studio-glass production from the 1950s to the 1990s. Featuring American, European, and one Japanese glass artist, the collection contains important works by many of the leading glass proponents working today. With a range of artists working in all of the techniques available now to the studio-glass artist, this collection affords an excellent opportunity to assess the state of studio glass at the close of the twentieth century.

Because of the material's magical qualities and gemlike appearance, historical objets d'art made of glass were highly prized. Up until the nineteenth century, display pieces made from glass and other more precious materials carried a value beyond their intrinsic worth. But when industrial processes were applied to the forming of glass, machine production of glass objects superseded the handmade methods of the previous centuries, and glass increasingly became associated with mundane and purely functional objects. As the century progressed, only minor glass objets d'art were made for the emerging middle class. By the middle of the twentieth century, just before the advent of the American studio movement, this shift from a material for fashioning fine objects to one used only for everyday items was complete, and the early artistic attainments of glass were a distant memory.

Marvin Lipofsky
American, b. 1938
Assisted by Gianni Toso

Serie Fratelli Toso — Split Piece, 1977–78
Blown glass, cut and polished
TWO PARTS
A: 7 x 13 x 10 inches (17.8 x 33 x 25.4 cm)
B: 14 x 16 x 18 inches (35.6 x 40.6 x 45.7 cm)
cat. 26

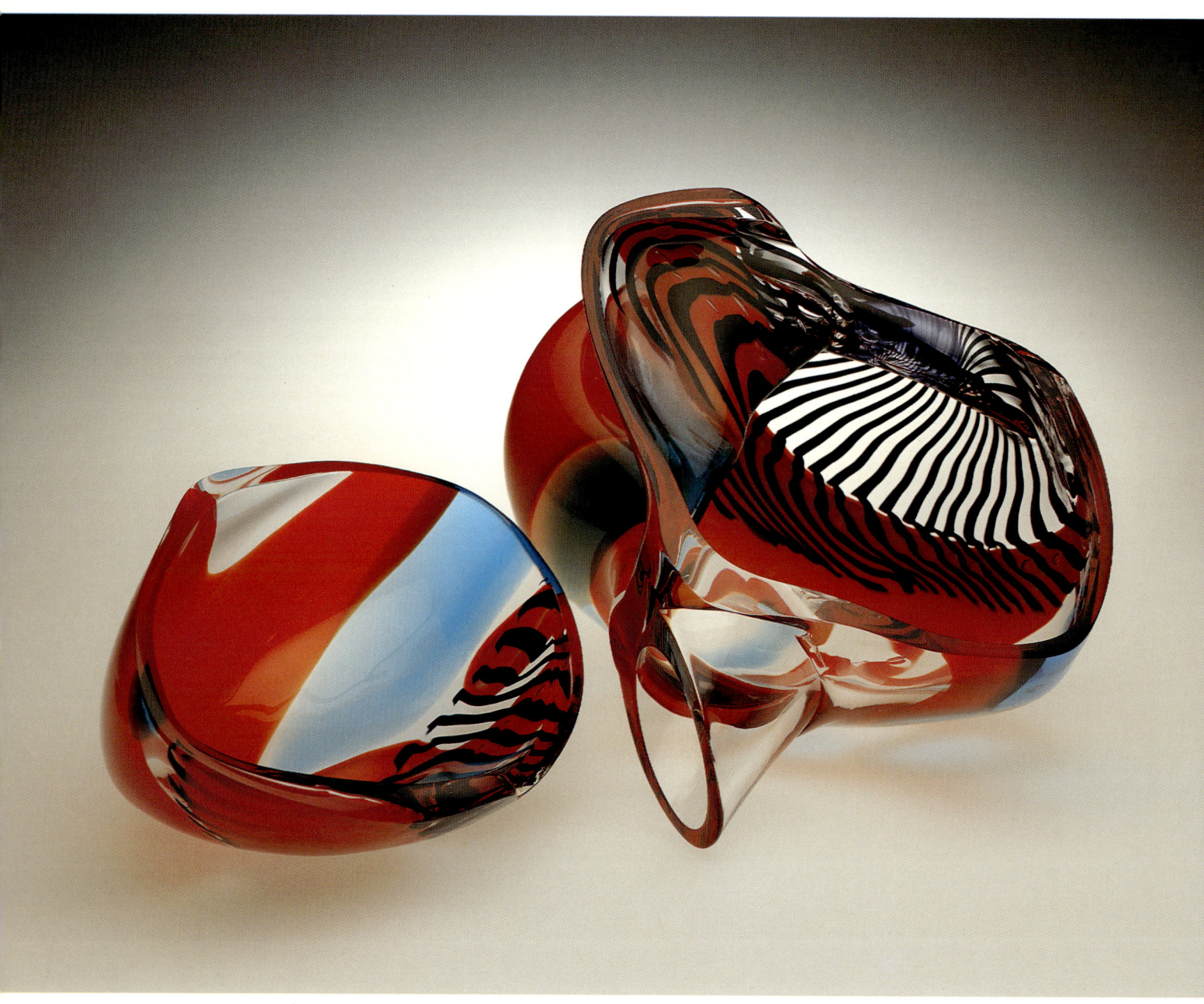

American factories, the new centers of glass production, focused on making utilitarian objects such as beakers, bottles, tubes, etc. Never termed art, these functional objects were made in factories because only large facilities could sustain the capital investment necessary to build and run the furnaces and annealing ovens. Supported by the marketplace, these plants trained their own workers and built the equipment necessary for their work. As a matter of economics, and eventually custom, small-scale glass furnaces and annealing ovens were not known.

Out of this system came a charming custom that could be termed an early manifestation of the studio-glass impulse. Due to the size of factory enterprises, fuel for sustaining the high temperatures needed to melt batch glass for forming amounted to a considerable cost. It proved most economical to leave the furnaces on at all times. This practice led the glassmakers to create off-hand glass objects (called "whimsies" or "friggers") outside of work time for their own amusement. While not conceived of as art by their makers, these works ranged from impressive displays of technical virtuosity to pieces that captured artistic expression. They also were glass objects formed without much concern for their utilitarian use.

Also from the factory culture came the belief that a team consisting of a minimum of six to eight workers was necessary for blowing glass. This belief, coupled with the practical economic and technological considerations, precluded attempts to establish small glassmaking facilities. Further, it was considered impossible to melt glass in small batches and even more outlandish for an individual alone to attempt to form objects. This deeply ingrained attitude fostered contempt for those who tried to be "amateur" glassworkers. Sidney Waugh, a designer for the Steuben Glass Works in Corning, New York, wrote in his 1947 book *The Making of Fine Glass*, that "[i]t must be emphasized that glassblowing, as described on these pages, is not within the scope of the amateur or even the most talented artist or craftsman working alone."[1] This attitude perpetuated the belief that glass-forming was possible only as a team process within a factory setting.

This cultural stance led to a split in the American glass-forming communities between the specialized knowledge needed for working glass that resided within the industrial community, and the interest in using glass as an expressive art medium that lay in the crafts and art communities. Although linked by a passion for the medium, these populations had little or no contact with each other.

The Evolving Definition of Studio Glass

The history of the studio-glass movement in the United States is really the history of the rediscovery of traditional handworking techniques and the renewal of interest in using glass as a medium for artistic expression. Because of the intercession of industrial processes, a technical disjuncture had developed during the nineteenth century that was perpetuated into the twentieth century. During the first third of the twentieth century, isolated proto-studio-glass artists formed objects out of glass for their own artistic expression. But it was not until 1962 that artisans came together with the factory community at the Toledo Workshops in a serendipitous melding of industry-based skills and art ambitions. These events ignited an enthusiasm for glass as an art medium and led to the emergence of the contemporary American studio-glass movement.

The definition of what comprises "studio glass" has been problematic and a source of considerable fluctuation and debate over the past fifty years. In general terms any studio craft is one in which functionally related objects are fabricated by an artist working with traditional techniques in a nonfactory setting. This definition implies that a single artistic sensibility is responsible for the creation, fabrication, and, often, the marketing of the objects produced. But in the case of studio glass, this definition does not hold.

First, the word "studio" when applied to glassmaking may refer to a setting that employs one person working alone or to one that features a team of craftsmen guided by a master designer. Both are legitimately referred to as producing studio glass. Clearly, stipulating the number of people involved in the creative and/or forming process does not establish a definition for the term "studio glass." Secondly, the term "movement" also has definitional problems. As it is understood from the larger-art-world contexts of painting and sculpture from which it is drawn, the term implies that there is a unified set of goals, usually put forth in a written manifesto, supported and adhered to by members of the group. But there is no uniformity of vision within the studio-glass movement as relating to artistic goals, usage of technologies, or even how many craftsmen can work in a studio. The only unifying element is the raw enthusiasm for the material itself and, according to this larger-art-world criterion, this does not constitute a true movement. Lacking a manifesto to communicate their intent to the general art community, the studio-glass movement has invited dismissal by the larger art world as mere technical wizardry with little artistic potential.

This problem has also led to the categorizing of glass art by the techniques employed to form it, rather than by more relevant, content-based distinctions. Working with a seductive medium, most familiar as a material for everyday objects, with no central manifesto, has led some glassmakers to define themselves as craftsmen who work in glass and prompted others to style themselves as artists who happen to work with glass. This complex classification system hinders the assessment of contemporary glass as a serious art medium, but does not negate the talent and skill that glass artists display.

Interestingly, these definitional problems have haunted the American studio-glass movement's emergence during the mid-twentieth century. The confusion has directly affected the

Harvey Littleton
American, b. 1922

Green Loop (from the "Loop" series), 1978
Pulled and cased glass, with glass base
16¾ x 13½ x 5 inches (32.4 x 15.2 x 12.7 cm)
cat. 28

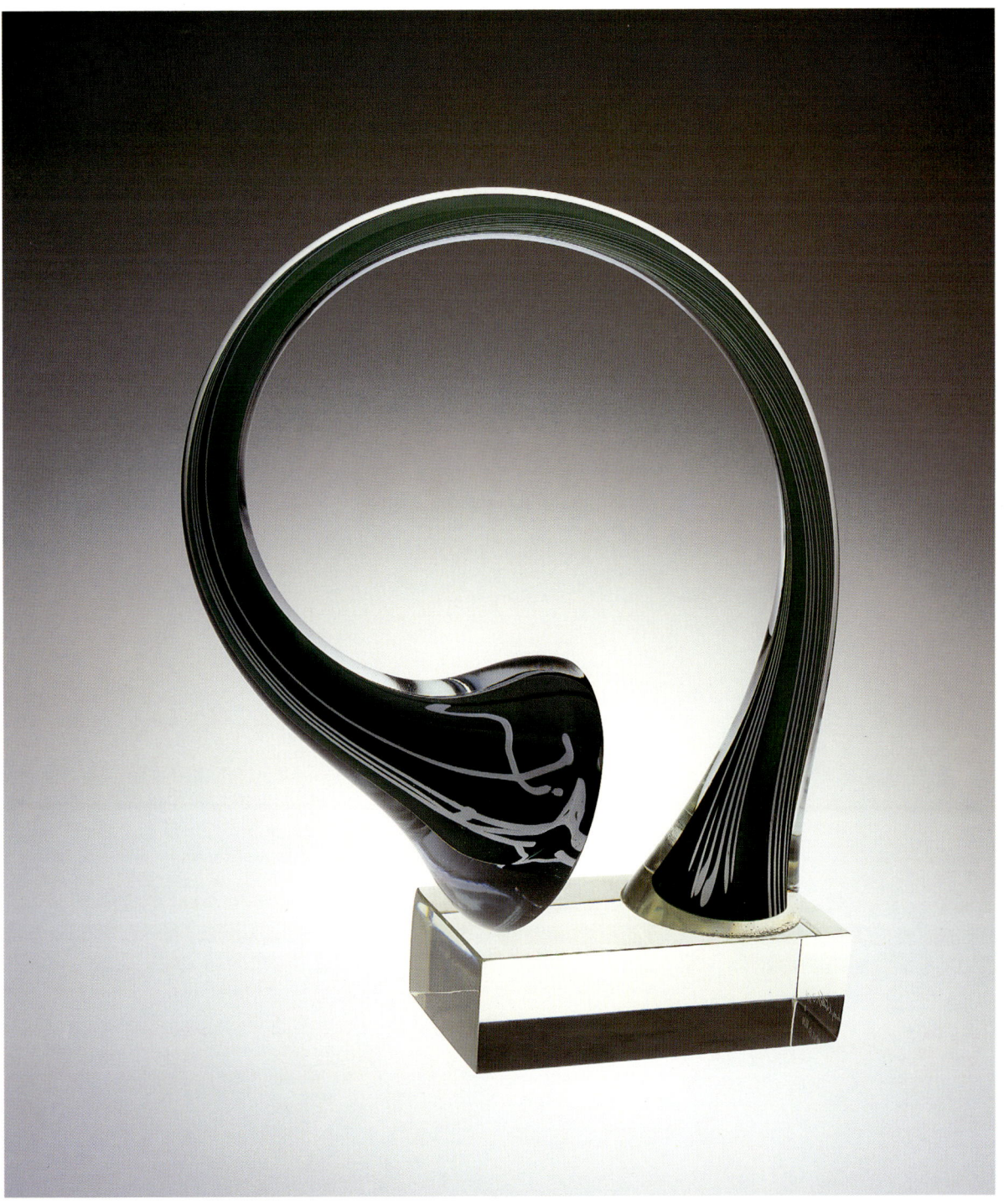

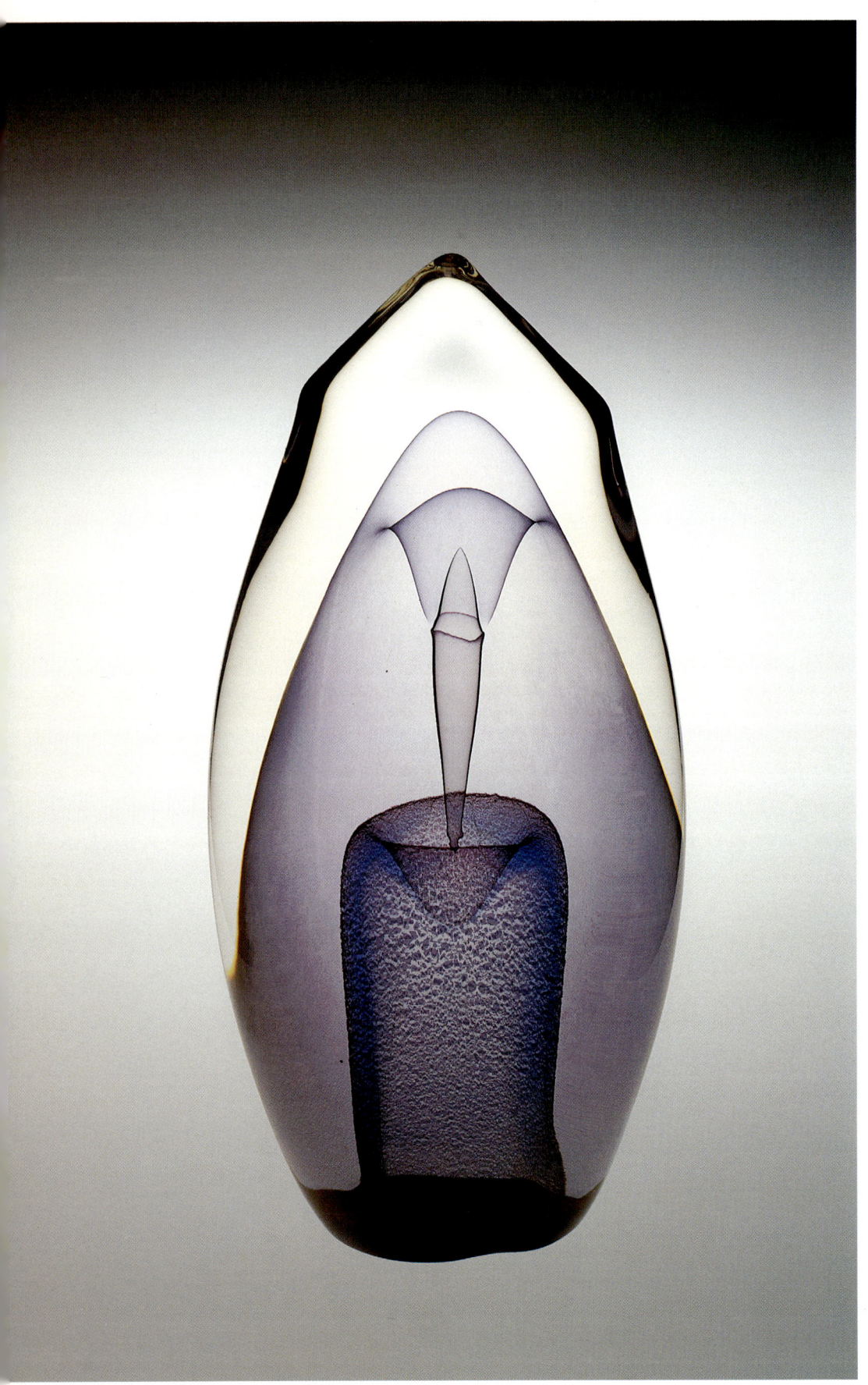

Dominick Labino
American, 1910–1987

Untitled (from the "Emergence" series), 1
Clear glass with dichronic veiling and cas
crystalline iridescence
8½ x 4 x 3 inches (21.6 x 10.2 x 7.6 cm
cat. 22

canon of acceptable glass-forming technologies that are rightfully included under the umbrella of studio glass. Since the proto-studio artists began their work in the 1930s and 1940s, the list of acceptable techniques has fluctuated. Through intentional manipulation, hot glass has been privileged over other forming methods. In the review that follows of the emergence of the American studio-glass movement as it relates to the Glick collection, this manipulation of inclusion and exclusion is critical to understanding that the selection of glass-forming methods used by the artists over the past four decades reflects a return to technologies that once were discredited and excluded from the term "studio glass." Ironically, many of these "newer" methods were ones used by the proto-studio-glass artists to launch the studio-glass movement.

European Factory Versus Early American Industrial Glass

To understand the history of the American studio movement, one must review the story of European and American glass. European factories were structured differently from those operating concurrently in the United States. Positioned between the definition of "factory" in the American sense and the term "studio" in the contemporary sense, there did not exist in European glassmaking traditions any privileging of hot glass over warm or cold glass-forming techniques.[2]

During the nineteenth century, French art-glass manufacturers Emile Gallé and René Lalique worked as professional designers and sketched designs that were then executed by a glassmaking team. As the team worked, the designer would come through the work area and alter or augment the gaffer's work. The price structure for these glass items reflected the amount of individual work provided by the gaffer and the relative closeness that master designers Gallé or Lalique had to each individual piece. This touch of the designer's hand justified marketing the works as high-end "art glass." Representing an early manipulation of the language and a linking of the terms "art" and "glass," French art glass was, in fact, manufactured in quantity to set formulas and was the product of a largely anonymous group making forms with repetitious factory techniques. In the United States, during the same period, a similar pattern was seen in the work of Louis Comfort Tiffany. Although his promotional literature referred to his production as "studio" glass, it was, in fact, formed in a factory setting. Tiffany designed and made limited-edition Art Nouveau and Arts and Crafts glass in a manner analogous to the small art-glass factories of Gallé and Lalique. Both Tiffany and the French factories exemplify the notion that glass could be an art medium and that glass art objects were commercially viable. They also further muddled the meaning of the word "studio" as applied to glass.

American Studio Glass: Pioneers and Trailblazers of Warm Glass

In the United States, by the early twentieth-century, cracks in this factory-system hegemony were developing. One of the earliest to challenge the strict factory approach was the Englishman Frederick Carder (1863–1963), who founded the Steuben Glass Works in 1903 in Corning, New York. Known for his innovations in the development of glass color and composition, he oversaw the manufacture of Steuben's production. Carder sought to produce art glass in the same vein as the European factories. Intrigued by the potential of glass's beauty, from the 1930s until the 1950s Carder worked at the small kiln in his office/studio developing a lost-wax glass-molding technique. Due to his industrial position, Carder's interest in the potential of glass was very significant. Although he was sheltered by factory support, his efforts moved the cause of studio glass one step closer to realization.

The backbone of factory glassmaking was glassblowing in large quantity. Usually used in tandem with molds to form objects, this technique necessitated large furnaces and vast quantities of fuel to reach and maintain the high temperatures required to melt glass. Maintaining medieval European guild practices, factory glass was always formed by teams of workers, usually eight to a team. But other techniques did not involve such high temperatures and were available to those interested in making glass in small studios. They offered the earliest opportunities for the studio-glass artist.

Three of these "warm-glass" techniques were flameworking (lampworking), glass fusing, and glass slumping onto molds.[3] While lampworking was most often seen in the service of paperweight-making in factories, the technique was possible in small studio settings. John Burton and Charles Kaziun were two mid-twentieth-century American flameworkers who made work in their own studios. Knowledge of flameworking techniques was jealously guarded by factory practitioners, so Burton and Kaziun sought independent training. Burton taught himself how to make his eccentrically decorated vessels and considered himself an artist. Kaziun during the late 1950s built his own furnace and cased his flameworked forms inside glass ingots. Artist Paul Stankard (cats. 58 and 59) experienced similar roadblocks when he wanted to acquire technical information. Ginny Ruffner (cat. 56) was also attracted to flameworking as the structural element of her sculptures and as an armature for her paintings.

The techniques of fusing and slumping could also be accomplished at relatively low temperatures. Using equipment scavenged from ceramics applications, four pioneer fusers actively made objects in their studios during the 1940s and 1950s. Swiss-born Maurice Heaton supported himself through his glassmaking business. Heaton had been trained by his father and grandfather who made Arts and Crafts glass in England.[4] The family moved to New York in 1914, and

Toots Zynsky
American, b. 1951

Untitled (from the "Exotic Bird" series), 1986
Glass threads, fused and kiln-formed
7 x 10 x 9 inches (17.8 x 25.4 x 22.9 cm)
cat. 69

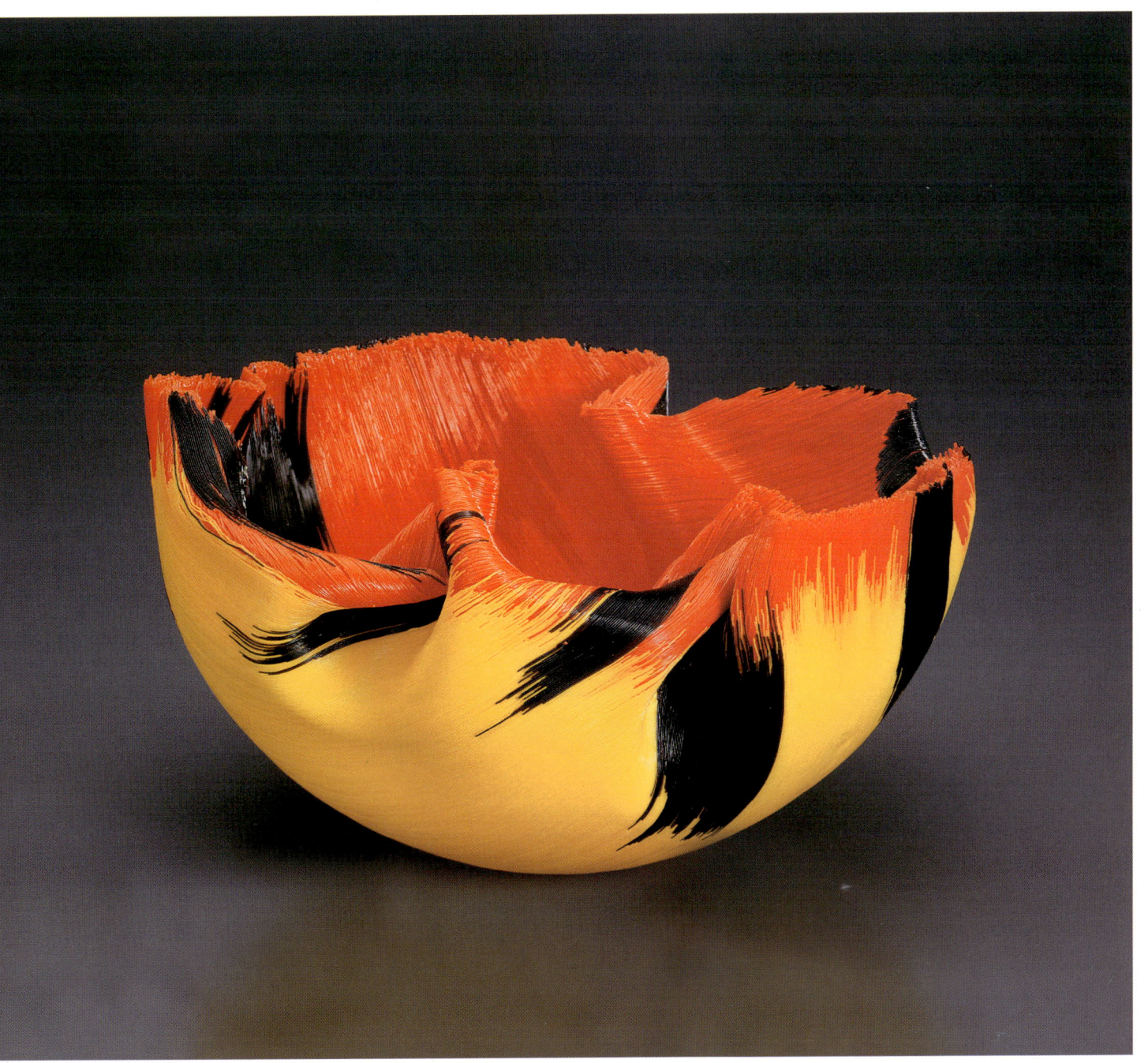

Dale Chihuly
American, b. 1941

Untitled (from the "Soft Cylinder" series), 1987
Blown glass, shards, with small blanket drawing
by Flora Mace
10 x 7 x 7 inches (25.4 x 17.8 x 17.8 cm)
cat. 8

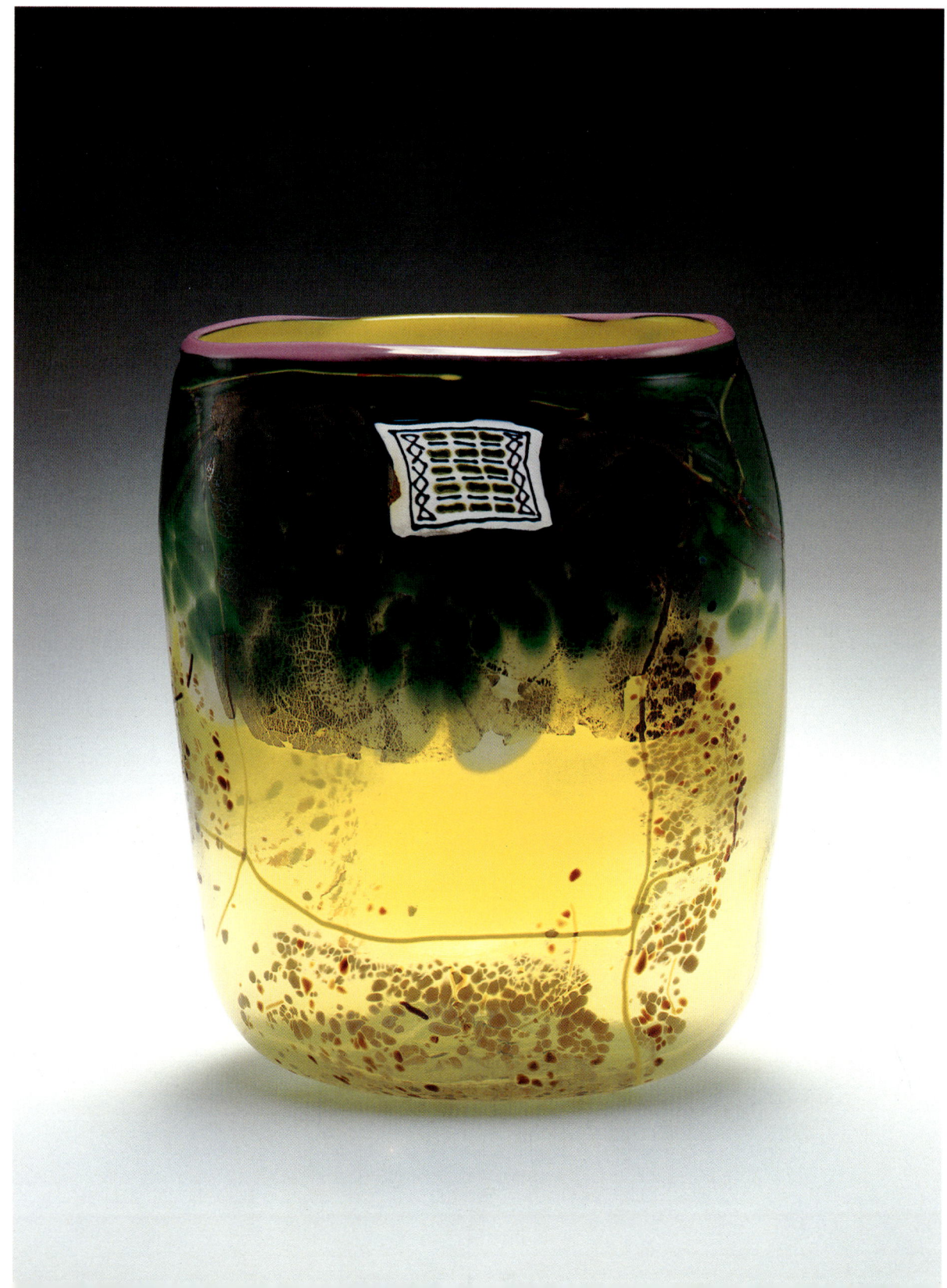

by the early 1920s, Heaton had committed himself to glass. He made lighting fixtures, wall sconces, screens, and tableware. In 1932 Heaton completed a commission for a large mural depicting the career of Amelia Earhart that was installed in the women's lounge of Radio City Music Hall in New York. His later work uses powdered-glass enamels arrayed in intricate patterns on glass sheets that he then fused and slumped in a kiln. Similar contemporary enamel work can be seen in the work of Robert Carlson (cat. 5).

A second proto-studio-glass artist was Edris Eckhardt. As with many glass trailblazers, Eckhardt worked first as a potter. During the 1950s she experimented with making her own glass from batch in her basement studio. She cast glass in lost-wax molds to form plaques and freestanding sculptures, such as *Archangel* (1965), which was featured in the important survey exhibition "Glass 1959," mounted by The Corning Museum of Glass, Corning, New York, and is now in their permanent collection.

The last two pioneer artists comprised husband-and-wife team Michael and Frances Higgins. Their interest lay in fabricating tableware decorated with brightly colored glass enamels, which they applied in geometric patterns. By 1962 the Higginses were fusing glass into large sheets to make screens, panels, and sculptures.

The work of these trailblazers was known to other craftsmen at the time. In fact at the First Annual Conference of American Craftsmen of the American Craftsmen's Council at the Asilomar Conference Center, Pacific Grove, California, in 1957, Eckhardt and the Higginses spoke about their work and shared their enthusiasm for glass as an art medium.[5] All four pioneers set the stage for later inquiries into other glass-forming technologies, such as blowing, casting, and assembling, but their warm-glass techniques of fusing and slumping are used to great advantage today in the works of, among others, Sydney Cash, Klaus Moje, Mary Shaffer, and Toots Zynsky (cats. 6, 35–37, 57, and 69 and 70). A further advancement in this technology came with the rediscovery in the late 1970s of the nineteenth-century fusing method known as *pâte de verre* through the work of artists such as Karla Trinkley (cat. 62).

There also were a few pioneers who worked part-time in glass using simple ceramics kilns (made and designed with the aid of such manuals as Bernard Leach's 1941 *A Potter's Book*). While working as the ceramics instructor at the University of Southern California in Los Angeles, Glen Lukens slumped glass into the molds he used for his clay pieces. This example of technique shifting was typical at mid-century. These explorations in small studios, not factory settings, fit the definition of studio glass as it is now understood.

A common thread that has linked all of the pioneer glass artisans was that they had to learn their techniques from industry sources or by trial and error. While some information was available from trade schools (and even at the university level from Alfred University, Alfred,

New York), these skills were considered technical and not applicable to artistic endeavors. This division between the technically skilled factory worker and the artistically inclined but unskilled artist was underscored by the University of Georgia instructor Earl McCutchen in his article for *Craft Horizons*. He illustrated the paucity of information available to the artists by suggesting that glass batch could be obtained from cast-off industrial sources.[6] Some forms of preworked glass ran the risk of not forming or annealing properly, nor would they melt well in the lower-temperature, small studio furnaces.

Technological breakthroughs in working glass at all temperatures had to be conquered before the dream of a small studio could be realized. With only mid-temperature methods currently accessible, the two workshops held at The Toledo Museum of Art in 1962 focused on the challenge of melting and then blowing molten glass. This shift in focus redefined the term "studio glass" to mean that which was blown. This privileging of hot glass over warm (or cold) effectively cut out the pioneering efforts of these earlier fusers and slumpers, and removed them from inclusion as genuine studio-glass artists.

Critical Mass: Harvey Littleton, Dominick Labino, and the Toledo Workshops

In the early 1960s Harvey Littleton (cats. 28 and 29) served as a catalyst for the emerging American studio-glass movement. His enthusiasm for glass as an art medium and his ability to gather around himself a group of committed glassblowers attracted a broad audience of both practitioners and supporters. Equally important, Littleton facilitated the institutionalization of the discipline within college-level curriculums. Littleton had energy, passion, and good timing—for the period was marked by a developing antiestablishment attitude, and consequently, interest in using nontraditional mediums for artistic expression.

Born in the glass town of Corning, New York, where his father was the director of research at the Corning Glass Works, Littleton knew firsthand the capabilities of glass. He sensed a danger in the increasing factory automatization and feared that important craft skills were being lost. Echoing the proto-studio-glass artists before him, Littleton felt that glass could become an art medium only if it could escape the factory and be made by artists in small studios. In Littleton's mind the key to wresting glass from the factory resided with the hot-glass technique of blowing. These thoughts and ambitions led him to organize the famous Toledo Workshops of 1962.

Two other individuals were crucial to mounting these workshops: Dominick Labino (cats. 21 and 22), then vice president and director of research at Johns-Mansville Fiber Glass Corporation in Toledo, and Dr. Otto Wittmann, the director of The Toledo Museum of Art. Wittmann had hired Littleton to teach evening crafts courses at the museum; Labino was a student in these classes.

For studio glass to become a reality, art and technology needed to be reconnected. Having the workshop on the grounds of The Toledo Museum of Art, albeit in a gardening shed, added an art gloss to the proceedings. Moreover, Labino's glass-forming expertise, derived from years of experience in industry, supplied the technology. This combination of skills and interests brought art and technology together and studio glass one step closer. Held from March 23 to April 1, 1962, the first workshop was attended by seven participants. A second workshop, in June, had twelve participants.[7] They focused on the practical (technical) requirements for building a small glass furnace and annealing oven, and melting glass cullet and keeping it at a temperature appropriate for blowing. It is important to note that the workshops would not have been successful had Labino not brought his knowledge of materials. Labino found that #475 Johns-Mansville fiberglass marbles were an adequate mettle for blowing and they became the workshop's first melt. Although it was not perfect, the attendees were able to form and anneal simple objects, thus making the workshops into galvanizing events that marked the reinvigorating of the glass movement and brought glassblowing into the repertoire of the studio-glass artist.

Challenges of the Early Decades

As a result of the Toledo Workshops, interest in glass expanded and the movement was dubbed "studio glass." Focusing on blowing and learning by trial and error to master the technical aspects of glass-forming, the early practitioners needed to develop a daunting range of expertise. Building furnaces, selecting the right glass cullet, mixing and melting the batches, finding appropriate colorants, learning how to use traditional tools, inventing new tools when necessary, and then successfully blowing forms were all adventures into the unknown.

During this first decade, most glass used for blowing was produced from the same #475 fiberglass marbles introduced by Labino. This material had a green tint that muddied most colorants and restricted the palette. In time new glass formulations would emerge, thereby increasing the range of colors, type of optics achievable, and available methods of forming. Artist Mark Peiser (cats. 52–54) took up this challenge and became a pioneer in formulating a good, clear, glass mettle.

As was to be expected, the form vocabulary used by the early glassmakers was limited. Because the easiest shape to free-blow is the bubble, many of the early pieces are bubbles that were altered while still warm. So pervasive was this form that ceramics artist Robert Arneson wrote in 1967: "If I see another drippy glass bubble, I'm going to blow my mind."[8] Additionally, many of the forms that emerged in this first decade are vessel-based, because this form also was created easily on the end of a blowpipe, and many early glassmakers had absorbed a vessel sensibility from their studies in clay.[9] Littleton and artist Dan Dailey (cats. 10 and 11) both had been potters. These types of forms were not

Joel Philip Myers
American, b. 1934

Untitled (from the "Contiguous Fragment" series), 1988
Blown glass, cased, with inclusions
16 1/2 x 22 1/2 x 4 inches (41.9 x 57.2 x 10.2 cm)
cat. 48

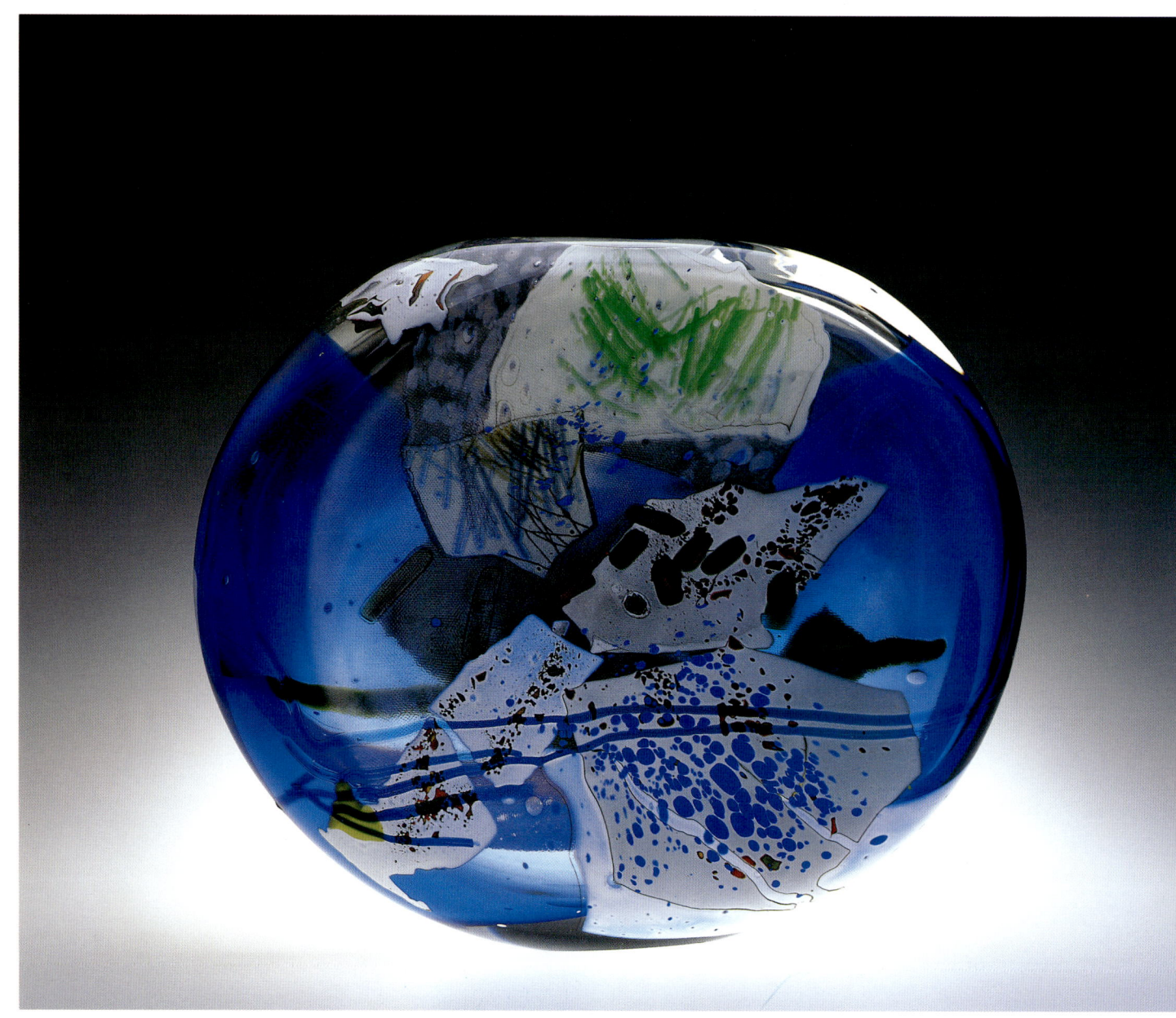

very different from those produced by factories and it would take time for studio glass to establish its separate visual identity. Eventually the vocabulary matured to incorporate "a whole series of complex blown, broken and collapsed pieces,"[10] but technical issues still forced aesthetics to take a subsidiary position. Sculptural forms (usually not blown) would come later.

This early period of technical exploration led to a series of interesting and important features that soon became hallmarks of the studio-glass community. Setting up a studio was a group effort because funding was limited: teachers starting new programs called upon students to build the furnaces and kilns for annealing. Studio space and supplies were inadequate, and artists such as Marvin Lipofsky (cats. 25–27) and Joel Philip Myers (cats. 39–49) used ingenuity to work around these problems.

Another studio-glass pattern was the around-the-clock working habits. Because melting glass took many hours, furnaces were run day and night to conserve fuel and save time, thus making forming also a twenty-four-hours-a-day activity, ironically repeating the pattern seen in factories. Additionally, at this time glassblowing was a mostly male activity, although several women had attended the Toledo Workshops. The decidedly male tone of the movement would remain until the mid-1970s, when the women's movement led to women entering the field. Blowing glass is hard, heavy, hot work; men who participated enjoyed the team structure and the technical challenges of the activity.

Finally, the glass movement emerged during the anti-Vietnam War period of the late 1960s and early 1970s. For members of the first American generation to take college for granted to opt instead to practice the artisanal activity of glassblowing was one of a number of antiestablishment stands that marked the times. The revolutionary changes that were taking place in the glass world mirrored the larger counter-cultural lifestyle and profession shift.[11]

By the second decade a larger group of glass devotees had developed and as the fascination with glassblowing faded, other techniques became accepted as part of the studio-glass movement. This shift was facilitated by greater exposure to European studio and small factory work, and the entrance into glassmaking of those who were not attracted to the labor of furnace work. Consequently, in the late 1970s, cold-working, fusing, casting, and painting on glass were returned to the canon of appropriate studio-glass activities; more recently kiln-forming, *pâte de verre*, and bead-making have been rehabilitated.

This change in direction away from an emphasis on blowing may be seen in the careers of many artists represented in the Glick collection. Mark Peiser (cats. 52–54) began as a glassblower in the Littleton mold, but in 1981 he turned to cast and polished work. David Huchthausen (cats. 17 and 18) and Michael Glancy (cats. 14–16) also abandoned glassblowing. As the result of an injury, Dale Chihuly (cats. 7 and 8) now has others blow his work, as does Kéké Cribbs (cat. 9). The circle has been completed: studio artists now relegate the blowing to skilled subordinates and focus instead on orchestrating the total work of art. Dale Chihuly and Dan Dailey both work in this manner, which is reminiscent of European factory practice and again blurs the definition of the term "studio glass."

This need to conquer technique led to one of the core controversies within the glass movement: is technique or content more important for the glass artist to address? Littleton, believing that content was the only route for glass to pursue, made his famous dictum "technique is cheap" in 1972 at the National Sculpture Conference in Lawrence, Kansas. This statement opened the way for technique to be downplayed, with the emphasis turned toward issues of content. But only with technique finally in hand as a result of the first decade of experimentation could the making of art become the focus of 1970s and 1980s glass. This development can be seen in the Glick pieces that date from 1962 into the late 1970s. After that time the methods used for working glass and the subject matter addressed expanded rapidly.

Glassmaking at the Universities

The tenuous acceptance of glass by the larger art world would not have occurred without the inclusion of glass in college-level art programs. All of the American glass artists represented in the Glick collection are college-educated; the majority received a graduate art degree with specialization in glass. The drive to have glass training available at the college level began even before the Toledo Workshops.[12]

In 1956 glass artist Robert Willson received a National Study Grant to conduct research at The Corning Museum of Glass on the historical and technical background of glass in art, architecture, and crafts worldwide. In order to understand the European approach to glass education, Willson collaborated with Alfredo Barbini and other craftsmen in Murano, Italy, and made glass sculpture. As the result of his experience, Willson urged support for the training of artists to use glass as an art medium. Willson's work and enthusiasm joined that of Littleton and helped to move glass into the mainstream of art education.

Consequently, in the early 1960s, glass programs, usually focused on glassblowing, appeared in a number of universities. In 1962 Alfred University ceramist André Billeci started an independent-study course in glassblowing. Harvey Littleton set up his own independent course for the study of glass techniques and established his Art 176 course at the University of Wisconsin, Madison, in September 1963.[13] Dominick Labino led three workshops at his studio under the auspices of The Toledo Museum of Art School of Design in 1966 and 1967. Glassblowing programs subsequently spread to colleges throughout the United States.

Many of the early teachers were either attendees of the Toledo Workshops or Littleton's students. Among them were Marvin Lipofsky (cats. 25–27), who taught at the University

Michael Glancy
American, b. 1950

Master Gem, 1988
Blown glass, sandblasted, with electroplated copper
5½ x 9 dia. inches (14 x 22.9 cm)
cat. 14

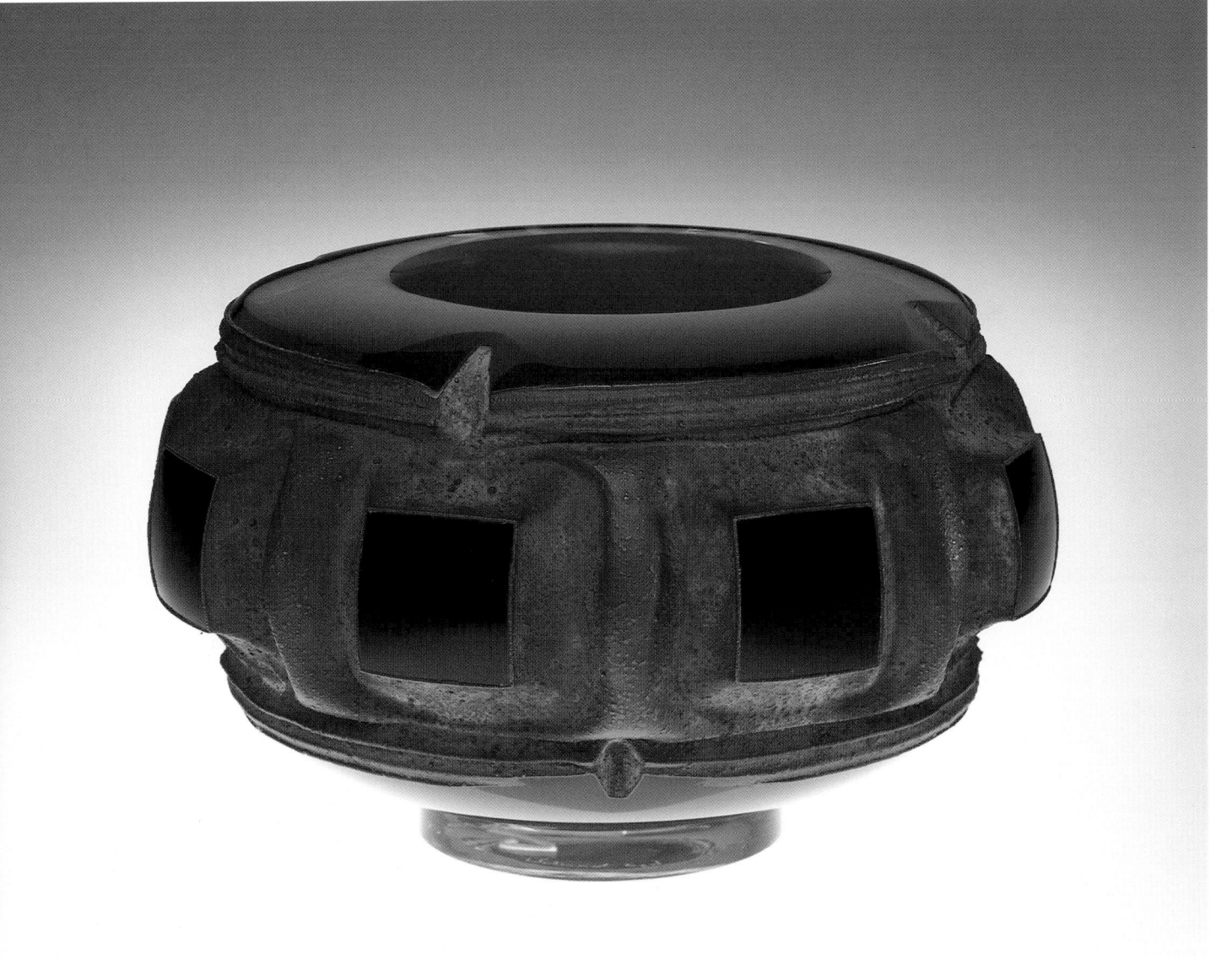

Klaus Moje
German, b. 1936

Untitled, 1990
Fused and slumped glass with wheel-ground surface
2 x 13$\frac{1}{2}$ dia. inches (5.1 x 34.3 cm)
cat. 37

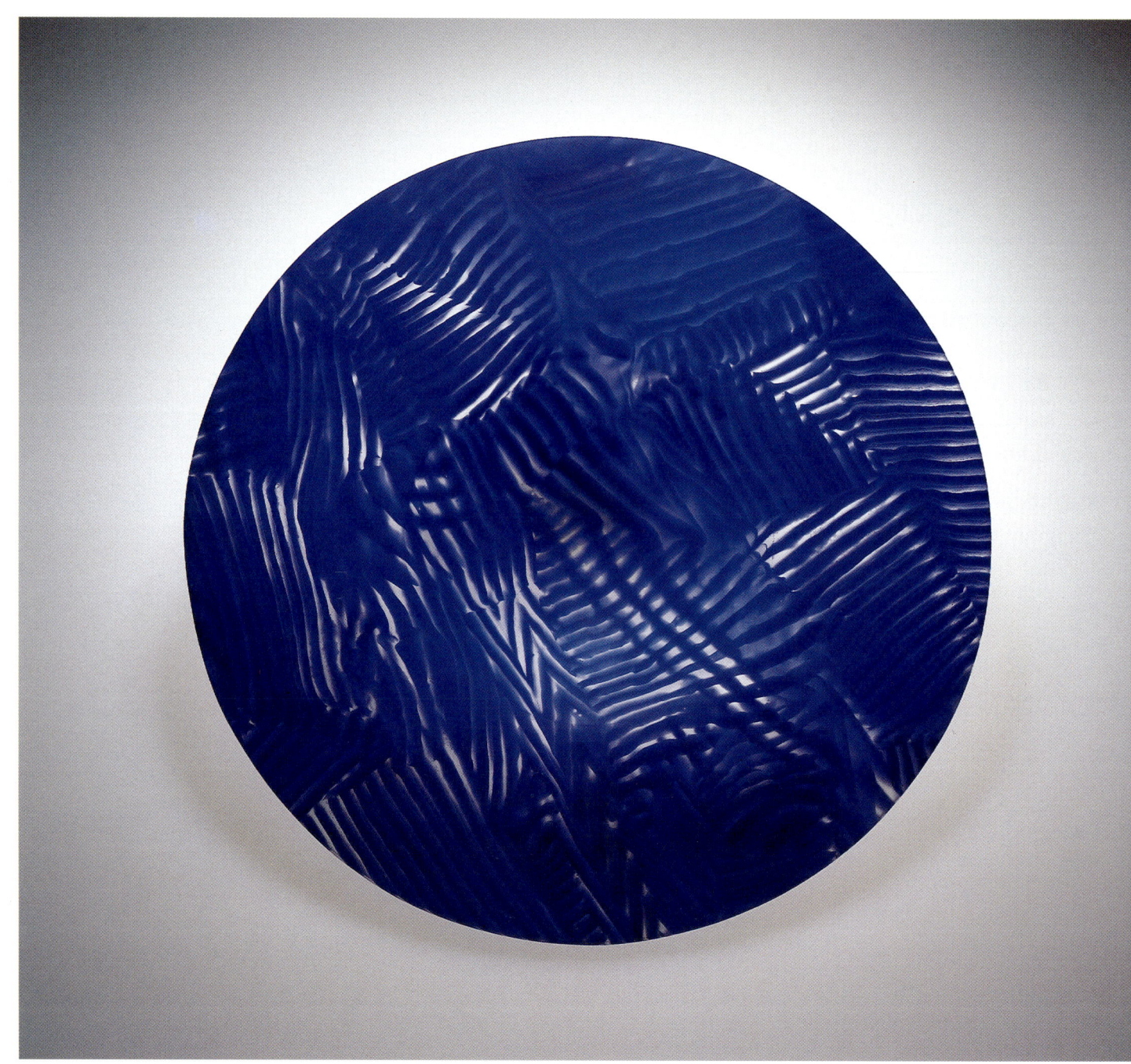

of California, Berkeley, and later at the College of Arts and Crafts in Oakland, California; and Toledo Workshop staff member Norman Schulman, who in the fall of 1965 founded the program at the Rhode Island School of Design, Providence, where his assistant was Dale Chihuly (cats. 7 and 8). Joel Philip Myers (cats. 39-49) graduated from Alfred University, New York State College of Ceramics, with a degree in ceramics in 1963 and became director of design for the Blenko Glass Company, Milton, West Virginia. He left Blenko in 1970 to establish the glass program at Illinois State University in Normal.

There also developed a group of seasonal schools that catered to glass artists, as well as other crafts practitioners. Among them were Haystack Mountain School of Crafts on Deer Isle, Maine; the Penland School of Handicrafts, near Asheville, North Carolina, where Mark Peiser (cats. 52-54) received the first hot-glass artist residency. Later this pattern would be repeated on the West Coast with the founding of Pilchuck Glass School outside of Seattle in 1971 by Dale Chihuly (cats. 7 and 8) and Ruth Tamura on land donated by John and Anne Gould Hauberg. These schools provide opportunities for glass artists to work on projects, interact with their colleagues, and solidify the glass community. Even international artists Erwin Eisch, Klaus Moje, and Bertil Vallien (cats. 12, 35-37, and 63 and 64), for example, have attended Pilchuck Glass School.

By 1973 *Glass Art Magazine* listed in its "Guide to Glass Instruction" seventy educational programs. These university programs established the fundamental character of the movement: glass artists received the same education available in the more sanctified areas of painting and sculpture. Exposed to the fine arts, this new generation, although working in a traditionally crafts-oriented medium, acquired larger-art-world ambitions.

International Studio Glass: Czechoslovakia, England, Hungary, Japan, and Australia

Exchanges between studio artists in the United States and those trained and living in Europe have been mutually advantageous. Perceived as incorporating a freer approach, not hobbled by the confines of traditional European delineations of artisanal versus artistic, the American approach has been described as predominantly enthusiastic with lagging technical skills; the European approach has been referred to as technically fine, but in need of energizing.[14] Europeans, captivated by American enthusiasm and loosely structured working situations, in their turn imparted a respect for the medium and knowledge of traditional techniques. Cross-pollinations occurred as artists from around the world traveled either to attend or teach courses devoted to studio glass. Marvin Lipofsky (cats. 25-27) has served as unofficial ombudsman for glass since the mid-1960s.

The productive interaction between Europe and the United States was seen early on, for example, in 1964 at the World Congress of Craftsmen held at Columbia University, New York.

There European glass artist and long-time Littleton friend Erwin Eisch demonstrated glassblowing with Norman Schulman and Marvin Lipofsky using a portable furnace and annealing oven provided by Dominick Labino (cats. 21 and 22).[15] Their work impressed even the European attendees with its "can do" ethos; and the Americans were excited by Eisch's emphasis on content over technology.

Conferences such as the ones sponsored yearly by the Glass Art Society have also fostered international interaction, beginning in the 1960s. European glass maintained a distinctive aesthetic, but time and mutual exposure softened these demarcations. Bulwarked by an increasing international literature about glass,[16] studio glass has become so international that a number of artists represented in the Glick collection have felt comfortable working outside their countries. Jane Bruce, Klaus Moje, Yan Zoritchak, and Toots Zynsky (cats. 4, 35–37, 68, and 69 and 70) have all moved to other lands.

But glass education in Europe is artisanal in nature and involves an apprenticeship period of several years. The goal has been to train designers and cold-work artists for industry. Craftsman status is attained only after the completion of a series of skill-based tests. Glassmaking has taken place in large factories and also in small factory settings such as those found in Italy. A time-honored relationship exists between training in factories, trade schools, and some art schools, where cutting, engraving, enameling, sandblasting, and kiln-forming are taught by masters. Only glassblowing had remained within the province of the factory, and because of this connection, in contrast to American programs, art schools were hesitant to introduce hot glass into their curriculum.

The success of Czechoslovakian glass since World War II is the result of a fine school system implemented between World War I and II. Glass artists were taught art and design as well as how to form glass. Small furnaces were established around the traditional glass center of Železný Brod.[17] Although this development prefigured the American glass movement, war disrupted the expansion and later political tensions continued to interfere with the growth of Czech art glass.

After World War II, Czech glass sculptors Stanislav Libenský, Jan Kotík, René Roubíček, Václav Cigler, and Vladimír Kopecký rose to prominence. Support for their work was evidenced by the 1945 exhibition entitled "Exhibition of New Glass," which featured works made in the factory setting by art-trained glassmakers. In time this marriage of factory facilities and artistic endeavor led to new ideas about cut-glass forms (seen in the work of Roubíček) and to experiments in transparent enamels and vitreous glass by Libenský and Jaroslava Brychtová (cats. 23 and 24).

In the postwar period Professor Josef Kaplický headed the glass department at the School of Applied Art (later the Academy of Applied Art) in Prague where Libenský studied. Libenský later created the curriculum for the newly founded Secondary School of Glass Making in Železný Brod.[18] Its eight-year course of study featured both technical expertise and artistic creativity. In time this school (and others like it) became linked with the Academy of Applied Art and constituted a formidable educational structure. With schools located near industrial-glass producers, Czech artists worked with industry to establish an understanding of the material and its artistic potential. The American dichotomy of artistic expression versus factory hegemony did not exist for the early Czech glass artists.

But the Czechs had a complicated political situation to deal with. After the Communists took over the government, they decided that glass was a good propaganda tool. Consequently, unlike many artists working in other mediums, glass artists were allowed to travel to the West and, at least in the beginning, to earn hard currency. This favored position helped to protect the schools and the artists, even when funding for other arts was cut.

In England during the 1930s, Stourbridge College of Technology and Art established a small industrial furnace that created designs and produced blanks for the students. Technicians ran the furnaces and did the forming, but students were allowed to do cold work. By 1959 London's Royal College of Art's small furnace for melting lead crystal offered similar student opportunities. Subsequently the Royal College established a course with the help of American glass artist Sam Herman. Jane Bruce (cat. 4) studied with him and so did Colin Reid (cat. 55), who took a technical course offered through England's continuing-education scheme.

Postwar studio glass in Hungary developed relatively independently from the other studio-glass movements. Most of the work was cold-formed because there were relatively few hot-glass studios. Architectural applications, rather than the vessel tradition, predominated. In 1966 György Z. Gàcs (1914–1978) founded the School of Applied Arts in Budapest. Although he was trained as a painter, he enjoyed the new effects that were possible when glass, cement, and steel were activated by light. He was also intrigued by the technical challenge of making large pieces that incorporate a number of mediums. His star student was Zoltán Bohus (cat. 3), who succeeded Gàcs as the head of the glass department.

In Asia glass has never been as popular as pottery, lacquerware, wood, and bamboo. During the Edo Period (1603–1868), European glass brought to Japan by Portuguese traders became the model that the Japanese strove to emulate. Glass production centers were located in Nagasaki, Osaka, Kyoto, and Edo (later Tokyo). Using a glass with high lead content, the Japanese favored European techniques over the Chinese method of carving forms from blocks of glass.[19]

In the 1920s a group of Japanese glass artists traveled to Europe for the first time. Searching for technical expertise in engraving and cutting glass, Kozo Kagami (1896–1985) studied with Willem von Eiff (1890–1943) in Stuttgart. Upon his return to Japan, he founded Kagami Crystal. A relative of Kyohei Fujita (cat. 13), Toshichi Iwata (1893–1980) founded his own company in 1931 after receiving a degree in painting and metals from the Tokyo Institute of Fine Arts.

Bertil Vallien
Swedish, b. 1938

Calendarium, 1990
Sand-cast glass with inclusions and copper-foil elements
5 x 77 x 6 inches (12.7 x 195.6 x 15.2 cm)
cat. 64

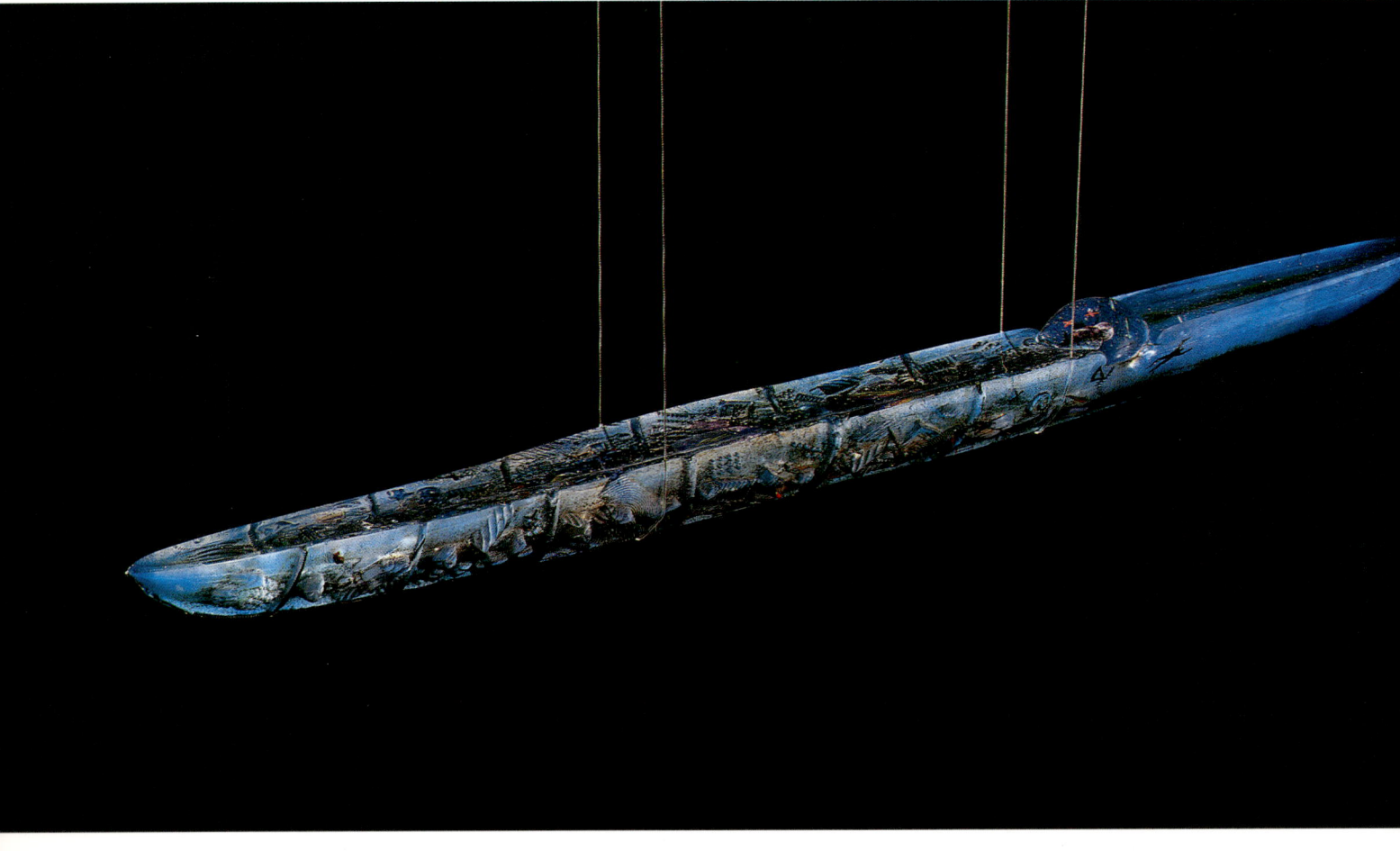

Exhibiting internationally, "he called [his works] something roughly translatable as 'garbage glass.'"[20] It was left to Fujita to firmly establish studio glass as a viable medium with a unique Japanese aesthetic.

In Australia the development of the studio-glass movement parallels that seen in the United States, only occurring about a decade later. During the early 1970s an informal group of about six glassblowers were living and working in Perth and New South Wales. Member Stephen Skillitzi's public demonstration of glassblowing in 1972[21] may be described as the beginning of the Australian studio-glass movement. An infusion of American enthusiasm and expertise followed when Sam Herman, fresh from a stint in England, and artists Richard Marquis (cats. 30–34) and William Boysen held workshops in Australia.

Australian glass went through three stages, again roughly analogous to those seen in the American development. The first phase, during the early 1970s, focused on the gaining of technical skills; the second, from the end of the 1970s until the middle of the 1980s, featured the inclusion of kiln-forming and saw the split of concerns between making art versus conquering the craft. Since the middle 1980s, the preoccupation has been with originality of concept and expression coupled with competent execution. When Klaus Moje (cats. 35–37) arrived in late 1982, he furthered this development by stressing content over technique. Currently there are two glass centers, one at the Sydney College of the Arts and the other at the Canberra School of Arts.

Glass 1980–90s: Craft or Art? The Cross-Over Artists

As the issue of technology versus content and the definitional problems of studio-glass orthodoxy have stabilized in the last ten years, more important questions for the movement and its future viability have arisen. Chief among them is whether glass can be assessed as an art medium. Much as its admirers urge this acceptance, the larger art world is still uneasy with a medium that has ties to craft skills and utilitarian forms. But perhaps such rigid categorization is itself a distortion. Strata of quality exist in all mediums: painting ranges from a hobby activity of painting by numbers to the artistic challenge of painting free-hand. Because glass does not consistently live up to its highest potential should not exclude it from the pantheon of art. Only time will clarify these questions; until then each piece should be assessed in the light of history and knowledge of the field.

HOWARD BEN TRÉ

American, b. 1949

Howard Ben Tré is the preeminent sculptor of cast glass in the United States. Born in Brooklyn, Ben Tré attended high school at Brooklyn Technical, then spent a year at Missouri Valley College, Marshall on an athletic scholarship (1967–68), and a second year at Brooklyn College (1968). Dropping out of school, he traveled to Europe and then ended up on the West Coast where he attended Portland State University, Oregon. There he received a Bachelor of Fine Arts degree in ceramics (1978), and two years later he received his Master of Fine Arts in glass sculpture from the Rhode Island School of Design, Providence.

Ben Tré had always shown an interest in art. His father, a carpenter, had studied art at Cooper Union in New York.[22] Thus conditioned to value physical labor as well as art, Ben Tré was at home on construction jobs and working in factories. In fact, demanding physical effort became integral to his art and knowledge and affection for machines are seen in his work.

The artist dates his mature work from 1977 when he was still an undergraduate at Portland State University. Included in the prestigious 1978 "Americans in Glass" exhibition at the Leigh Yawkey Woodson Art Museum in Wausau, Wisconsin, Ben Tré stated that "Glass as a medium allows me to explore the merging of organic and geometric qualities in form and decoration. I am particularly interested in sand casting of glass because the process gives a timeless feeling to contemporary shapes and frees me from the limitations of the blown form."[23] During the 1980s Ben Tré worked at the Blenko Glass Factory, Milton, West Virginia. On a trip he took to England, the architectural glass at Tintern Abbey made Ben Tré aware of the monumentality of architectural imagery. He began and continues to explore in a clearly structured manner issues such as the continuum of time.

Much of the impact of Ben Tré's work is derived from his use of cast glass. As with plate glass, the thick "white" glass[24] he uses to make his rough-textured "green" pieces has a green tinge unless it is obscured through modifications to the batch chemistry. In Ben Tré's case, he prefers the material to remain murky and dense. Its glow and pattern of imperfections impart an intriguing timelessness.

Ben Tré begins his artistic process with a gestural drawing to establish the general sense of the piece. He then makes an orthographic projection (full-scale mechanical drawing) to help establish

Howard Ben Tré

Pilaster #8 (from the "Pilaster" series), 1983
Cast white glass with patinated copper inclusions
30$\frac{1}{2}$ x 10$\frac{1}{2}$ x 5$\frac{1}{2}$ inches (77.5 x 26.7 x 14 cm)
cat. 1

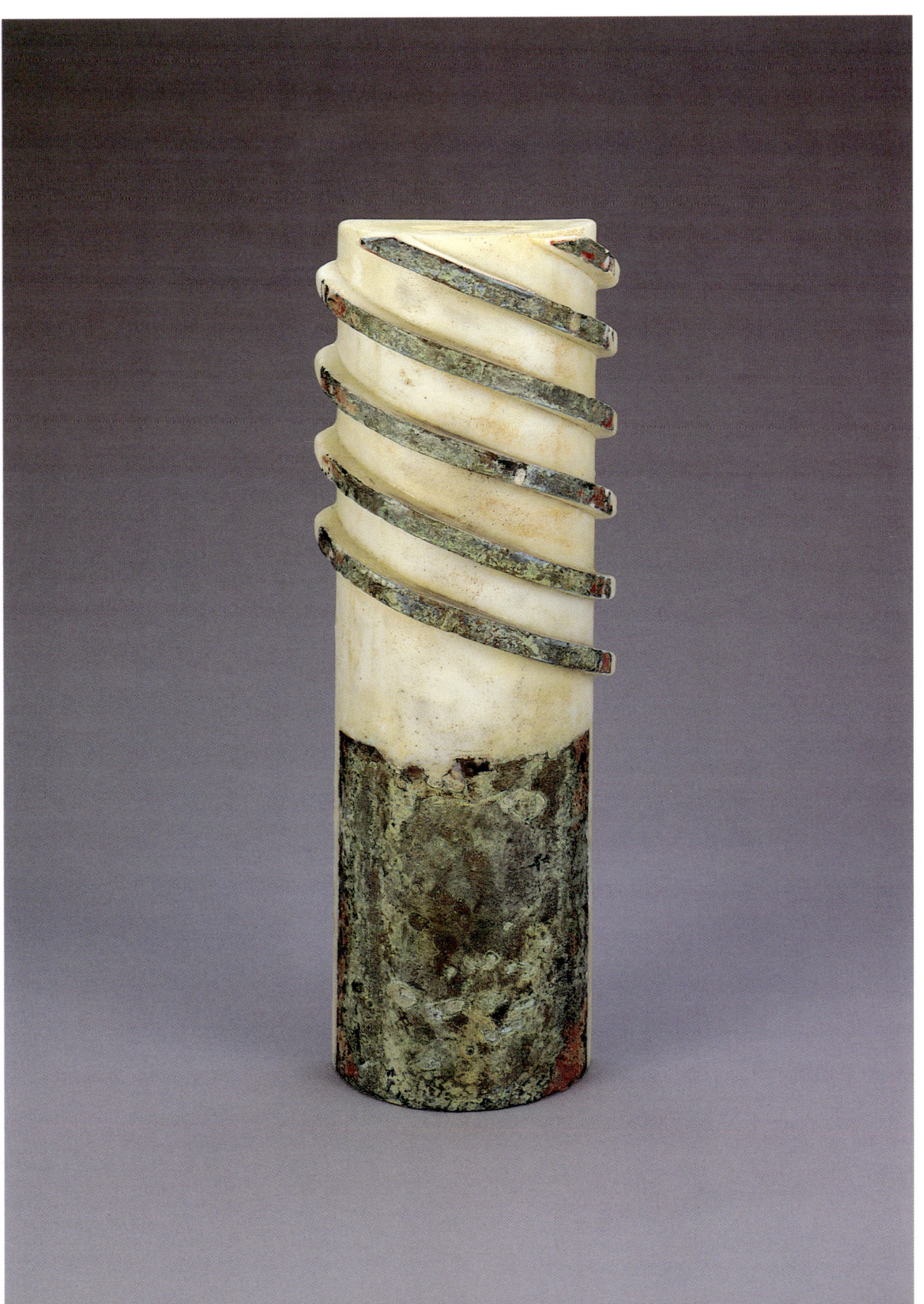

Howard Ben Tré

Second Vase, 1989
Cast glass with gold leaf and bronze
71 1/2 x 23 3/4 dia. inches (181.6 x 60.3 cm)
cat. 2

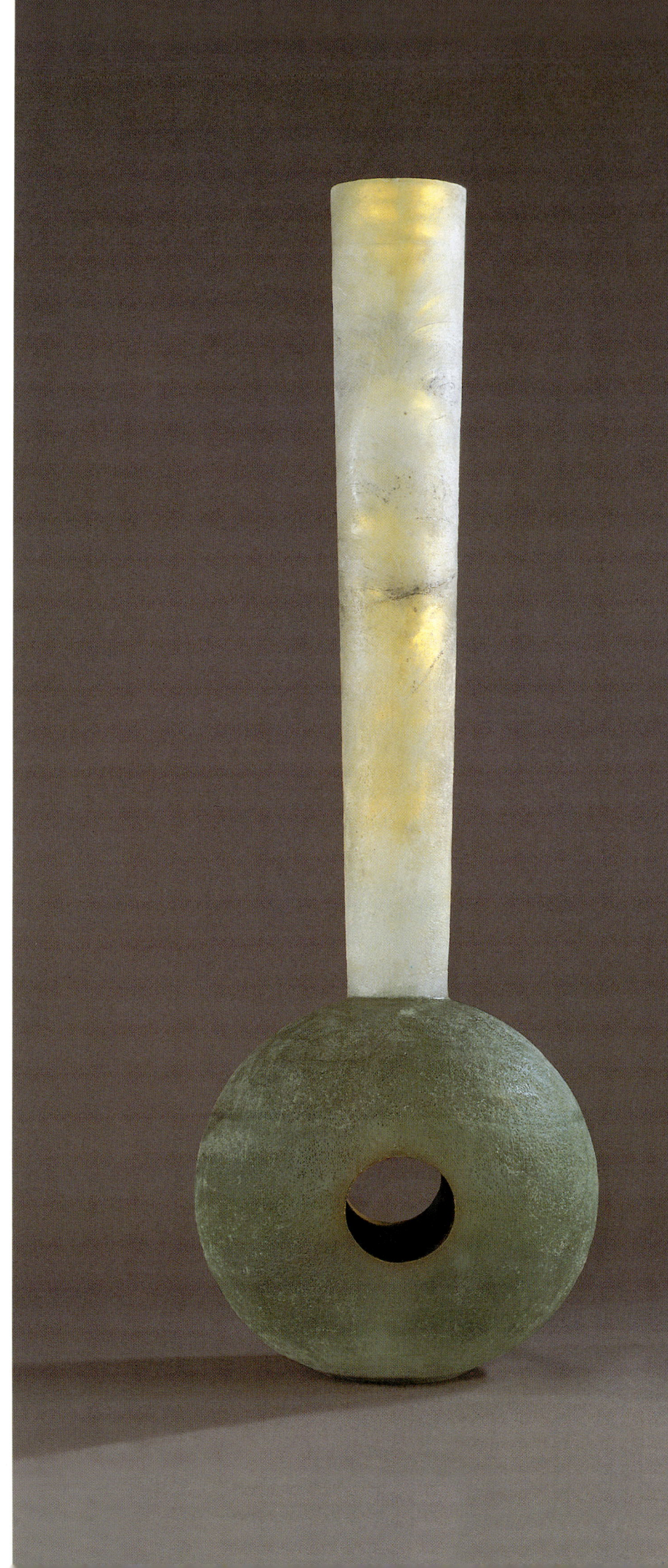

the scale and proportions that are key to his work. After establishing a family of shapes, he selects a few to be transferred into full-sized patterns made of rigid polystyrene board and cardboard. Once all modifications have been made, Ben Tré and his assistants take the patterns to the bronze-casting foundry where resin-bonded molds are made around the patterns. These molds are formed from sand mixed with chemicals that cause them to harden to a concretelike consistency in one to two hours. Then the polystyrene is scooped out, leaving a negative space. The heavy molds next are moved to the nearby glass factory where twenty to fifty dippers of hot glass are ladled into them. The molds and their contents are placed in annealing ovens for about six weeks. Ben Tré then takes the annealed pieces back to his studio to grind, cut, and embellish with additions of metal.

The Glick collection has two works by Howard Ben Tré. *Pilaster #8* (from the "Pilaster" series) (1983), made at the Blenko Glass Factory, is number eight of ten in the series that was begun in 1982 and finished in 1987. The Glick piece was cast in white opal glass with the copper sheet details placed in the mold before the glass was ladled in. Imbued with Ben Tré's knowledge of architectural traditions and nomenclature, this work suggests a dialogue between classical forms and contemporary industrial imagery.

Second Vase (1989), made of cast glass, gold leaf, and bronze, is a full-scale sculptural work. Consisting of a circular form out of which rises a long neck, *Second Vase* evokes an ancient ritual object. The complementary and perfectly integrated shapes have a Cycladic clarity and totemic mystery. The glass tones from pale green to ocher, embellished only with gold leaf that runs down the center of the neck. The work is a masterpiece of restraint: the rough cast glass, its surface imperfections balanced by prefect proportions, demonstrates the powerful combination of art and archaeology that invigorates Ben Tré's work.

Howard Ben Tré is one of the few glass artists widely accepted by the larger art world. This recognition was spurred by Ben Tré's relationship with a well-known New York gallery, the Charles Cowles Gallery, during mid-1980s. Supported by gallery publications and museum shows (including the prestigious Phillips Gallery in Washington, DC), Ben Tré was introduced to collectors who usually purchased only paintings and sculpture executed in the more mainstream mediums. Ben Tré's powerful, intelligent, and beautiful works continue to be appreciated by both the studio-glass community and the larger art world.

Zoltán Bohus

Parabolic Composition, 1988
Laminated and metalized sheet glass, cut, and acid-etched
TWO PARTS
A: 6 x 7 x 12 inches (15.2 x 17.8 x 30.5 cm)
B: 10½ x 7½ x 7 inches (26.7 x 19.1 x 17.8 cm)
cat. 3

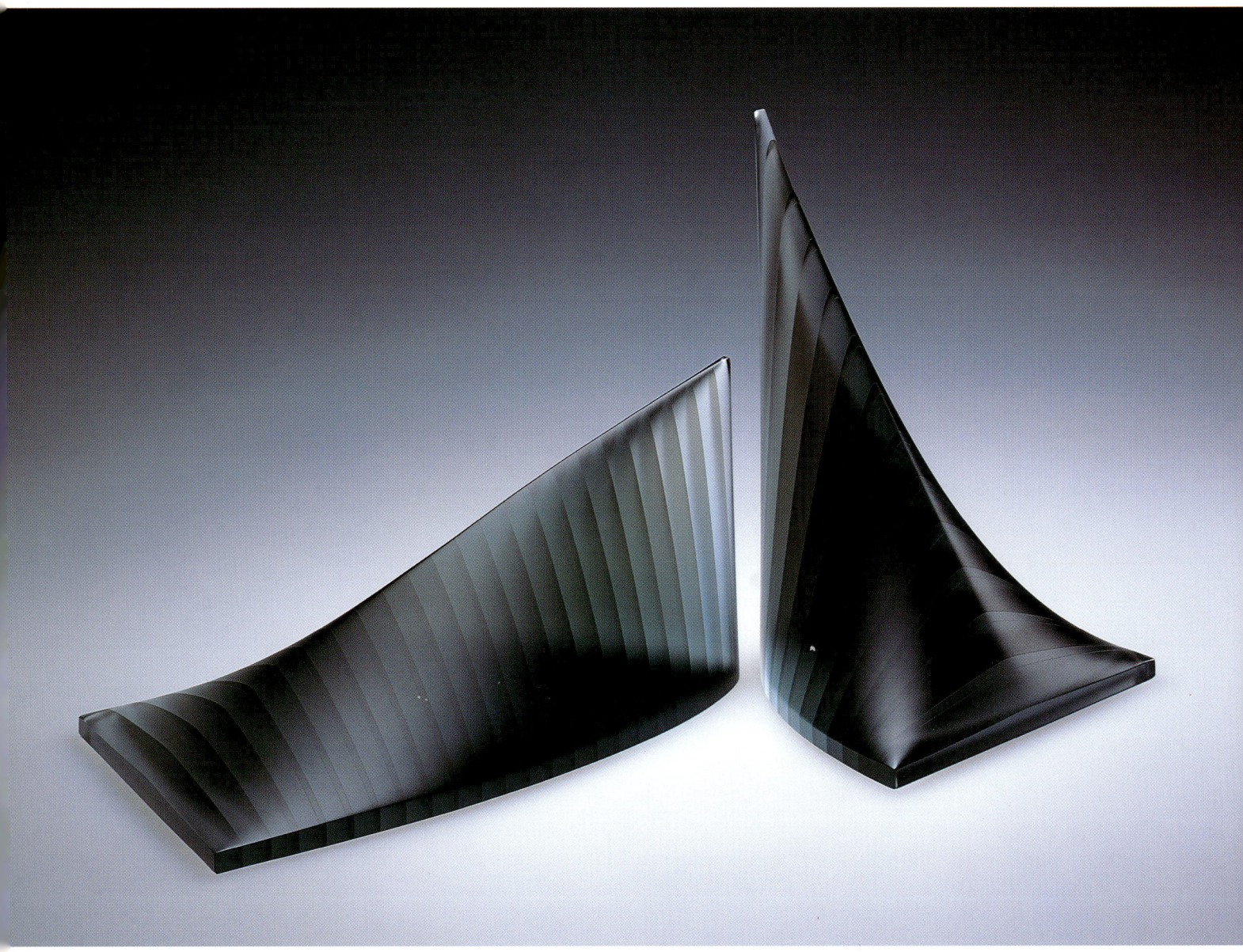

ZOLTÁN BOHUS

Hungarian, b. 1941

In his cold-worked glass sculptures, Zoltán Bohus explores inner and outer spaces as he embraces ambiguities of form and optics. One of the premier artists of Hungary, Bohus was a student of György Z. Gàcs (1914–1978) at the School of Applied Art in Budapest. There Bohus was exposed to Op, Minimalist, Constructivist, and kinetic art and these influences can still be seen in his work. Hot-glass shops are few in Hungary and this is reflected in Bohus's use of the cold-working techniques of anodizing, laminating, cutting, and polishing. His method also preserves the optical purity of the glass.[25] Working exclusively in sheet glass since 1968, Bohus embraces a Modernist approach that makes use of industrial materials and processes. His laminated structures investigate issues of shape, structure, proportion, and space, all within the matrix of inside/outside dichotomies.

Working in series, which in itself implies an analytical stance, Bohus manages to keep his pieces from being clinical. Although the forms are mathematically derived, the softness of their finish and the translucency of the glass infuse the sculptures with a sense of mystery. In his inquiries into inside/outside, Bohus derives his curves and contours from the Möbius strip, the nineteenth-century topologist's tool for rendering inside as outside.[26] This apparent denial of visual logic softens the flow and augments the mystery of Bohus's rigorous forms.

In *Parabolic Composition* (1988), Bohus created a dialogue of form between two related sections that come together to complete a whole. Bohus roughly cuts sheet glass to reveal the color and approximate the shape desired. Then he laminates the sheets together layer by layer with glue. Once the adhesive is dry, he uses a grindstone to smooth the contours. Finally he sandblasts and polishes the exterior. The layers of laminated glass operate as a never-ending hall of mirrors that is stabilized by its velvet exterior. Taking advantage of the green tinge inherent in sheet glass, Bohus reveals subtle nuances of color that range between the lightest tones to the darkest chromas. While heavily handcrafted, Bohus's works are emptied of all personal content and focus instead on the material, the play of inside/outside, and, in true Modernist fashion, make reference only to themselves.

JANE BRUCE

English, b. 1947

Jane Bruce describes her art as "a search for a place, both mental and physical; to create and through that to find and define a self."[27] She uses the vessel form for this self-exploration. An artist linked to three continents, Bruce was born and educated in Buckinghamshire, England. She then immigrated to the United States to stay for a decade and now lives in her third country, Australia. In 1970 she received her diploma in three-dimensional design and interior design from the City of Leicester Polytechnic, England. She planned to work in films and be a theatrical designer. However, a chance visit to her school by American studio-glass artist Sam Herman led to the installation of a glass furnace at the school and the appointment of glass artist John Cook to develop a glass program. Out of curiosity Bruce ventured into the glass studio and subsequently changed her goal to the study of glass.

Bruce applied for graduate work in glass at the Royal College of Art in London, and was turned down. With no other facility at her disposal, she began blowing glass at the newly established Glasshouse on Neal Street, London, which had been founded by Graham Hughes in 1969 as a place where graduates could work before setting up studios. Bruce applied again to the Royal College and was accepted in 1971.

At the Royal College, Bruce studied under Sam Herman who was working as a senior tutor in glass. Although she disliked him and his work— especially his "drop-it-on-the-floor-school-of-glass"— forming,[28] the antipathy helped her to establish her own sensibility. An exhibition of Finnish artist and designer Oiva Toikka's clean, fresh work was influential and established the foundation blocks for Bruce's own art.

While continuing to make hot glass at the Glasshouse, Bruce soon became involved in the running of the facility. Becoming part of a five-person ownership team, Bruce worked there from the early 1970s until 1977 when the Glasshouse moved to larger premises. Keeping the place growing and thriving was fun for Bruce, but after it became properly established, the challenge was gone and she wished to move on. In 1979 Bruce went to Alfred University, New York, to study as a special student with André Billeci, who urged her to move into sculpture. This transition was aided by exposure to works by James Turrell, Vito Acconci, Walter de Maria, and the Earth Art and Non-Sites of Robert Smithson. Not all of Bruce's time was spent on glass: she also worked with ceramist Wayne Higby, who helped to hone her vessel-form sensibility.

Bruce moved to New York and became attached to the New York Experimental Glass Workshop as an artist-in-residence. Once again she became involved with management and in 1992 she was named education director. But by 1994 Bruce was again restless; she accepted a position as a lecturer in glass at the Canberra School of Art, Australia. What began as a four-to-five-month stint matured into a three-year contract with an option for another three years. This opportunity at the leading glass school in Australia offered a steady job, a good location to complete her own work, and the collegial support of fellow faculty members and glass artists.

Positive/Negative (1990) is from Bruce's New York period. This classically pure vessel of blown glass is part of a series begun in 1979 that explores "vesselness." Bruce says that she had "deconstructed the vessel to its essential components: history and context, form and decoration, and I comment on each of these with oil paint, wheel-cutting, and engraving and gold leaf. The result is content that explores reality, vesselness, and random effects."[29] Using only cutting and gold leaf to decorate and articulate this form, Bruce encircled its belly with a frieze of baluster vases. Set on a register of gold, they shimmer and dance on their frosted background. The table-sized work has an elegance, intelligence, and clarity of vision that delight the eye and force the mind to contemplate the nature of a vessel.

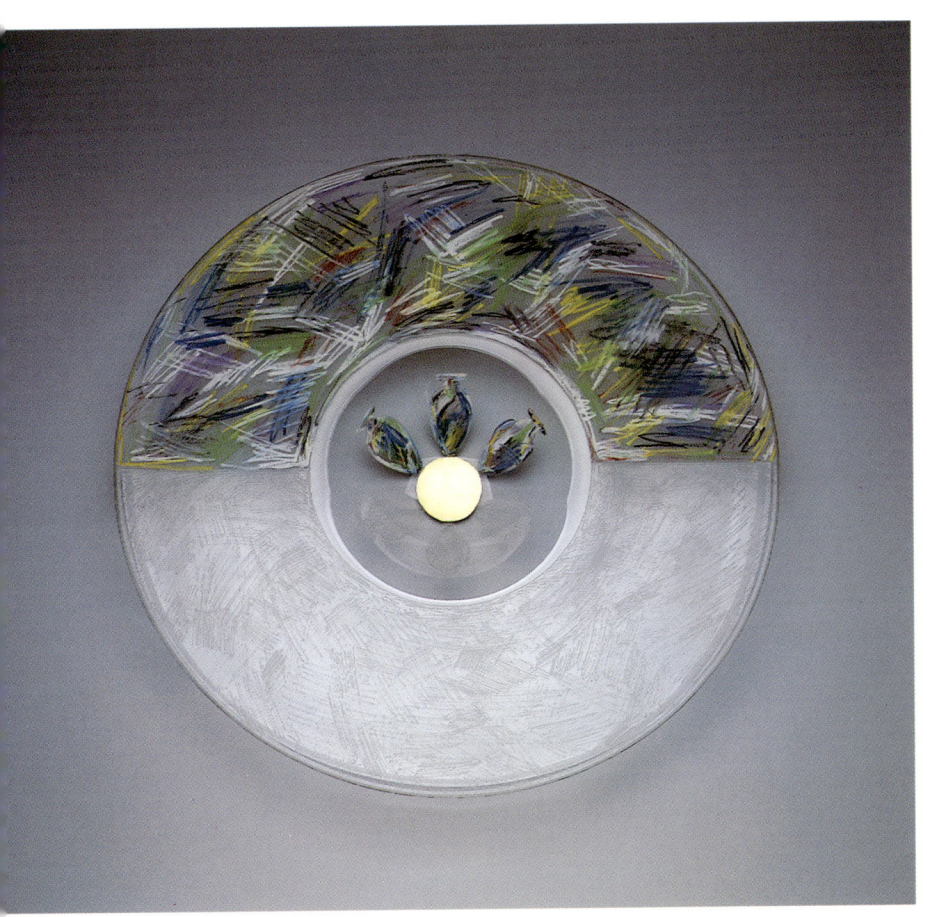

Jane Bruce

Positive/Negative, 1990
Blown glass with engraving, oil paint, and 23-karat gold leaf
3 1/2 x 28 1/2 dia. inches (8.9 x 72.4 cm)
cat. 4

ROBERT CARLSON

American, b. 1952

Robert (Bob) Carlson describes his blown and painted glass sculptures as "soulwork."[30] Carlson attended City College of New York from 1970 to 1973. Eight years later he began to make glass, taking in 1981 an apprentice position for glassblowing with Tom Philabaum in Tucson, Arizona. By 1983 he had become a partner in the Philabaum/Carlson studios where he remained until 1986. Also in 1981 Carlson traveled to Pilchuck Glass School in Stanwood, Washington, where he studied under glass artists Flora Mace and Joey Kilpatrick. During a later visit in 1983, Carlson worked with artist Bertil Vallien (cats. 63 and 64), from whom he learned how to blow into sand molds. This technique became Carlson's main forming method. Later he would add enamel painting to his work.

Enamel painting on glass is an old technique. By adding the further refinement of painting in reverse (*verre églomisé*), Carlson creates images that are intended to be seen from both the inside and the outside. He applies these painting methods to an underlying glass armature that he blows or casts with pulled-glass additions.

While he was not trained as a painter, Carlson's love for that medium comes from his decorating of plastic models as a child.[31] Because he layers pigment in intricate patterns and builds up images that interrelate, Carlson's work seems obsessively driven: all surfaces must be covered to complete his drive for expression. Carlson has been working in this labor-intensive method since 1985; his output is seldom more than ten pieces per year.

Carlson derives his conceptual imagery from a number of sources, chief among them the writings of pioneering psychologist Carl Jung and the explorations of mythologies and folklore by Joseph Campbell. He also has studied religious texts of both Western and Eastern origin. His own personal cosmology teases the viewer into parsing his work to decipher its meaning. Striving to find his voice and likening himself to a mystic, Carlson states that his work is the result of "a struggle to unite with [my] deep self. It is out of this mystic struggle that my work emerges. In a sense the work creates itself, wishes to express itself through me."[32] This quest began when Carlson saw the "primitive" works on display at the Museum of Anthropology in Victoria on Vancouver Island.[33] They seemed to Carlson to be a perfect expression of the unity of the spiritual and the real, and he has tried to capture these same elements in his own work.

The Glick collection's *Apis Arcana* (1988) is a complicated, two-part house form named for the *axis mundi* or the "central axis of the world." The base is decorated with enamels and gold leaf. The crowning gilded and painted obelisk is fashioned from blown glass shaped in one of Carlson's unique breakaway sand molds. Carlson has expanded the suggestion of a temple to encompass the notion of the temple of the body: the door and windows correlate to ears, eyes, and mouth. Taken a step further, they represent "ideas, emotion, intuition, instincts."34 As the *axis mundi* is the central point in existence, it is also known as the still point of the world. For Carlson the cacophony of color and forms presented creates a peaceful unity—a contradictory notion that appears almost Hegelian in its melding of two antithetical ideas to create a dichotomous synthesis.

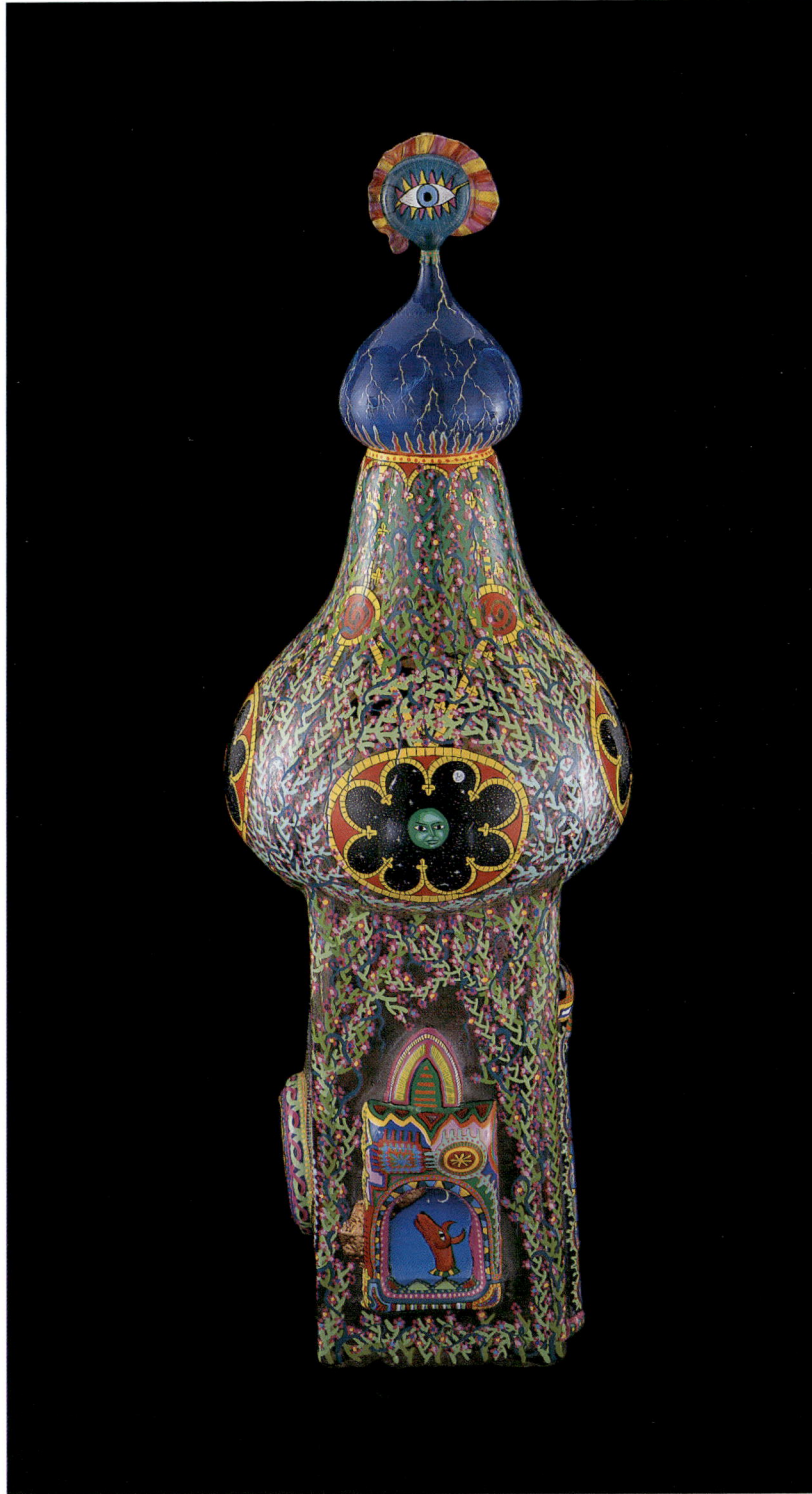

Robert Carlson

Apis Arcana, 1988
Free and mold-blown glass with painted decoration
30 x 9 x 9 inches (76.2 x 22.9 x 22.9 cm)
cat. 5

SYDNEY CASH

American, b. 1941

Sydney Cash kiln-slumps glass into forms that track the transformation of glass from a solid to just short of a liquid state. Born in Detroit, Cash received his Bachelor of Science degree in mathematics from Detroit's Wayne State University, where he also studied metallurgy and physics. Shortly after graduating he started a business reproducing architectural details and ornamental oddities. Moving to New York's Greenwich Village in 1970, Cash developed a line of decorative mirrors that incorporate architectural elements as frames, which he marketed through his wholesale shop, Gargoyles. Although he viewed himself as a hippie—and still relishes being "far out"—Cash had a conventional fascination with the impact that technical inventions have on everyday life. As a child he had loved visiting the Henry Ford Museum in Dearborn, Michigan, and was especially drawn to the Wright brothers' work benches, which he would touch when the guards were not looking.[35]

One day while fitting a mirror into its frame, Cash decided to curve the mirror by applying heat. Needing technical advice, he contacted pioneering glass artist Maurice Heaton,[36] who provided guidance and showed Cash how to build a kiln. Bedazzled by the transformation of glass from a liquid to a solid state, Cash soon became aware of the potential of glass as an art medium. With no formal glass education or specific art training, he set out to explore its mutability.

At the end of 1977, Cash had his first glass show, at the Hundred Acres in Soho, New York. By this time he had closed his production business and devoted himself full-time to glass. He was also increasingly aware of its ability to express both a spiritual and psychic sensibility. His early works, such as *Untitled* (1983), feature slumped-glass forms "frozen" at a point that implies a continual evolution toward a liquid state. Formed by slumping glass over a wire frame, this small piece achieves its drama by "freeze framing" the glass as it moves from a solid to a taffylike state. Here the blue glass, mysteriously held in place, allows the heated material literally to drip into a sculptural form.

Cash's later works of the mid-1980s were made possible by a technical breakthrough. Using computer-graphic imagery applied first to the industrial material FLUTEX, and then to commercial plate glass,[37] Cash created optically kinetic works that rely on graphic, linear precision and the play of oscillating lines. Often constrained in rigid frames that serve as foils to his optical wizardry, these later works are activated optically when the viewer moves around them. Here Cash felt that he was approaching his goal of being able to espress the ineffable. An injury to his right hand in 1993 interrupted his progress and led to a period of enforced reflection that resulted in the recognition that his "work now feels less bound to [his] ego—[and that] anything seems possible."[38]

Sydney Cash

Untitled, 1983
Sandblasted plate glass with wire armature
11 1/2 x 5 1/4 x 6 inches (29.2 x 13.3 x 15.2 cm)
cat. 6

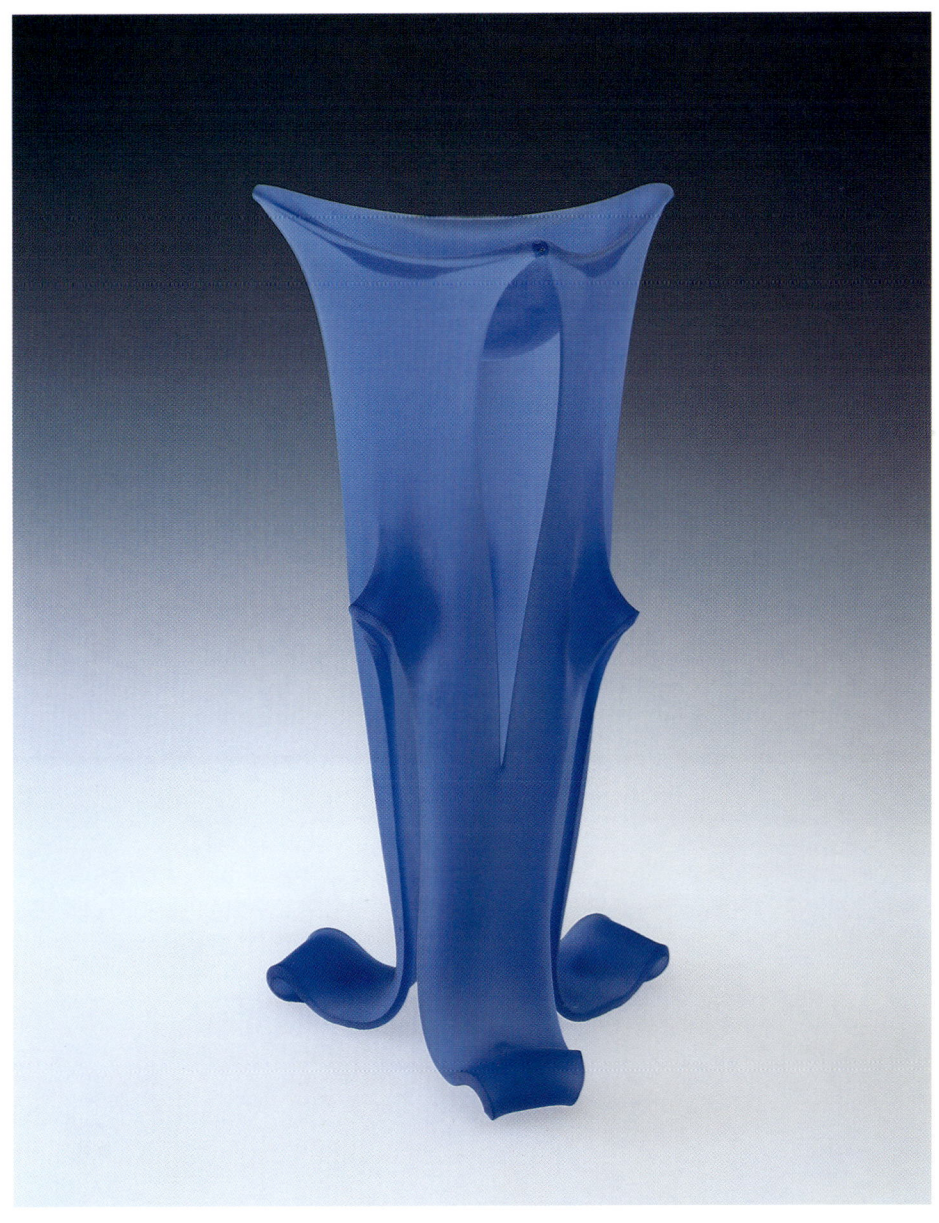

Dale Chihuly

Untitled (from the "Macchia" series), 1982
Blown and altered glass
9 x 15 1/2 x 14 inches (22.9 x 39.4 x 35.6 cm)
cat. 7

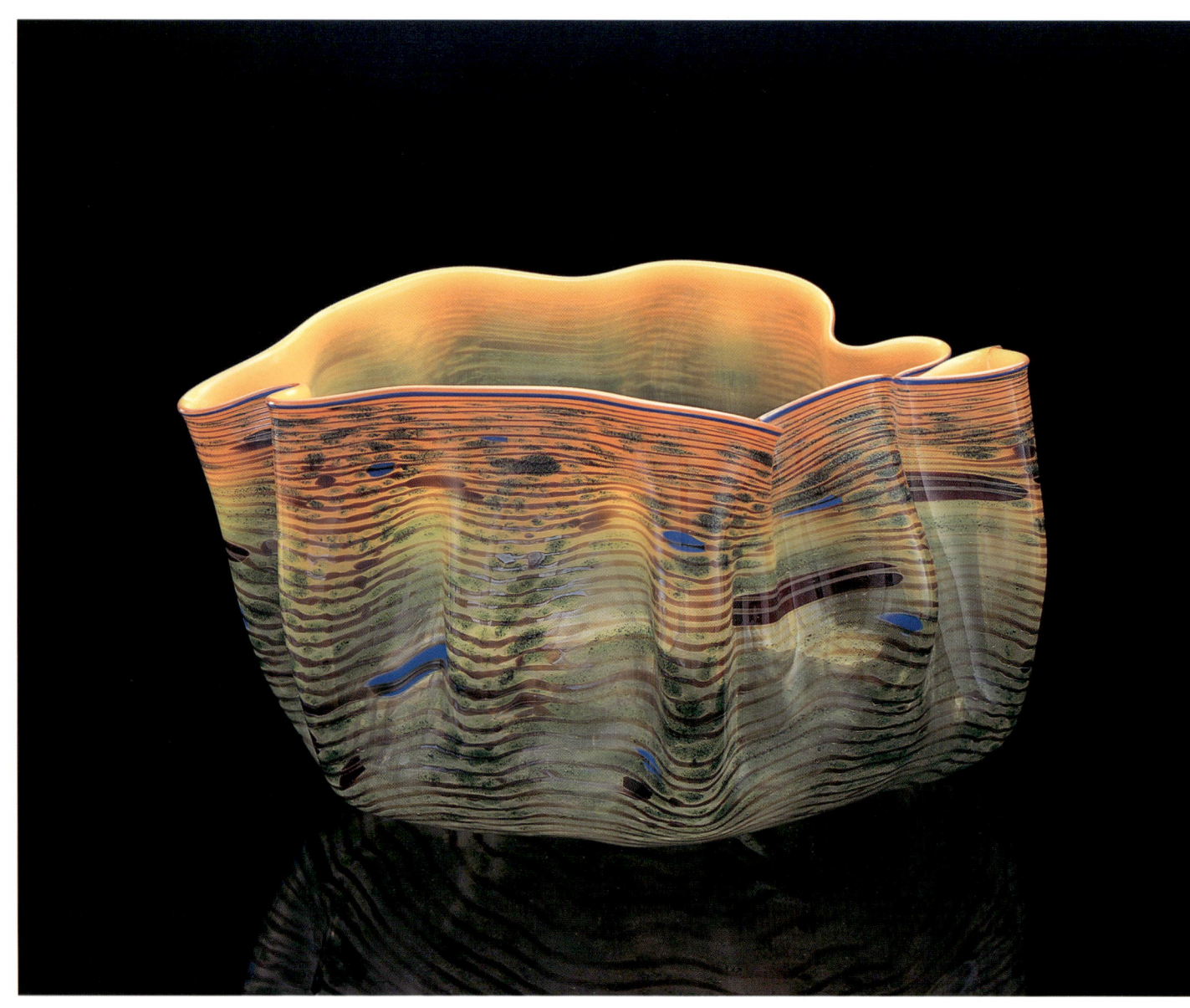

DALE CHIHULY

American, b. 1941

Dale Patrick Chihuly is a charismatic glass artist who makes lushly colored, blown biomorphic objects. His high-energy personality has been responsible for the broad international acceptance of both himself and the American studio-glass movement. Born in Tacoma, Washington, the son of a butcher who was an ardent union supporter, Chihuly came to glass in the mid-1960s just as American glass was being invigorated by the Toledo Workshops. After studying interior design at the University of Washington, Seattle, Chihuly took a year off and traveled to Europe and the Middle East. In 1962 he reentered school and began experimenting with glass, weaving wall hangings that incorporate glass filaments.

In 1965 Chihuly began work as a designer at John Graham Architects in Seattle, but his interest in glass continued and with the encouragement of fellow artist Russell Day, Chihuly received a scholarship to study with Harvey Littleton (cats. 28 and 29) at the University of Wisconsin, Madison. To earn the necessary money, Chihuly worked on a commercial salmon trawler in Alaska during the summer before he left for Wisconsin. Finishing his Master of Science degree in 1967, he moved on to the Master of Fine Arts program at the Rhode Island School of Design, Providence, where he received a teaching assistantship. At this time most of his work was in neon and environmental installations, but in Providence he met the Italian glass artist Italo Scanga and his love affair with Italian glass techniques began in earnest.

Upon completion of his master's degree in 1968, Chihuly received an award from the Tiffany Foundation in recognition of his glassmaking to date and a Fulbright-Hays Fellowship to study glass in Italy. While at the prestigious Venini Glass Factory (Venini e C.) on Murano island, he designed objects that were not put into production. During the summer Chihuly taught at Haystack Mountain School in Maine, returning in the fall to travel throughout Europe. Among others he met artists Jaroslava Brychtová and Stanislav Libenský and Erwin Eisch (cats. 23 and 24 and 12). He then returned to the Rhode Island School of Design to head up the glass department. Joined by glass artist Jamie Carpenter, Chihuly spent the early 1970s collaborating with him and continuing with neon and installation art.

It was at Haystack that Chihuly realized the importance of ongoing glassmaking opportunities for the glass artist. He dreamed of establishing a facility like Haystack in the West. In 1972 he and Ruth Tamura, chairman of the Glass Department at the California College of Arts and Crafts in Oakland, received a $2,000 grant from the Union of Independent Colleges of Art to establish a summer program in glass. With the additional support of art patrons John and Anne Gould Hauberg, Chihuly and Tamura established the Pilchuck Glass School on the Haubergs' tree farm near Stanwood, north of Seattle.[39] Starting as a ragtag adventure with sixteen students sleeping on the ground, Pilchuck now provides a venue for glass artists from all over the world to meet, work, and learn from each other.

In 1975, in addition to his neon and installation work with Carpenter, Chihuly started a series of smaller pieces (working with Kate Elliot and Flora Mace) called "Blanket Cylinders." Incorporating imagery drawn from Navajo blankets and later Native American baskets, these forms are loose and colorful, charged with a spontaneity Chihuly had seen in Italy. As luck would have it, three of the next "Blanket series" were acquired by Henry Geldzahler, then curator of Contemporary Art at New York's Metropolitan Museum of Art. This acquisition gave Chihuly welcome acknowledgment and larger-art-world exposure. In the late 1980s Chihuly returned to the cylinder concept. *Untitled* (from the "Soft Cylinder" series) (1987) is from these later iterations (ill. p. 24). As with all of this series, there is drawing by Flora Mace.

In 1976 an automobile accident cost Chihuly the sight in his left eye. Unable to establish proper depth perception, he was forced to cease blowing glass. However, because he had always worked in a collaborative manner, his production was not affected. By being "the guy up front with the baton"[40] and working with the best gaffers, Chihuly moved in a new direction for his glassmaking: controlling the outcome proved more gratifying than being just one of the group.

Two aspects of working glass have been important for Chihuly. The first was breaking the tyranny of the blowpipe. Most blown forms have a relentless sense of center, but Chihuly disrupts that logic and creates off-centered forms. Secondly, he has a brilliant and daring sense of color, which he expresses through glass' miraculous ability to transmit hues. These two qualities allow Chihuly to express his theatrical nature, evident, for example, in *Untitled* (from the "Macchia" series) (1982).

"Macchia" is Italian for "stain" or "spot." This series consists of vessels constructed of layers of glass, with the interior flesh-colored and the exterior executed in vivid colors modulated with daubs (spots) of color. Blown into open molds with patterned interiors (optic molds), the forms are loose and casual, appearing to be soft and inviting to the touch. This illusion of tactile accessibility is one of Chihuly's hallmarks.

Chihuly has been described variously as having a "Warholesque genius for self-promotion," and of being a "glass leprechaun" and a master of theatricality who provides "if nothing else…pretty good theater."[41] While not all of the comments are complimentary, Dale Chihuly has brought American studio glass to the attention of a large public and given them a name that they remember. He has also been accepted by the larger art world and is one of only two American glass artists who have had solo shows at the Musée du Louvre in Paris.[42] His energy, art, and showmanship have expanded the presence of the American studio-glass movement internationally.

KÉKÉ CRIBBS

American, b. 1951

Kéké Cribbs is a multimedia artist who uses glass as an integral part of her polymorphous playthings. Born in Colorado Springs, Colorado, Cribbs is a largely self-taught artist. Difficulty in school led to a sense of isolation that bred a passion in her for artistic expression. With few friends, she came to depend on her fantasy world for companionship.[43] In 1966, when she was fifteen years old, Cribbs and her family moved to Ireland where her mother studied the poetry of William Butler Yeats. During the ten years of European travel that followed, the family enjoyed art museums, concerts, avant-garde literature, and other cultural activities. This eclectic education made Cribbs comfortable with diverse cultures and open to inspiration by all media, styles, and idioms. She returned to the United States in 1976 and in 1979 moved to Santa Fe, New Mexico.

Cribbs was enthralled by Santa Fe's adobe architecture and Native American and Spanish culture. She particularly liked such festivals as the Zozobra, which celebrates happy times by burning a large effigy of "old man gloom."[44] At this time, when Cribbs was considering writing children's books, she became aware of the art of the Mimbres Indians and their joy in honoring the everyday acts of life. The exposure helped to clarify her thinking and moved her toward constructing narratives through pictures and decorative elements. Adapting the Mimbres graphic style, Cribbs drew everyday items such as skateboards, laundromats, and lounging cowboys, transforming the mundane into the emblematic. In her first art show, at Dewey Kofon Gallery in Santa Fe, Cribbs was part of a two-person exhibition with Fred Myers entitled "Mimbres and Moderns." While the show was on view, Cribbs was offered a commission for glass designs for use in a kitchen.[45] Intrigued by the project and the material, Cribbs discovered glass to be a compelling medium.

While not formally trained in glass (or any other mediums), Cribbs needed to acquire basic skills in order to complete the project. She first explored blowing glass, but the method did not come naturally to her and she also experienced resistance to her entering that male-dominated world. Instead, by the early 1980s she had developed supportive friends within the glass movement, especially Therman Statom and Richard Marquis (cats. 60 and 61 and 30–34). Statom shared

Kéké Cribbs

Baudino (from the "Scarecrow" series), 1992
Carved and painted wood with canvas and sandblasted plate glass
41 x 24 x 5 inches (104.1 x 61 x 12.7 cm)
cat. 9

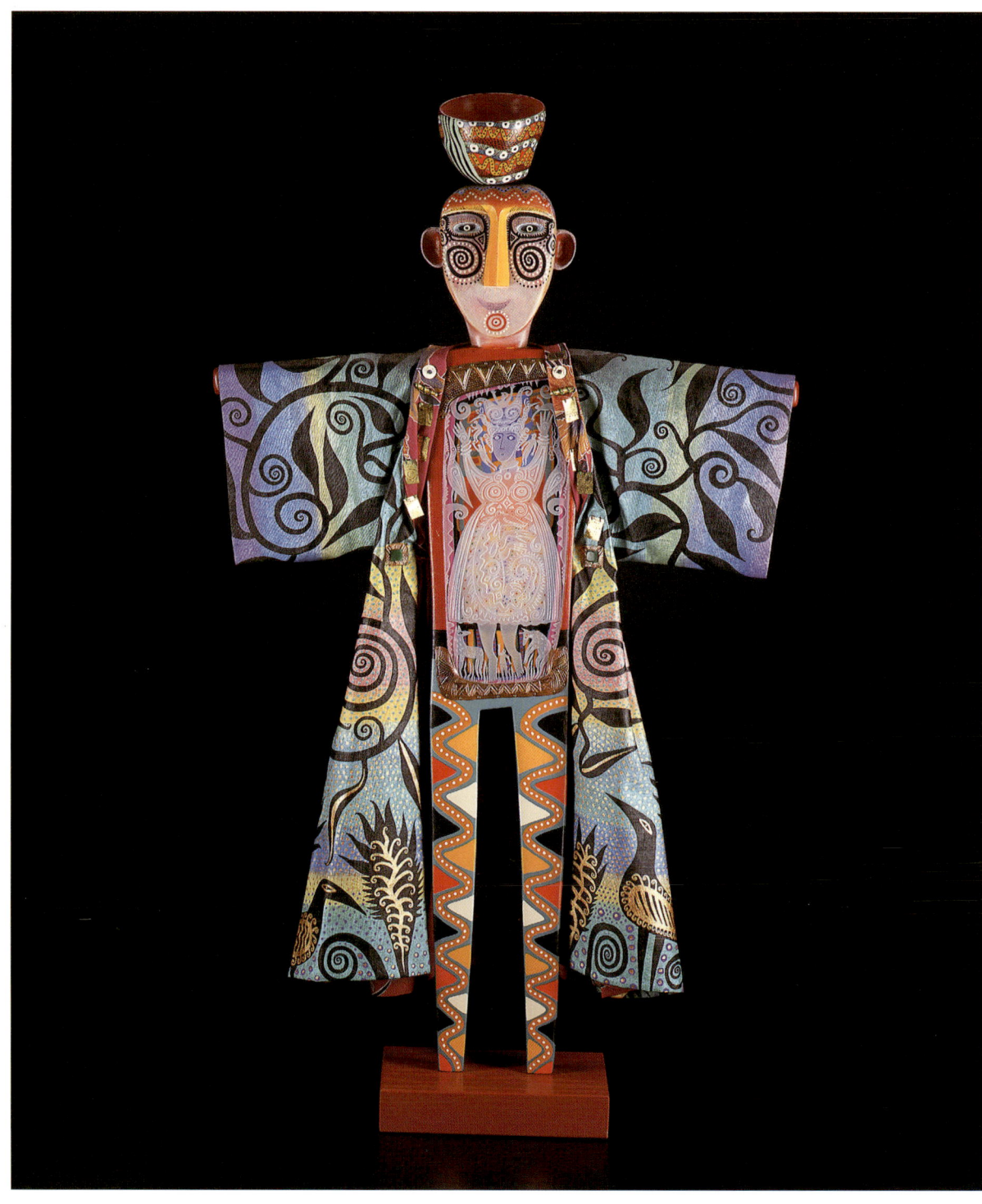

Cribbs's sensibility and Marquis's glassblowing gave her the building blocks for her art. Cribbs was also inspired by artists Klaus Moje, Dan Dailey, and Bertil Vallien (cats. 35–37, 10 and 11, and 63 and 64).[46] In 1985 she had a show at Foster/White Gallery in Seattle, and a year later was invited to teach glass at the Swain School for Design in Bedford, Maine. During her three years there, she honed her skills in metal and woodworking. She also began to incorporate plate glass in her work.

Having worked on a series of multimedia boat forms, Cribbs began to make figurative sculpture. The early abstracted ovoids were inspired by New Guinea art forms. Subsequent experiments involved placing sandblasted plate-glass images over painted grounds. Scarecrow forms followed. Cribbs explained that she "always thought crows had a rather bad rap...and scarecrows have the disagreeable job of standing lonely through the summer heat waves and dust storms desiring the wonderful bad company of crows, a sentry to man's overwhelming desire to conquer nature."[47] Over time the figures became more polished and personalized with integrated patterns and elaborate fabric robes.

Baudino (from the "Scarecrow" series) (1992) features a bowl balanced on its head and is dressed in a painted linen kimono. The figure is emblazoned with Cribbs's simple, nearly primitive, drawing style. The flat body is literally and metaphorically a window into the identity of Baudino. Leaving the viewer to a personal interpretation of symbols, this piece presents two contrasting self-images, the decorative exterior and the more complex interior "window." The inner window is rendered by stage blasting (or depth carving) images into plate glass that has been covered with contact paper. By cutting though successive layers, the image is slowly built up. Drawing from form vocabularies seen in ancient art, Chinese, folk, and ethnographic art, Cribbs builds her work into a richly patterned play of shapes that delight the eye and bring a smile of recognition and amusement to the viewer. In 1995 Cribbs began painting on glass in conjunction with her engraving and sandblasting of nature-derived images.

Dan Dailey

Athena (from the "Mythology Head Vase" series), 1989
Blown glass with applied elements
18 1/2 x 11 x 11 inches (47 x 27.9 x 27.9 cm)
cat. 10

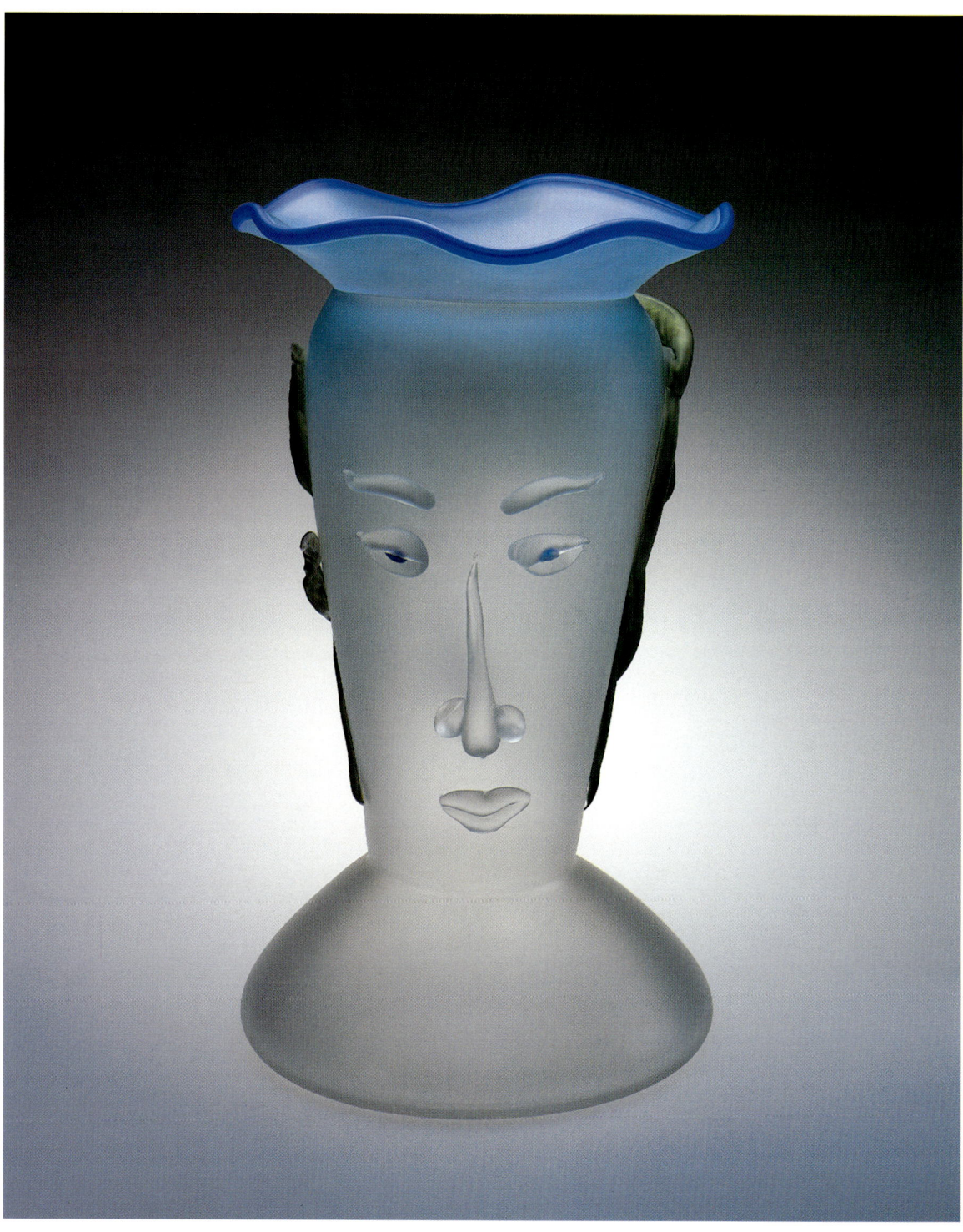

DAN DAILEY

American, b. 1947

Dan Dailey's elegant, refined works chronicle the foibles of human nature. A Philadelphia native, Dailey worked in ceramics from 1967 until 1969 at the Philadelphia College of Art where he studied with William Daley and Richard Reinhardt. Dailey absorbed the former's geometric sensibility, which accorded well with his own predilection for sophisticated, graphically rendered images. While still in school and working in ceramics, Dailey received a grant to set up a glass studio, which involved building most of the equipment. Once the project was completed, Dailey made the transition to glass and was "hooked on glass; no going back."[48]

The lure was multiple. First, glass has a deluxe quality that the rougher clay could not equal. Also, many clay-working techniques were transferable to glass: for example, throwing a pot harnesses centrifugal force and gravity—the same two factors at work when forming glass on the end of a blowpipe. Aesthetically Dailey preferred glass because of its shine and sparkle, qualities that attracted him to his other favorite medium, metal: "I suppose it's similar to the reason I like drawing in ink over drawing with a crayon; I don't find the clarity that I'm looking for in the line. I believe there is a certain quality of form that I can achieve with glass that I can't with clay."[49]

Because Dailey began working in glass when studio glass was in its infancy, there was little relevant technical expertise for him to rely on. Consequently, he observed anything formed out of glass to see if he could figure out how it was made. This intense process of looking made Dailey realize the potential that glass had for personal expression.

After receiving his undergraduate degree, Dailey did a stint drawing for Zap Comics. His ability to capture the essence of a thought, emotion, or action became the backbone of his art (see fig. 2). This also honed his skill at effectively conveying his ideas to a staff of assistants.

Seeking additional art education, Dailey went to the Rhode Island School of Design in Providence for his Master of Fine Arts degree, becoming the first to graduate from the nascent glass program led by Dale Chihuly (cats. 7 and 8). Adept at combining diverse form vocabularies, Dailey found inspiration in the historical styles of Art Nouveau and Art Deco, as well as 1950s Italian furniture. To further expand his repertoire, in 1972 Dailey took a Fulbright-Hays Fellowship to

Dan Dailey

Study, 1989
Vitrolite with stainless steel and gold-plated brass
26 x 20½ x 5 inches (66 x 52.1 x 12.7 cm)
cat. 11

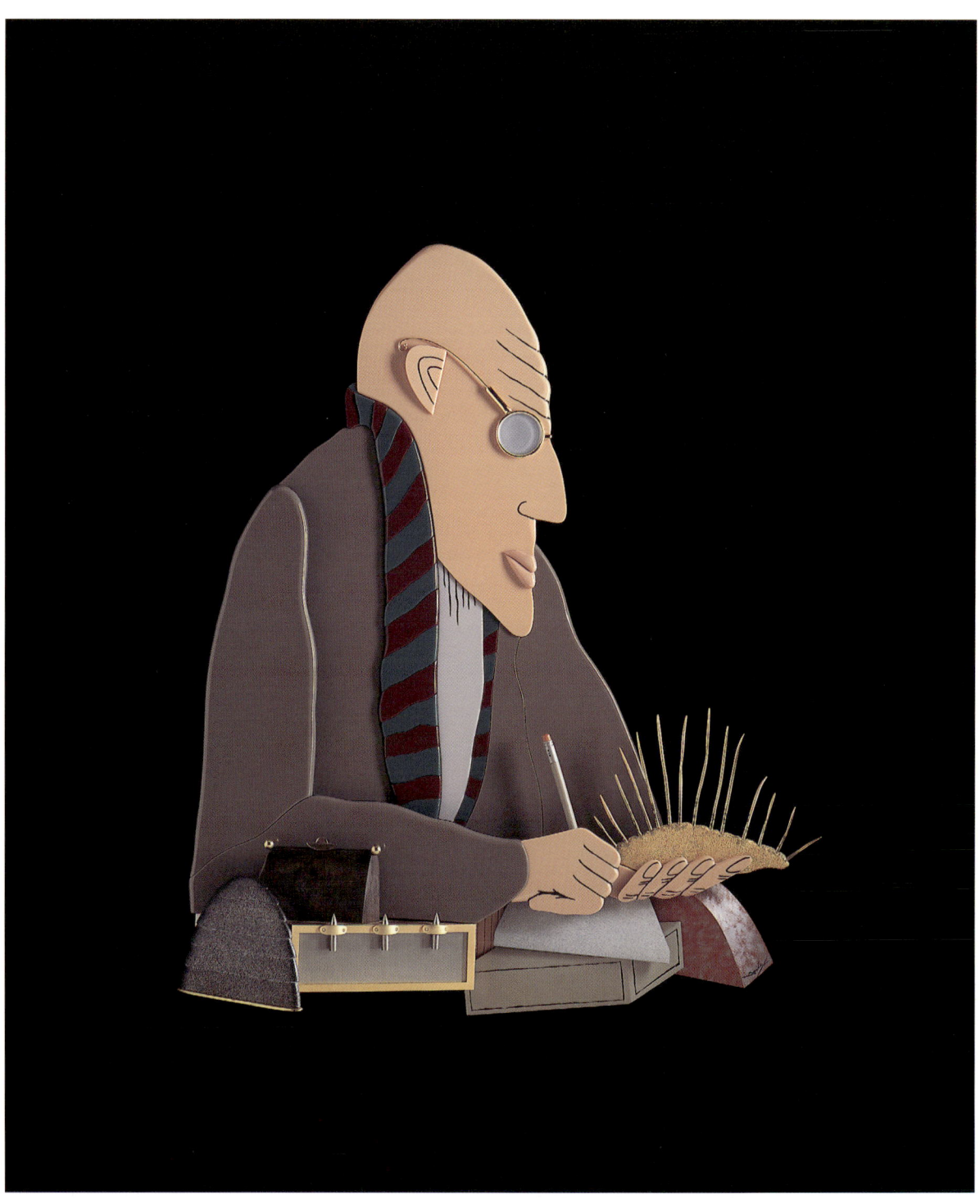

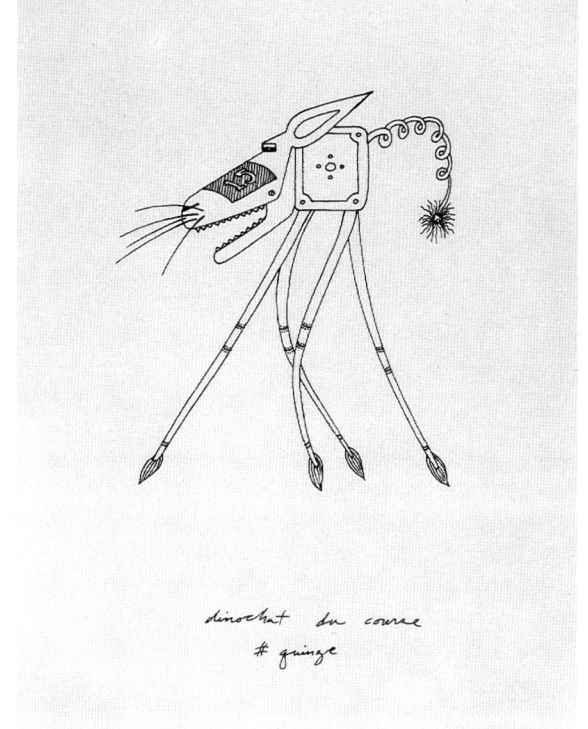

FIG. 2

Dan Dailey
American, b. 1947

Dinochat, 1996
Ink on paper
14¼ x 11 inches (36.2 x 27.9 cm)
Courtesy the artist

Murano, Italy, where he worked as a designer in the Venini Glass Factory (Venini e C.) in 1972. This trip and a subsequent one to France opened Dailey's eyes to the historical heritage and respect that glassblowing had within the European tradition. Two years later he again went to France and worked as a designer and independent artist for the Cristallerie Daum in Nancy. Known for its late nineteenth-century art glass, Daum made art-glass multiples that were based on designs by artists and designers. Most of their production features cased and colored glass and etching with hydrofluoric acid. The techniques learned there are evident in Dailey's work today.

In 1973 Dailey founded the glass program at the Massachusetts College of Art in Boston. Ten years later he left to concentrate on his own work. He describes himself as an observer, who notes the "oddities" of human nature that he sees around him.50 Dailey's restless, questioning spirit thrives on challenges: he is intrigued by translating new concepts into three-dimensional objects.

The Glick collection contains two pieces by Dailey from 1989. *Athena* is part of a twenty-two-piece series of "mythological" vessel-based forms made from 1989 through 1992. Unlike the previous "Head Vases," this group incorporates colored glass and features multicolor fades that mimic the liquid aspect of glass formation. Each sculptural glass "bust" represents a character from Greek mythology, filtered through Dailey's own late twentieth-century response to the original myths. Eschewing the layered meanings associated with Athena, Dailey turned the notion on its head and presented the viewer with a cartoon in glass.

Study (1989) depicts a balding, middle-aged man in a smoking jacket with a pen in his hand. Here Dailey has played on the several meanings of the word "study": a casual sketch, a place to enjoy a good cigar, and a character study. Dailey delivers all three in this work. This Vitrolite wall relief illustrates Dailey's skill and delight in working shiny, deluxe surfaces. Fabricated with stainless steel and gold-plated brass by Dailey's skilled assistants, the piece captures the self-satisfaction of the dilettante. While piquant in its commentary, the work relies on graphically rendered forms usually found in comics and other popular media; its technical virtuosity is leavened by Dailey's elegance and humor.

ERWIN EISCH

German, b. 1927

Erwin Eisch is a painter and a sculptor in glass. Born in the glassmaking town of Frauenau in Bavaria, Eisch came from a family that had made glass for 270 years. During World War II, Eisch had served for three months in the army when he was captured by the British and spent the rest of the war as a prisoner. After the war he returned to Frauenau and studied engraving with his father Valentin Eisch, a noted glass engraver, and attended the school for glassmaking in Zweisel. By 1949 he had completed a seven-year program and passed his journeyman's examination. Wishing to expand his artistic expression, Eisch attended the Akademie der Bildenden Künste in Munich (1956–59) where he focused on painting, sculpture, and industrial design.

His professors encouraged Eisch to embrace the Bauhaus philosophy which prized the machine aesthetic, abstracted forms, and the absence of color. Feeling that this aesthetic was linked to the contemporary sense of alienation, Eisch rebelled. For him the figurative, expressive, and colorful were life-affirming attributes of artistic expression.

In 1952 Eisch began working with his brothers to blow the blanks needed for their factory production. Preferring to work as a master designer in the factory, Eisch knew the various forming technologies, including blowing. Always aware of the larger-art-world trends, Eisch belonged to the *Spur* group in Munich and eventually helped to found the related *Radama* group.[51] An advocate for the return to the human roots of art, Eisch at one of his exhibitions in Munich placed a sign on the wall that read: "Don't let yourself be lowered by a thing's purpose or function."[52] Eisch believes that glass is about human expression, not technique.

In 1962 Eisch met Harvey Littleton (cats. 28 and 29) during Littleton's early European travels. As Eisch recounted it, Littleton found him "with glass in one hand and poetry in the other."[53] This first meeting sparked a friendship that continues today. Both men believe in the sculptural potential of glass and were impatient with the focus on technical expertise. In 1964 Eisch came to the United States and spent six weeks in Madison, helping Littleton set up a new glassblowing department at the University of Wisconsin. Happy to be part of what Eisch termed the "Renaissance in glass art"[54] that was occurring in the United States, he has returned

Erwin Eisch

Buddha, 1988
Mold-blown glass with paint and gold leaf
21 1/2 x 7 1/2 x 7 inches (54.6 x 19 x 17.8 cm)
cat. 12

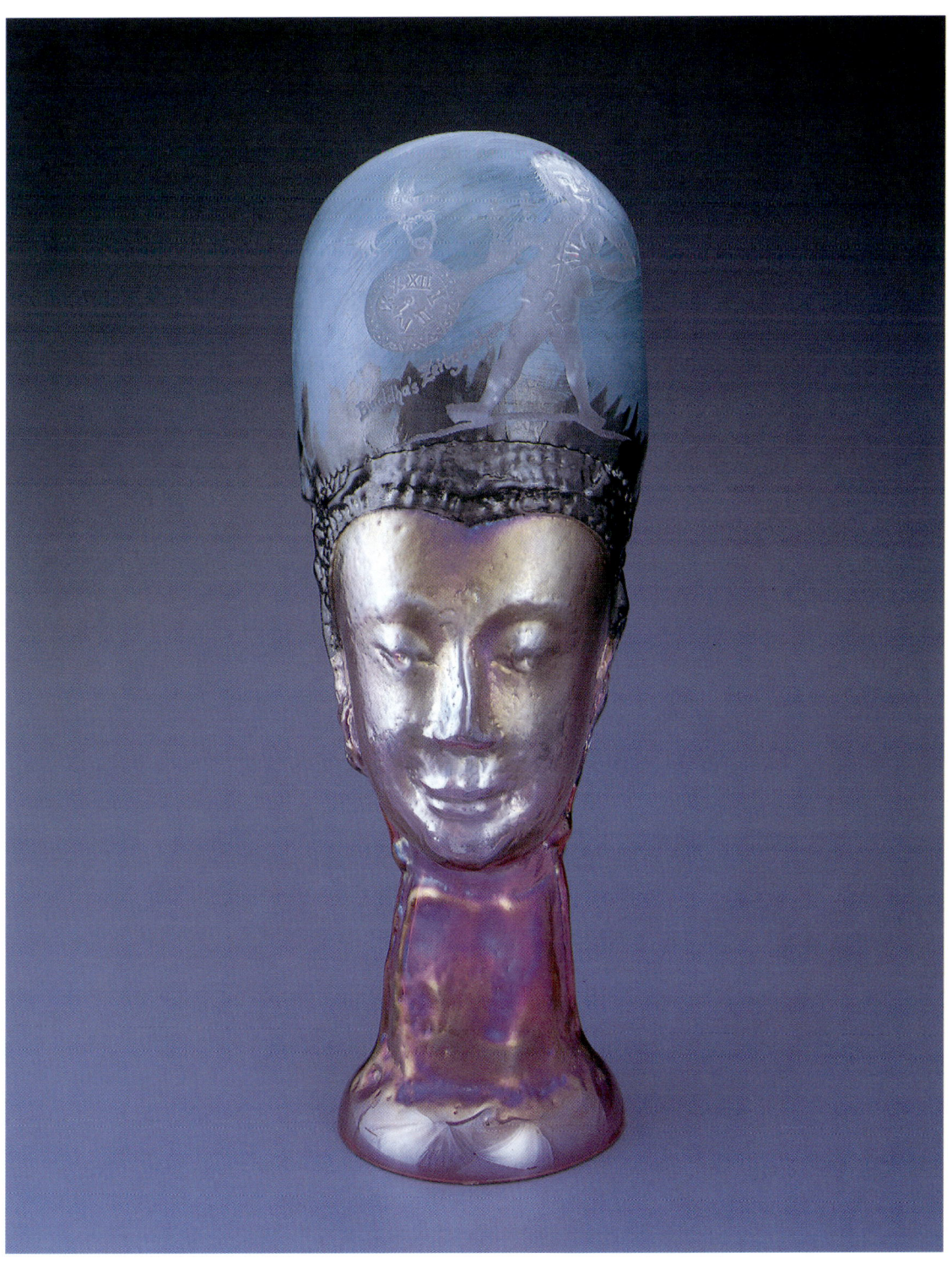

FIG. 3

Erwin Eisch
German, b. 1927

Telefon (Telephone), 1971
Mold-blown, manipulated glass with gold luster decoration
6 x 7 x 8 inches (15 x 17.5 x 20.2 cm)
The Corning Museum of Glass, New York

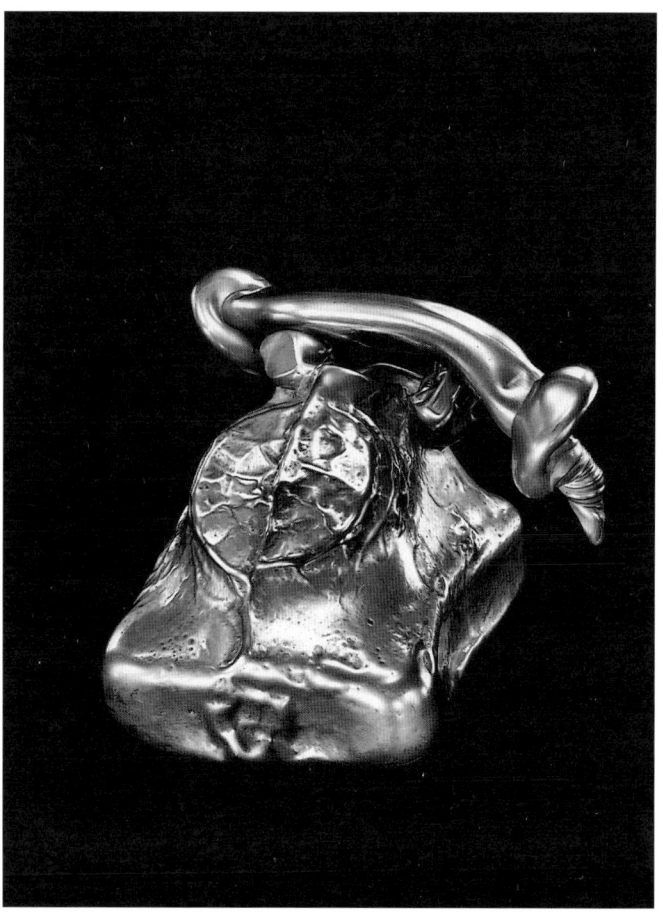

many times to work with Littleton and to teach American glassmakers.

Eisch's work reflects the tenets of German Expressionism and Surrealism. He uses figuration, vibrant color, and casually crafted forms; his glass sculptures of the early 1970s are Funk in sensibility and combine Claes Oldenburg's appropriation of everyday forms with the melting images derived from Salvador Dali (see fig. 3). In fact, Eisch's aesthetic is closer to that of the larger-art-world sculptors than to glass practice. He has not been seduced by the beauty of glass, but instead has chosen to obscure it by painting over its shiny surface. His passion for the human figure also reflects the long European tradition that has prized figuration over abstraction.

Buddha (1988), from a series of mold-blown portrait busts, uses a clay mold customized so that each blow creates a unique bust. Taking advantage of the fact that the mold is struck off the form while the glass is still soft, Eisch then alters the form. After annealing this piece, he engraved figures on the skull that depict men and women caught in the relentless cycle of life and death. The forms, shown at twilight, are suspended between light and dark. As with all of Eisch's work, whether lithographs, paintings, or glass sculptures, this piece is challenging intellectually, engaging visually, and addresses human issues that haunt us all.

KYOHEI FUJITA

Japanese, b. 1921

Kyohei Fujita, Japan's preeminent studio-glass artist, was originally attracted to glass while in junior high school, because "you can see results very quickly indeed."[55] Fujita received a degree from the Department of Metal Engraving at the Tokyo School of Fine Art. Related to the 1930s pioneer studio glassmaker Tochichi Iwata, Fujita is certain to have seen Iwata's works as a young man.[56] Appropriately, his first job after graduation was with the industrial-glass manufactory Iwata Glass Co., where he worked for two years.

Just before World War II, Fujita participated in the founding of the influential Mahani Craft Circle. The Mahani Circle believed in creative art objects that were also utilitarian. Fujita remained a member until 1956, leaving the group because he felt it was focused too tightly on traditional crafts at the expense of newer ones.

In 1949 Fujita opened his own independent glass studio, despite limited technical knowledge of glassblowing and no assured income. Slowly he taught himself a variety of glassmaking skills. As he worked to make beautiful and useful objects, he was rewarded with a one-person exhibition at the Matsuzakaya Department Store in Tokyo in 1957. The early vessel-format artworks were small, blown pieces that display a variety of decorative schemes including multicolored glass inclusions, gold-leaf sections, layers of casings, and contrasting trailed-glass festoons with captured metallic accents (see fig. 4). These intricate pieces were sandblasted to impart a soft texture.

By the mid-1960s Fujita was making vessel-based "ryudo" organic forms (see fig. 5), "that reference Roman cage cups."[57] "Ryudo" is a race against time in which the glass is brought to the melting point and then its movement is arrested. This interest in using glass' liquid-to-solid progression dovetails with the long-standing Japanese passion for the effects of "anima."[58] This technique was not attempted in American studio glass until a decade later. Only Erwin Eisch (cat. 12) rivals the range of technique and craftsmanship seen in Fujita's work. In the 1980s Fujita returned to the "ryudo" technique.

In 1975 Fujita was included in the "International Studio Glass" exhibition and conference held in Copenhagen. This first international exposure began a long series of contacts with the Western glass community and made American artists aware of the interesting work being done in Japan. In November 1977 Fujita traveled to Murano to

Kyohei Fujita

Red and White Plum Blossoms, 1990
Mold-blown glass, cut, polished, and acid-etched,
with platinum and gold foil, and sterling-silver
6 x 5 x 5 inches (15.2 x 12.7 x 12.7 cm)
cat. 13

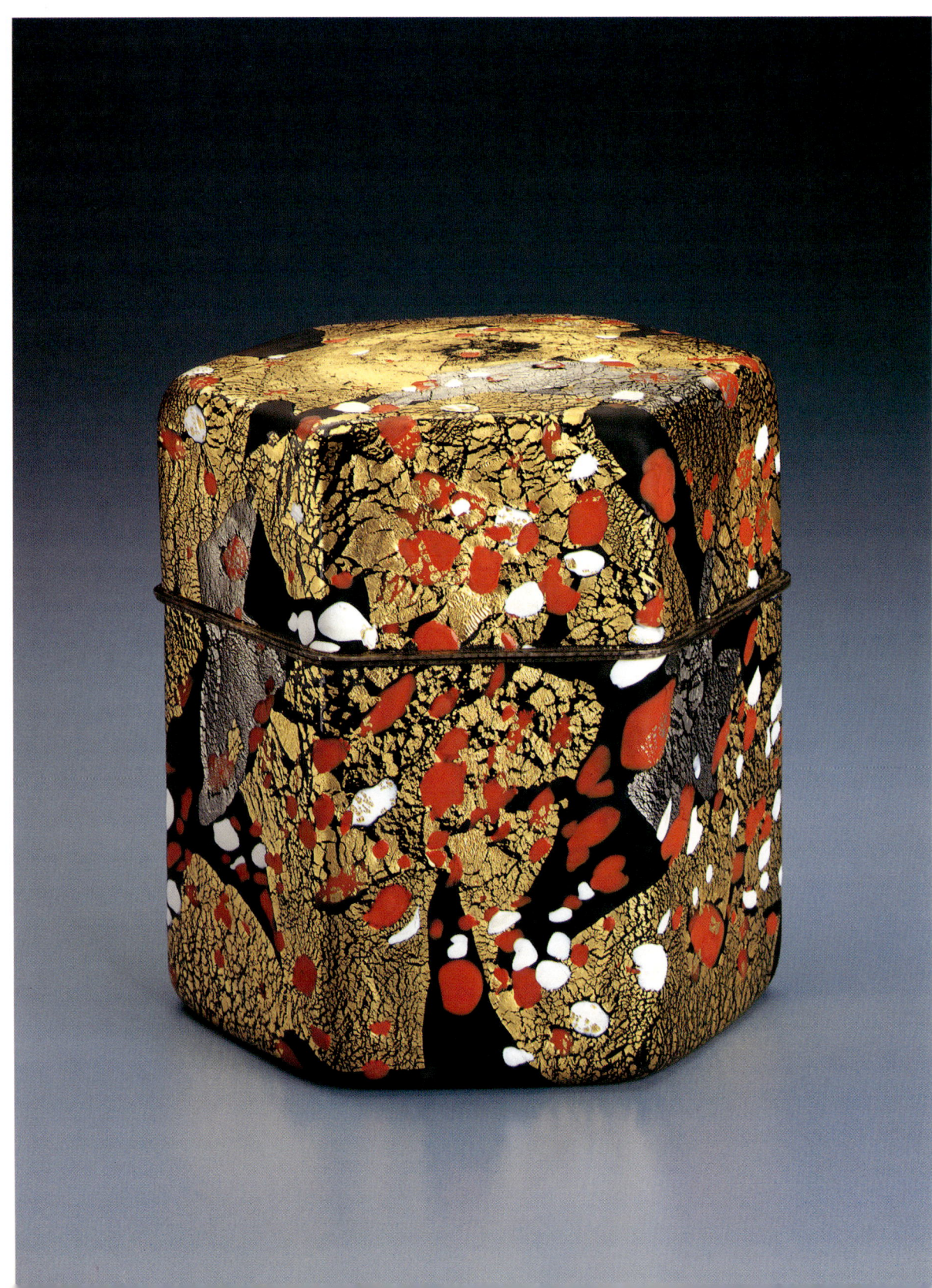

work with Italian master glassblowers. Italian glass factories are organized in a flexible manner. Although patterns are drawn from traditional forms, the designers often work side-by-side with the glassblowers to alter those forms and capture serendipitous events that occur during fabrication. This interactive and spontaneous method enlivens the finished product and gives Italian glass its distinctive character. In Italy, Fujita gained a renewed sense of color and form.

Red and White Plum Blossoms (1990) is part of the series begun in 1973 based on Kazaribako ornamented caskets, which are related to the lidded, hinged boxes originally made for reliquary or ornamental purposes. Fujita modified the form by merging it with another traditional form, that of tenth-century Heian Period Japanese lacquer storage boxes and inkstone cases. Fujita's updated iterations are decorated with abstracted and nature-based patterns cased in glass. Small scaled, they maintain a monumentality.

To fabricate these caskets, Fujita's team blows hot glass into separate molds for the top and bottom. Then he applies gold- or silver-foil inclusions and cases them again. After annealing, the glass sections are sandblasted and hand-finished. Metal mounts outlining the rim are added as part of the final assembly.

In *Red and White Plum Blossoms*, Fujita used decorative devices derived from the Rimpa School, founded by Sotatsu in the seventeenth century. This school favors asymmetrical compositions, simple silhouettes, and a variety of colors. As indicated in the title of the work, Fujita selected decorative elements that refer to red and white plum blossoms.

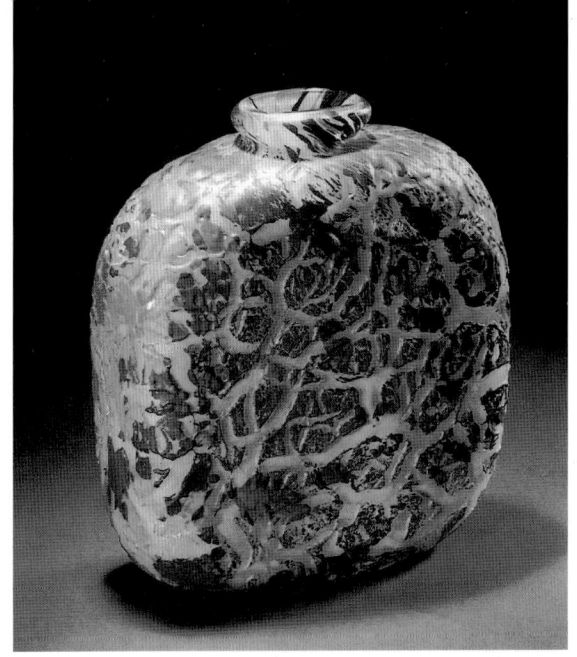

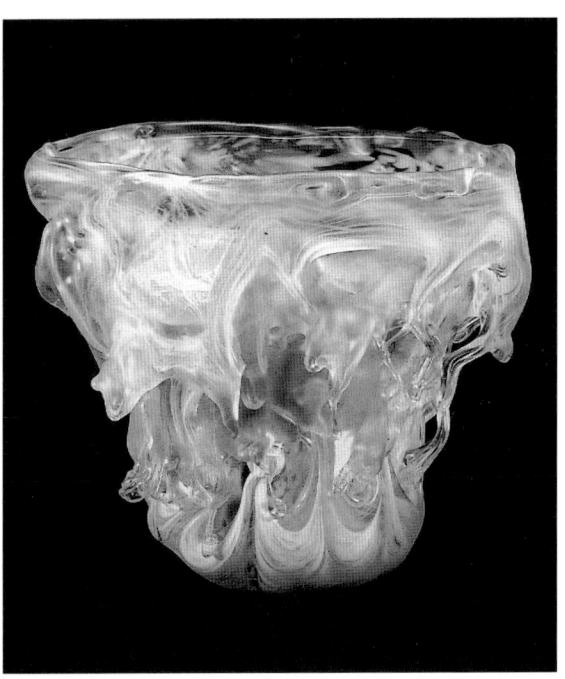

Kyohei Fujita
Japanese, b. 1921

FIG. 4

Vase (Early Autumn), 1960
Blown, frosted, and acid glass, with colored glass chips
9 1/2 x 8 1/2 x 4 inches (24 x 21 x 10 cm)
Courtesy the artist

FIG. 5

Vase (Rainbow Colors), 1964
Blown and acid glass, with colored glass chips and gold foil
14 x 15 inches (35 X 38 cm)
Courtesy the artist

MICHAEL GLANCY

American, b. 1950

Michael Glancy uses glass and metal to make mysterious, vessel-based forms. Raised near Detroit and educated first at the University of Denver and then at the Rhode Island School of Design, Providence, Glancy was drawn to glassblowing when he saw a demonstration while in Santa Fe, New Mexico. Although at the time he was attending business school and planned to join the family business, his interest in glass led to his asking glass artist Marvin Lipofsky (cats. 25–27) for advice about where to attend art school. Lipofsky urged Glancy to attend the Rhode Island School of Design.

There Glancy received both a Bachelor of Fine Arts (1977) and a Master of Fine Arts degree (1980). His timing was perfect, for he arrived at the school just as Dale Chihuly (cats. 7 and 8) and Jamie Carpenter were in the heyday of their collaborations. From them Glancy learned "the discipline of glass and the love of working with this most human [medium requiring] man's influence to bring out the refined brilliance of materials."[59] Glancy also learned the skill necessary for metal-forming from Louis Mueller. Mueller's work demonstrated how glass could be effectively combined with metal. Glancy additionally made drawings based on fantastical landscapes with sinister and futuristic overtones.[60] All these sensibilities would emerge in Glancy's later works.

The major historical influence on Glancy's early work was French glassmaker Maurice Marinot (1882–1960). Known for his thick-walled and acid-etched vessel-forms that communicate a spiritual intensity, Marinot was one of the first artists to make hot glass by himself. His blown and colored vessels are articulated with geometric etched forms (see fig. 6). Even the small works maintain a monumentality that belies their size and defined function. In time Glancy would pack similar power into his table-sized works.

Marinot also influenced Glancy's technical development. Marinot used hydrofluoric acid to etch deep patterns into his thick forms. This lethal but odorless liquid in time compelled Marinot to abandon this method of glass etching. Glancy modified his acid mix by adding sulfuric acid so that the presence of dangerous materials could be readily detected.

To further expand his repertoire of glass techniques, in 1977 Glancy went to Pilchuck Glass School in Stanwood, Washington, where he explored sandblasting. This technique permits a greater precision in application than acid work.

Michael Glancy

A Pert de Vue, 1990
Blown glass with electroformed copper
VESSEL: 2½ x 7 x 4 inches (6.4 x 17.8 x 10.2 cm)
BASE PLATE A: ¾ x 8 x 8 inches (1.9 x 20.5 x 20.5 cm)
BASE PLATE B: ¾ x 12 x 12 inches (1.9 x 30.5 x 30.5 cm)
cat. 15

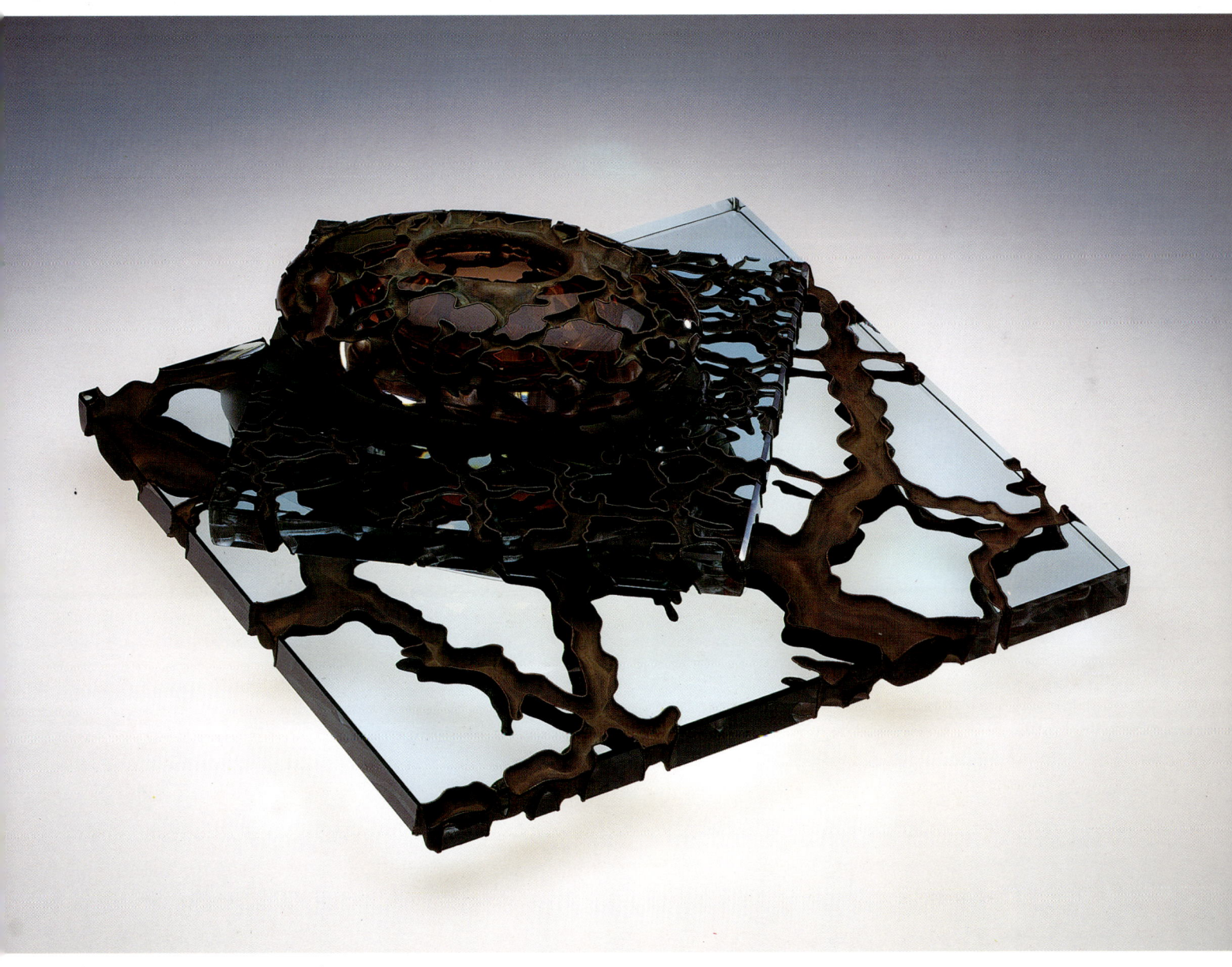

Michael Glancy

Ur Crustacean, 1990–91
Blown glass with gold foil and electroformed copper
6 x 9 dia. inches (15.2 x 22.9 cm)
cat. 16

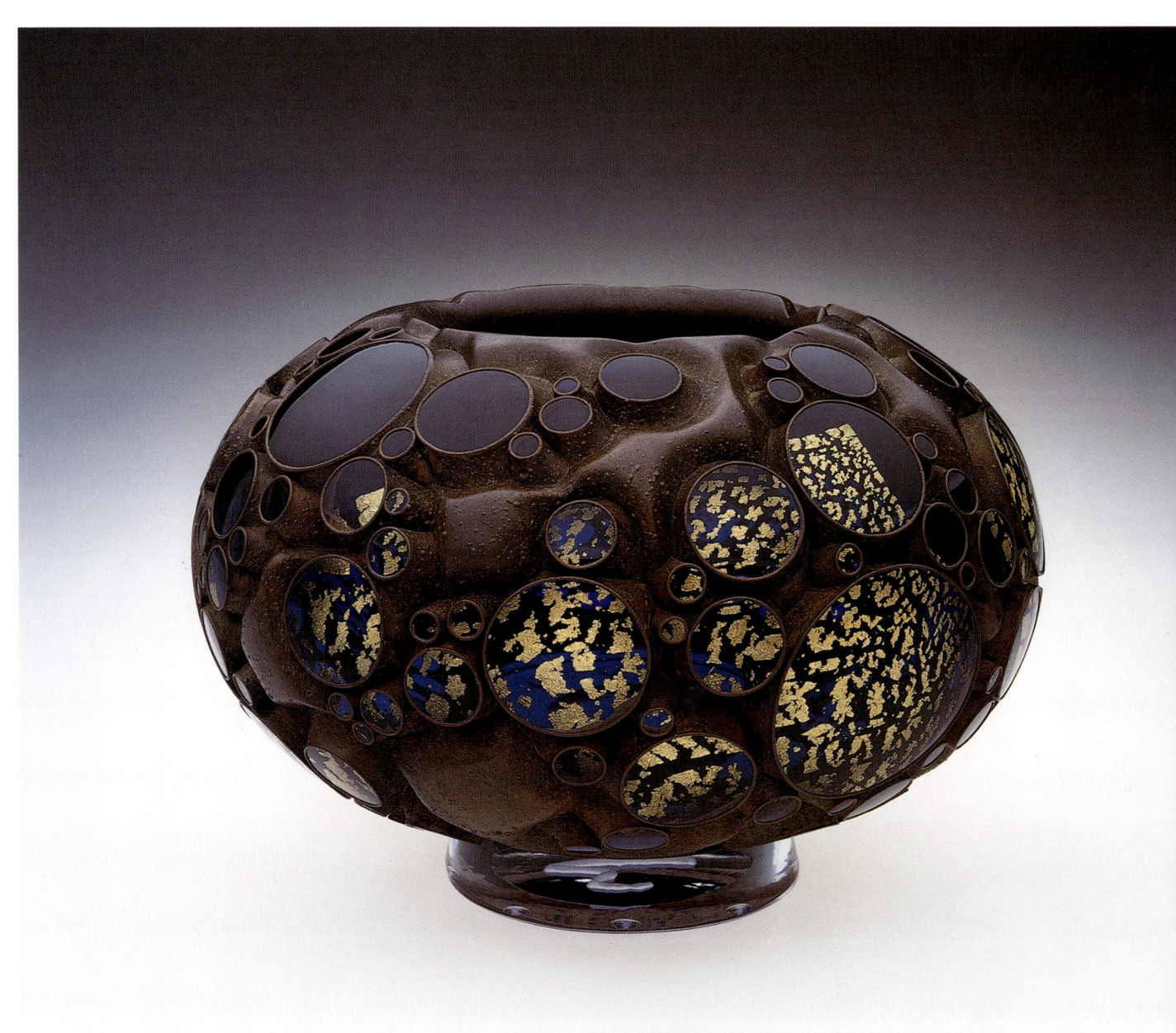

Glancy relies on both of these esoteric techniques to make work that is content, not technique, driven. He has ceased to blow his own forms and has come to use blanks blown for him by his Swedish colleague Jan-Erik Ritzman.

Glancy's earliest pieces were blown vessels, to which he soon added a partial metal "skin" to create a dynamic interplay between the two materials. He used a cartoon transfer method to apply his patterns, and subsequently incorporated the drawings themselves into his vessels as perfect horizontal planes on which to place the forms. They also led to a series of balanced contrasts: vertical vessels paired with horizontal plates, shiny glass countered by textured and patinated metal, and light areas set against dark. Glancy brought these qualities together in magical, gem-like pieces enlivened with the "pomp of orbs and scepters."[61]

Although Glancy's work manifests itself as intense radiance and a mysterious sensibility seemingly far from mundane existence, it is based in an aspect of our own world not visible to the naked eye. With the help of his friend Dr. Kenneth Miller, a biology professor at Brown University, Providence, Glancy gained access to an electron microscope. He transferred the engaging patterns of cell structures into the cool architecture of his work. The unfamiliar, but authentic, character of the forms lends an intuitive veracity to his works.

Master Gem (1988) (ill. p. 31) is a brilliant, blue glass vessel studded with large, bulging facets. Reminiscent of Islamic Persian glass, this table-sized work is monumental. Its metal patina evokes jewelry long buried in ancient tombs, and the work manifests the power inherent in reliquary vessels. *Ur Crustacean* (1990–91), also a vessel form, has circular facets with a sliver of

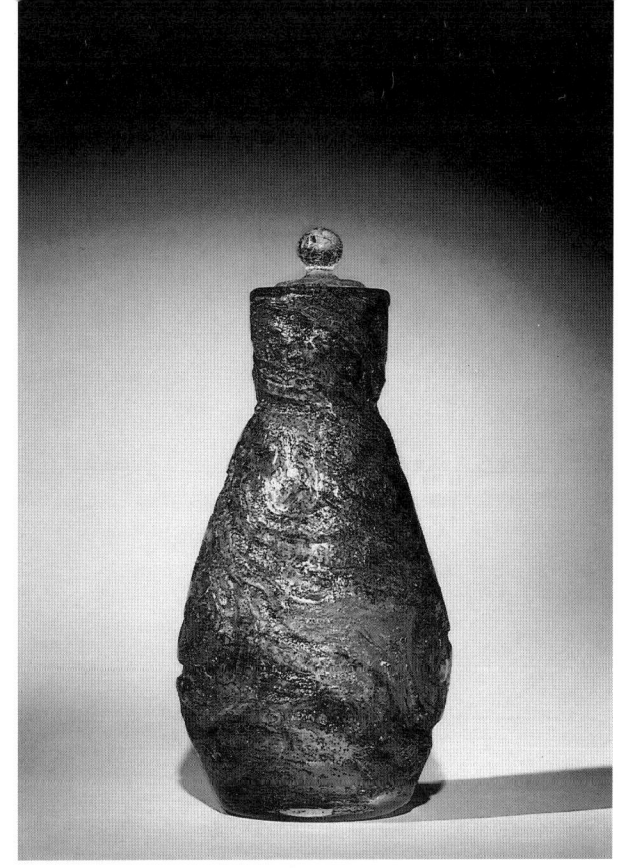

FIG. 6

Maurice Marinot
French, 1882–1960

Stoppered Bottle, c. 1930–35
Blown glass, acid-etched
10½ x 4½ dia. inches (26 x 9.8 cm)
The Corning Museum of Glass, New York
Gift of Evangeline B. Bruce

gold leaf suspended within their thick walls. Again Glancy exploited the contrasts inherent in glass and precious metal; the title suggests a jewellike object encrusted with meaning.

The third Glick work, *A Pert de Vue* (1990), is a multipart composition. Two angled plates of glass are supported by an invisible disk; on the top sits an orange glass and metal egglike form. The French title, which means "invisible," refers to the unseen potential within the egg. In this elegantly ambiguous object, Glancy has harnessed the carefully balanced opposites of thick glass and thin metal, vertical and horizontal, potential and fruition.

David Huchthausen

Alpine Landscape, 1977
Blown and cased glass with interior decoration
8 x 6 dia. inches (20.3 x 15.2 cm)
cat. 17

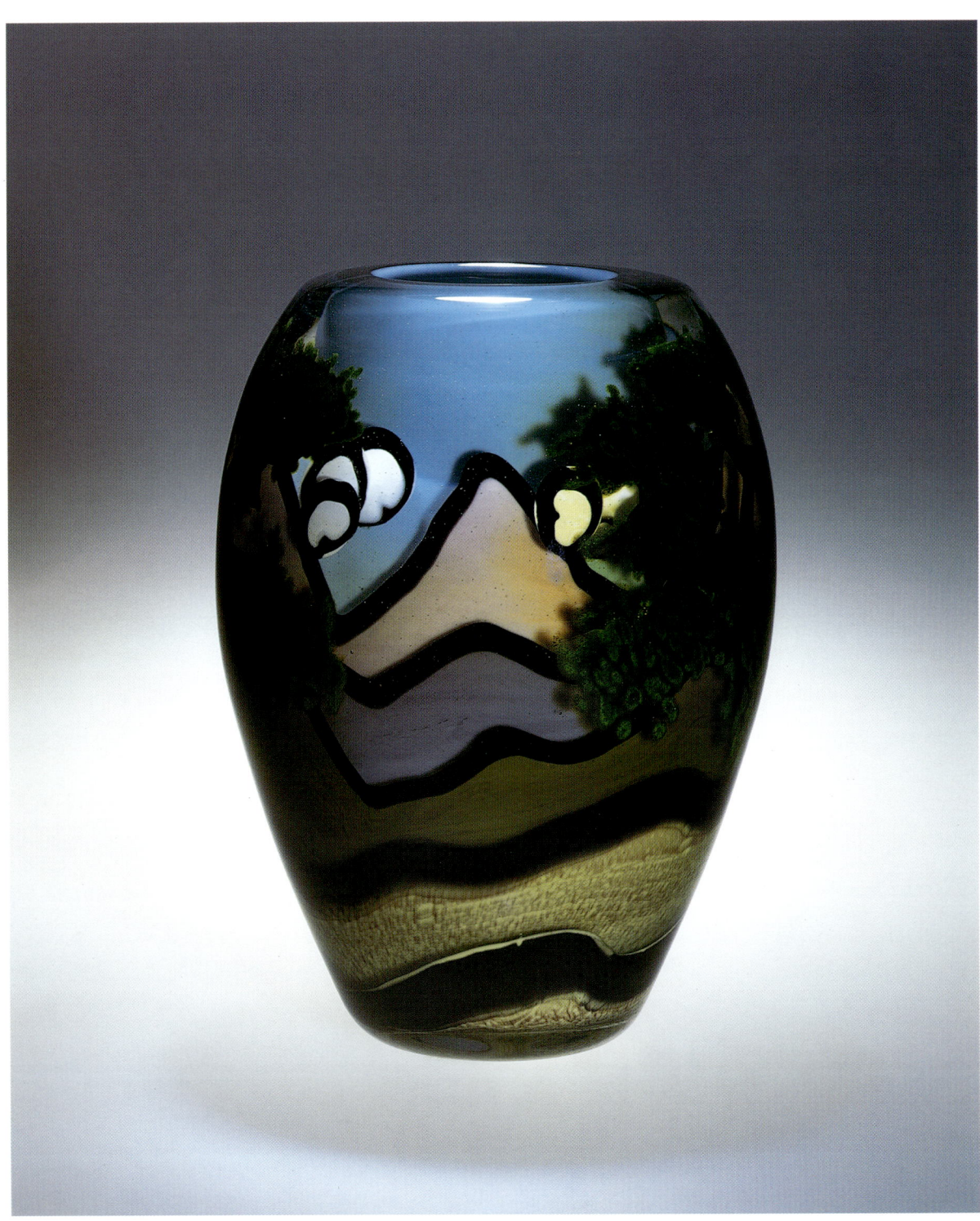

DAVID HUCHTHAUSEN

American, b. 1951

David Huchthausen, a cerebral artist who makes intellectual statements in glass, was involved early on in assessing the success of American studio glass. His perceptive essays in the "American Glass Now" exhibitions in the late 1970s and early 1980s express his concern about the long-term direction and importance of the glass movement. For example, in 1984 he addressed one of the central issues of glass: "[w]hen the success of a piece is reliant on the material alone, it will forever remain suspect on a conceptual level."[62]

Although initially interested in architecture, Huchthausen found himself attending art classes where he made sculptures of metal, wood, fiber, plate glass, and found objects. His art-school exposure to aboriginal art and Russian Constructivism appealed to his architectural sensibility and inspired his sense of the assembled form. In 1970 Huchthausen happened onto an unused glass furnace on the University of Wisconsin campus in Wausau. After making some repairs, he spent the next several months teaching himself how to work with glass.

Huchthausen heard about Harvey Littleton's glassblowing classes at the University of Wisconsin's Madison campus and relocated there in 1973; he soon became Littleton's assistant. While he was at Madison, Huchthausen met the painter Richard Dahle, who with others in his circle, urged him to move on to a more "appropriate" artistic medium. But Huchthausen wanted to work with glass.

Huchthausen's early works incorporate totemic forms relating to Olmec, Mayan, and African cultures, in pieces that were remarkable at the time for their large scale, often reaching four feet in height.[63] His experiments with laminated glass allowed him to accumulate a technical expertise and artistic vision that would reach its full expression in his later work. In 1975 he transferred to Illinois State University at Normal, where he became the graduate teaching assistant for Joel Philip Myers (cats. 39–49). Huchthausen's own recognition came with his inclusion in the 1976 "Modern Glass in Europe, America and Japan" exhibition sponsored by the Museum für Kunsthandwerk in Frankfurt.

Alpine Landscape (1977) is a "fantasy" vessel from this early period. Huchthausen had traveled to Vienna on a Fulbright-Hays Scholarship. Made at J. & L. Lobmeyr Studio in Baden (near Vienna), this blown and cased vessel is one

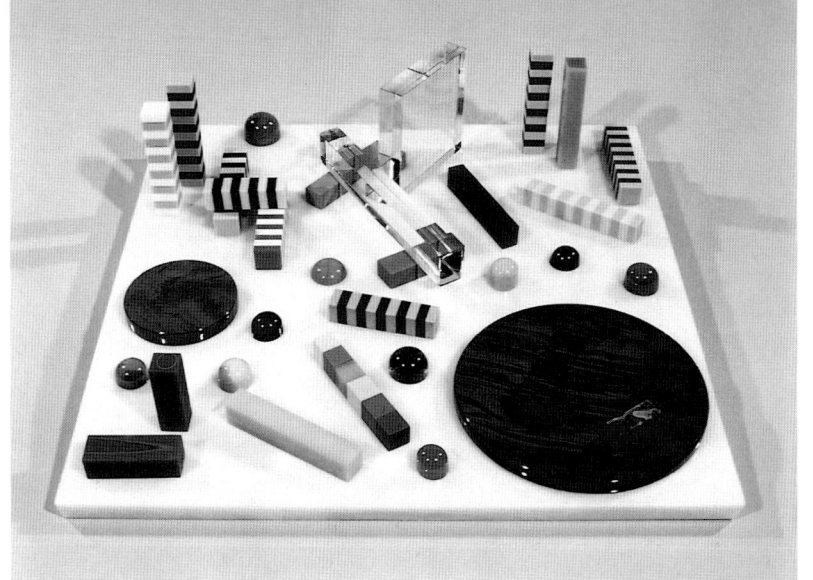

FIG. 7

David Huchthausen
American, b. 1951

Construction Field, 1981
Marble base with laminated, cut, and polished opaque glass pieces
5 x 24 x 24 inches (12.7 x 60 x 60 cm)
Courtesy the artist

of the best pieces from this technique-starved period in American studio glass. Limited by facilities that precluded his making large-scale sculptural works, Huchthausen invested this blown piece with a monumentality achieved through his layers of vividly colored, graphic forms cased between clear glass with passages of trapped air bubbles.

In December 1978 Huchthausen abruptly stopped blowing glass. Returning to New York, he resumed his exploration of laminated glass. A serious auto accident forced a fourteen-month hiatus in his work, and led in a roundabout way to his relocation to Tennessee, where from 1979 to 1981 he worked on a group of works entitled "Construction Fields," which were loosely based on Russian Constructivist concepts. Displayed in the "American Glass Art: Evolution and Revolution" exhibition held at The Morris Museum of Arts and Sciences in Morristown, New Jersey in 1982, this series of works includes cubes and rectangles of laminated Vitrolite placed randomly on a marble "floor." In among the angular pieces are less dominant rounded forms that function as structural counterpoints to the right angles (see fig. 7). These works invite the viewer to explore visually a variety of concepts concerning the interplay of form fragments. From these works flowed the later "Leitungs Scherben" series.

Leitungs Scherbe (c. 1987), is a sophisticated work. Activated by reflected light and the myriad accompanying refractions that occur as the viewer moves around the work, the top of the piece is a laminated glass grid suspended parallel to the supporting surface. Placed on top of jagged pink, shardlike legs, the Vitrolite grid functions both as a window revealing the pink glass legs and as a screen casting an Art Deco-inspired pattern. The title refers to the German word "Leitungs," meaning "guidance or control," with an underlying connotation of electrical conduction or transmission. Certainly this work has a circuit-board sensibility congruent with its being a simulacrum for electricity. The word "Scherbe" means "fragment," with the connotation of being in shambles; it also captures the precariousness of the piece, balanced as it is on glass shards of uneven heights. Only the pink color undermines the darker implications of the unsteady legs.

Huchthausen's finely crafted works are the result of numerous carefully calculated decisions. Icy in their sensibility, these works are glass art at its most intellectual. Huchthausen has recently completed a related series that explore matrices.

David Huchthausen

Leitungs Scherbe (from the "Leitungs Scherben" series), c. 1987
Glass, fractured, laminated, and optically polished
10½ x 17½ x 12½ inches (26.7 x 44.5 x 31.8 cm)
cat. 18

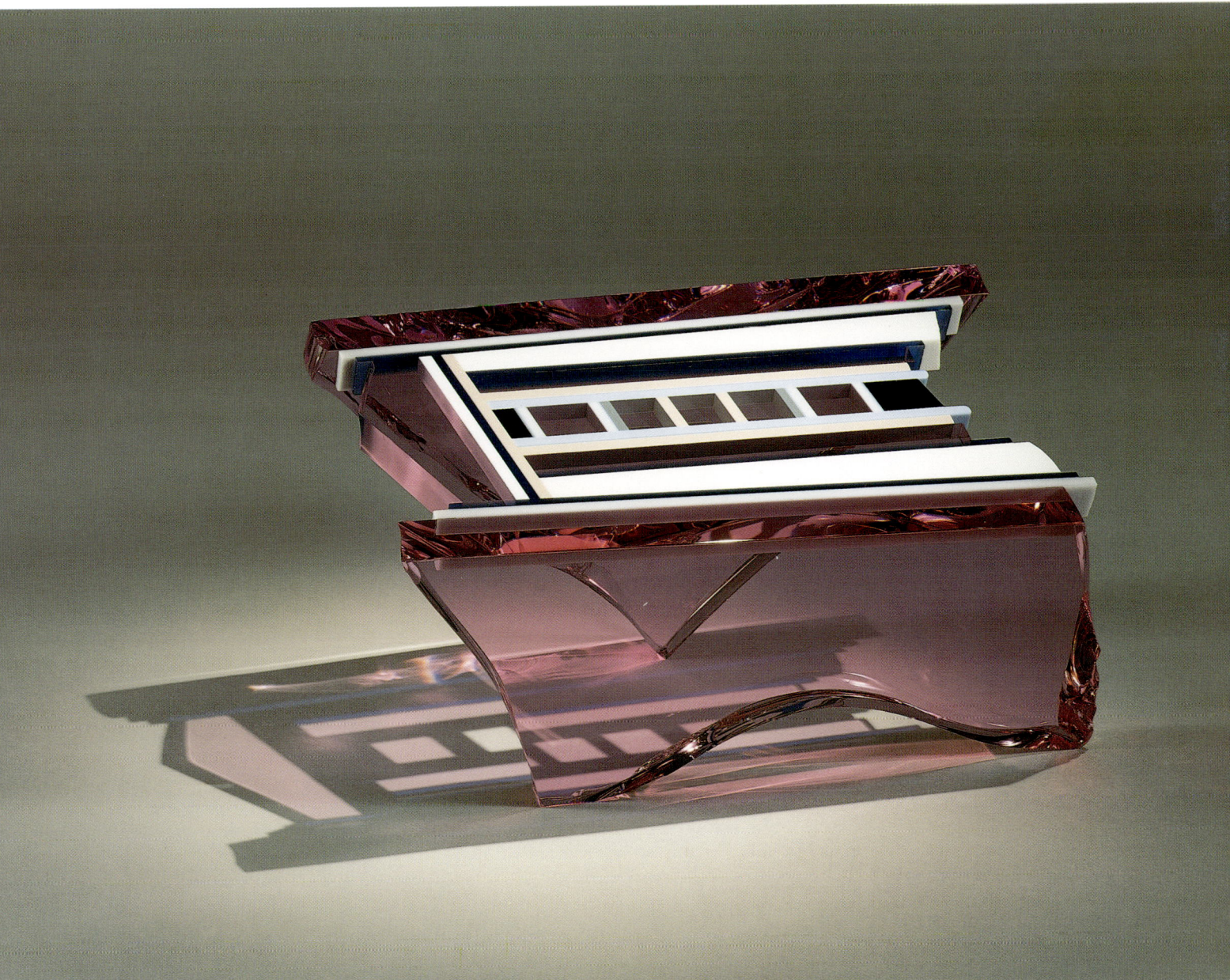

RICHARD JOLLEY

American, b. 1952

Richard Jolley is a master of figurative glass sculpture. One of the few glass artists to use the human form as his subject, Jolley creates a galaxy of fresh and entertaining characters. The son of a scientist, Jolley was born in Kansas, but his family soon moved to Oak Ridge, Tennessee. He completed the major part of his undergraduate work at Tusculum College in Greenville, Tennessee, where he was exposed to the liberal arts and to hot glass. He became intrigued by the crafts tradition of valuing the handmade object and specifically decided to create sculptural rather than utility-based forms.

Because his father's work had been devoted to abstract scientific inquiry, Jolley found himself drawn to the opposite camp of the literal and concrete. Feeling that industrialization promotes "dehumanization,"[64] Jolley abstracts his work only when it supports the content. He finished his Bachelor of Fine Arts degree at George Peabody College in Nashville, and then studied at the Penland School of Handicrafts, near Asheville, North Carolina. The fact that he did not study in a university-based glass program is seen in the originality of his work.

Jolley first explored vessel forms, but he soon added a signature technique: drawing on the surface of the vessel using contrastingly colored hot-glass canes. This technique is a modification of an ancient method used by Roman glassmakers. Because the molten glass is shaped on the end of a blowpipe with repeated reheatings to keep the metal pliable, and because each piece weighs up to twenty-five pounds, Jolley works with a team of four glass workers. The expressive line is accomplished by applying a thin cane of glass to the already formed sculptural glass armature. Metallic oxides create the intense hues.[65] Only at the correct temperature will the canes adhere and blend, but not mix in with the underlying shape. Working time for each passage ranges from forty-five seconds to one minute. In the final step the work is placed in an annealing oven for two to three days. Jolley uses a throughly contemporary form of gestural notation. His characters are lovingly modeled on ordinary people. His facial types recall Thomas Hart Benton's paintings from the 1930s. Jolley articulates each figure with charm and whimsy.

Female Bust with Leaves (1989) has been sandblasted and articulated with blue and green canes. Jolley's early works are narrative and executed in clear blown glass with bright red, yellow, and blue cane drawings; he later adopted the sandblasted addition. The surface treatment here marks a change in Jolley's work and brings it closer to a *pâte de verre* texture, denying the "glassiness" of the material and forcing the work to be assessed primarily on its composition and content.

One of the aspects of his work that Jolley relishes is the act of drawing, or as he terms it, the "making of a mark."[66] While he often makes preparatory drawings, Jolley feels that his best drawings are on the hot glass itself. In the future he would like to move away from themes based on everyday experience and to work without a team of glassmakers. To this end he has explored wood-block carving and investigated texture as part of a compositional whole.

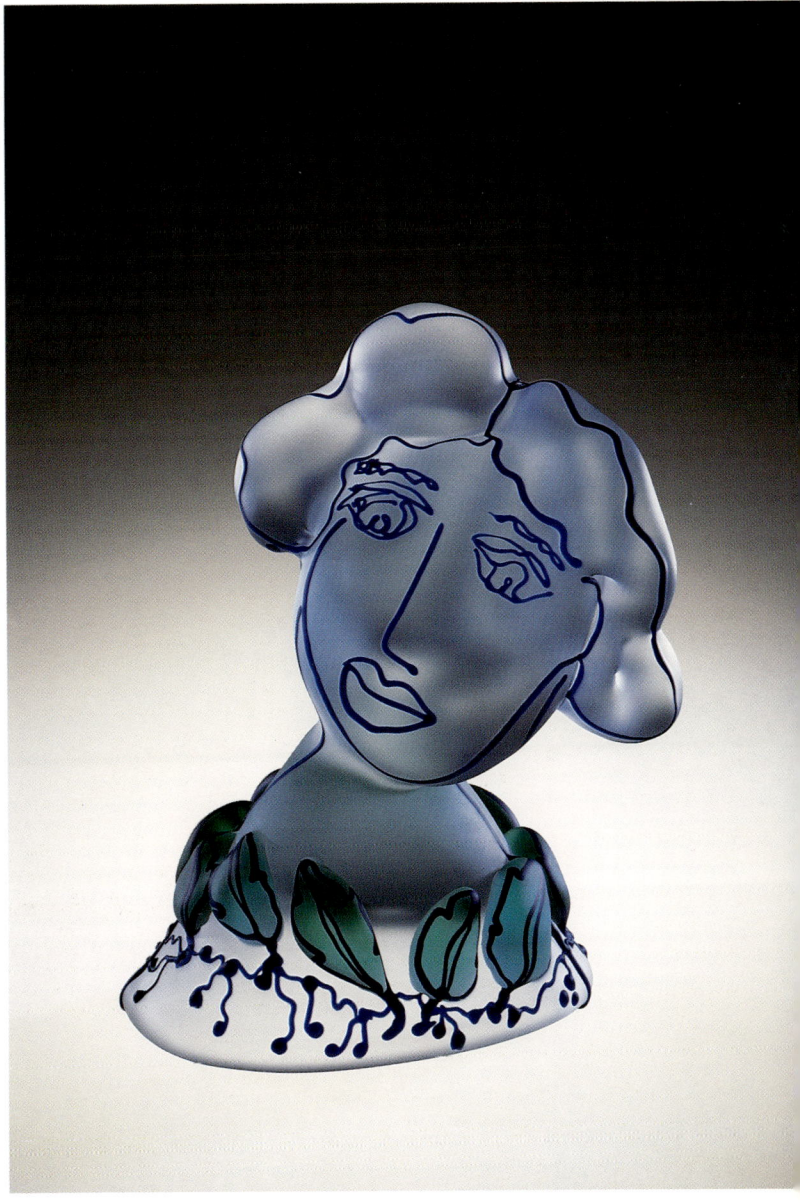

Richard Jolley
Assisted by Tommie Pratt

Female Bust with Leaves, 1989
Glass with cane drawing, sandblasted
13½ x 10 x 7 inches (34.3 x 25.4 x 17.8 cm)
cat. 19

Kreg Kallenberger

Period of Mystery (from the "Osage" series), 1989
Cast and polished optical crystal with oil paint
9 x 19¼ x 6 inches (22.9 x 48.9 x 15.2 cm)
cat. 20

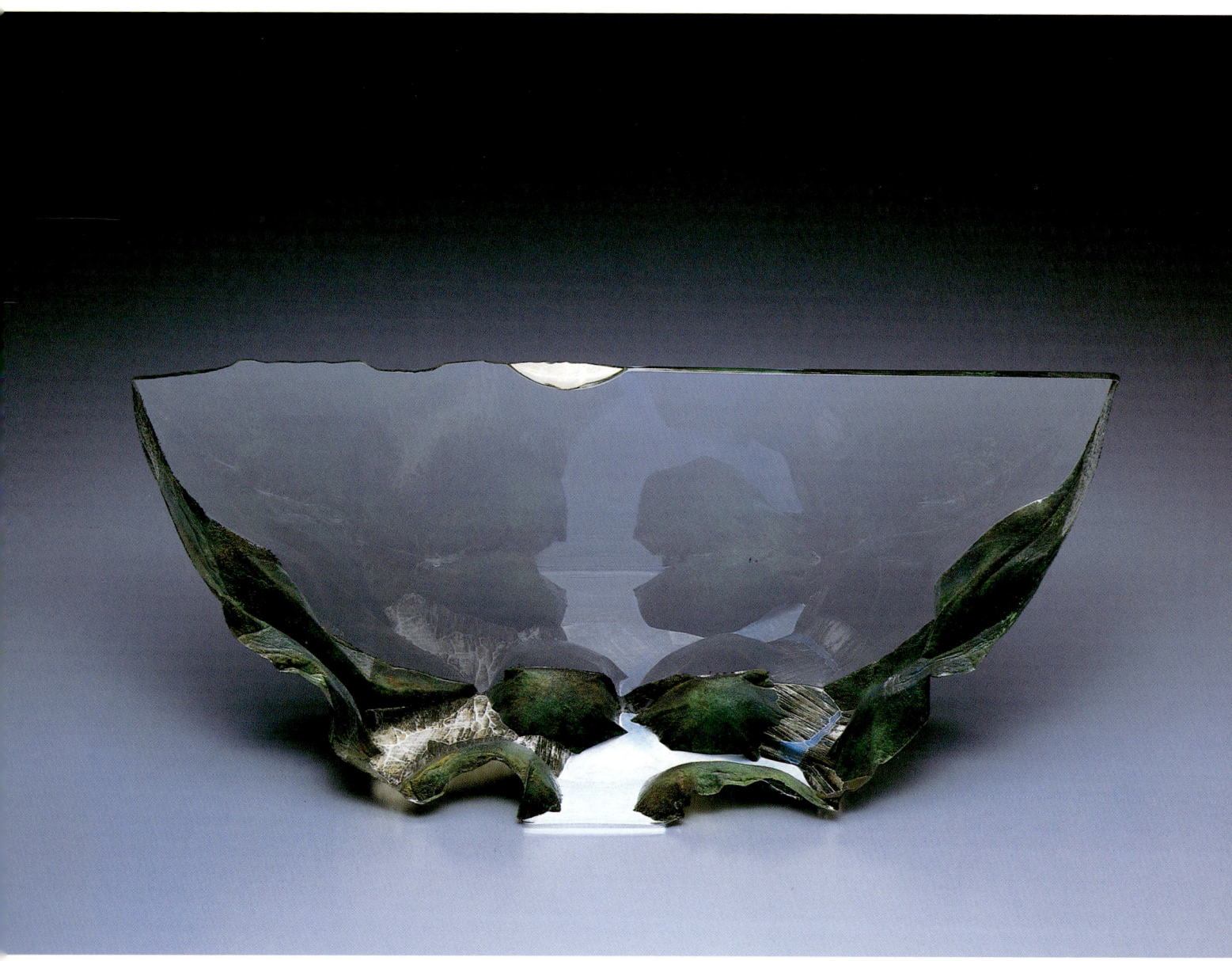

KREG KALLENBERGER

American, b. 1950

Kreg Kallenberger is a master of exquisite form. Kallenberger received his Bachelor and Master of Fine Arts degrees from the University of Tulsa, Oklahoma. He planned originally to study mechanical engineering, but switched to art and then focused on ceramics. He found clay to be too slow a process[67] and moved on to the faster medium of glassblowing. When a glass furnace was donated to the university (complete with glass marbles for the first batch[68]), he assembled it and began teaching himself how to use a blowpipe. Enticed by an offer to remain at the university, Kallenberger completed his degrees in ceramics by producing works in glass. After a brief hiatus working in the construction business, by 1978 Kallenberger was working full-time in glass.

His early blown works focus on formal issues. Thick-walled, architectural, and cool, these works were completed by being cut into smaller geometric shapes. Kallenberger eventually tired of working with up to forty pounds of glass on the blowpipe, and turned to cold-working techniques for finishing and cutting.[69] Adopting a serial methodology to tackle aesthetic issues in a progressive way, he completed his first series, "Cuneiform" and "Interlock." These early pieces deal with sculptural questions of scale, form, volume, and monumentality. In the later, transitional "Titanic" series, a narrative or anecdotal aspect entered the works. Each group builds on the previous series and continues the web of interlocking ideas and skills.

Period of Mystery (from the "Osage" series) (1989) was inspired by the Osage Hills near Kallenberger's home in Oklahoma. The series features cast optical crystal with oil-paint passages. Evocative of a "slice" of landscape, the slick beauty of the cast crystal serves as a foil to the undulating undersurface, which is left rough and finished with metallic paint. The mood of the work is serene and cool; subtle touches of iridescence and abstract color carry Kallenberger's spiritual meaning and his deep affection for the evocative beauty of glass.

DOMINICK LABINO

American, 1910–1987

Dominick Labino, a pioneer of the American studio-glass movement, was one of the first to successfully combine technological innovation and aesthetics. Trained as an electrical engineer at the Allegheny Vocational High School, Pittsburgh (1928), and then the Carnegie Institute, Pittsburgh, Labino had a lifelong love of tools and problem-solving. He also had a passion for artistic endeavors: as a child he carved wood and later designed jewelry and painted. As both scientist/inventor and artist, he worked with glass in commercial and artistic contexts for fifty years.

Between 1939 and 1982,[70] Labino received sixty patents for his work on formulas for high-quality, stable glass, honoring his research into glass composition, furnace design, and devices for glass-forming. His chief accomplishment was the invention of silica fiber for use in jet aircraft, which eventually led to his designing a machine that forms glass fiber into insulation for pipes. Three of his glass fibers were used for insulation in the National Space Agency's Apollo space capsules.[71] A true inventor, Labino felt that "machines were more beautiful than art because they are doing something, and they are doing it for a purpose."[72] To an inventor such as Labino, tools and inventions alike are works of art.

In the 1930s Labino was in charge of the Owens-Illinois Glass Co. milk-bottle plant. He had a small laboratory in which to formulate and concoct new glass metals. In 1940 Ben Alderson, Labino's predecessor at the plant, showed him how to blow glass. Although Labino enjoyed the experience, he did not pursue it as an art. When a friend retired in 1958, Labino did make a paperweight as a farewell gift in this small research studio. In 1960 he melted a batch of glass and fashioned a primitive blowpipe on which he blew bottles.[73]

Labino was a key figure in the success of the 1962 Toledo Workshops. He had met Harvey Littleton (cats. 28 and 29) when Littleton was teaching ceramics at The Toledo Museum of Art. When the first workshop was planned, Labino offered to provide technical advice about the construction of the furnace.[74] With this technical issue solved, the workshop could proceed, but the glass would not melt properly and Labino provided the #475 fiberglass marbles that could be melted. Labino again came to aid of the studio-glass movement in 1964 when he built the furnace used at the First World Conference of Craftsmen in New York, where he demonstrated glass-forming in a studio.

Always curious, Labino knew that many surviving examples of ancient glass were not understood from a technical point of view. He set about to investigate how the Egyptians had fabricated their core-formed glass vials and published his findings in the *Journal of Glass Studies*.[75] His 1968 publication *Visual Art in Glass* was one of the early books to connect the terms "art" and "glass."

Untitled (1968) shows Labino's passion for transparent colors. The vessel is free-blown, clear glass with gestural inclusions of bright orange. While not large, the work has a presence not always seen in early studio-glass pieces. For Labino, as with other glass artists, inquiries into the interplay between color and form were an enduring challenge. In his *Untitled* (from the "Emergence" series) (1982) (ill. p. 20), he made use of dichronic veiling and iridescence to establish forms within forms. Building on over thirty years of glass experience and his thorough understanding of the technical aspects, Labino's vessel forms are fine examples of first-generation studio glass.

By generously making technical information accessible, Labino opened the way for studio-glass artists. The invention of the top-burner furnace (which eliminated the need for a second glory hole), the creation of insulation materials that made annealing ovens more efficient, and his triple-hinged furnace door all have helped the artists who followed him. Oddly, it was the very availability of these advances that allowed technique to be discounted for a period by some of Labino's colleagues. But as the movement has matured and the artists have come to understand that technique is necessary to support their art, Labino's contribution has received its proper recognition.

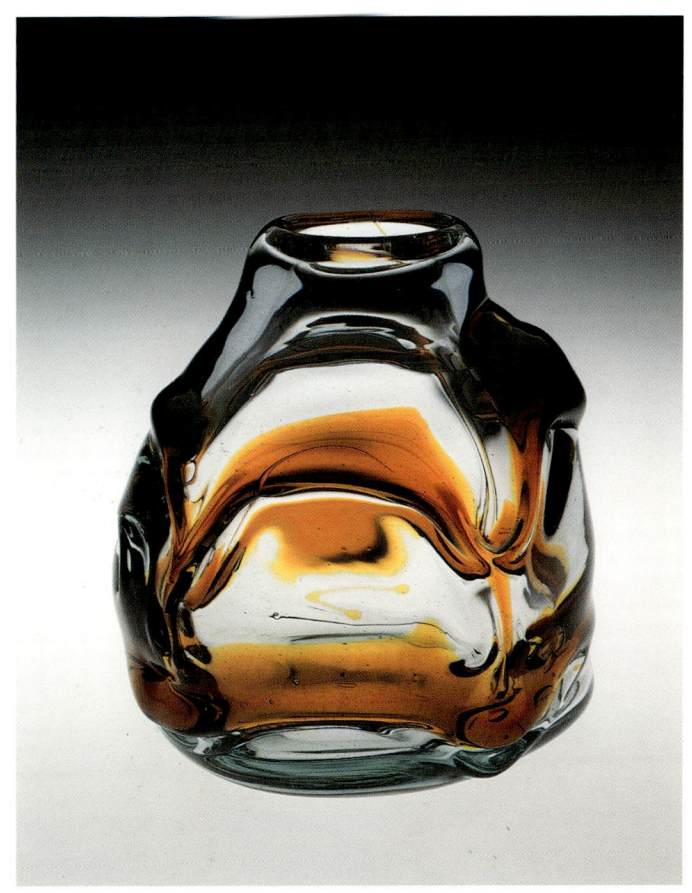

Dominick Labino

Untitled, 1968
Blown and manipulated glass
6 x 5 x 6½ inches (15.2 x 12.7 x 16.5 cm)
cat. 21

Stanislav Libenský
Jaroslava Brychtová

Head VI, 1986
Mold-formed glass, cut and polished
21 x 11¼ x 8 inches (53.3 x 28.6 x 20.3 cm)
cat. 24

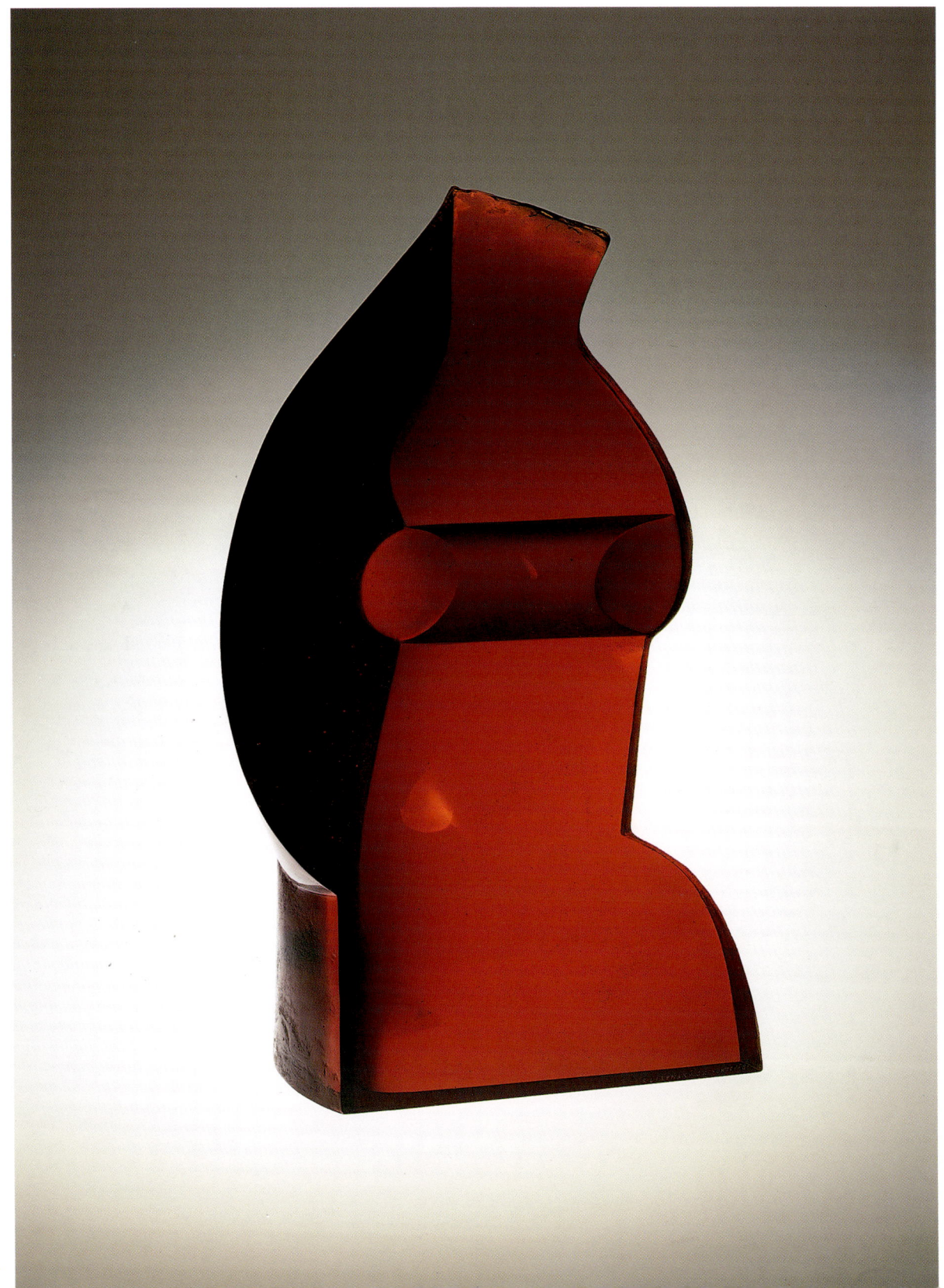

Czechoslovakian, b. 1921 | STANISLAV LIBENSKÝ

Czechoslovakian, b. 1924 | JAROSLAVA BRYCHTOVÁ

Husband and wife team of Stanislav Libenský and Jaroslava Brychtová are the preeminent glass artists of the Czech Republic. Both singly and together they are artists of great note and lasting international influence. Libenský has trained three generations of Czech glass artists; he and Brychtová together have affected many more through their monumental works.

Both artists were born at a time of turmoil. Their lives began during a democratic period, their young adulthood was spent under the Nazis, and their maturity under the Communists. Through it all they continued to work and maintain their commitment to glassmaking. Today, once again under a democracy, they are more productive than ever.

Libenský, the son of a blacksmith, was born at Sezemice near Mnichoro Hradiste. He began his formal art studies in 1937 at the technical college at Nový Bor, studying glassmaking, painting, and drawing. Because Czechoslovakia has a long tradition of glass as an art medium, it was an acceptable avenue to becoming an artist. Libenský entered the School of Applied Arts (later the Academy of Applied Arts) in Prague and studied painting and glass under Professor Jaroslav Holeček. But with the outbreak of World War II in 1944, male attendance was suspended.

Brychtová, born in the glass town of Železný Brod, was the daughter of Jaroslav Brychtá, a sculptor who received the Grand Prix in Paris in 1921 and the Grand Prix in Brussels in 1935 for his glass figures.[76] In 1945 Brychtová started at the Academy of Applied Arts where she studied cutting and engraving of glass and stone with Professor Karel Štipl. In 1947 she entered the Academy of Fine Arts to work with Jan Lauda. Libenský and Brychtová first met around 1954 over a collaboration at the Železný Brod Glassworks. Although they were drawn together by both personal and aesthetic attraction, both were married to others; only in 1963 did they marry and set up a home with her three children from her previous marriage.

After the end of World War II, when the Communist party took over Czechoslovakia, they supported a regeneration of Czech art as a propaganda tool. Postwar Czech glass, building on hundreds of years of tradition and large-scale castings that were the hallmark of the Czech glass aesthetic, was particularly suitable to the Communist sensibility.

Czech glass manufactories had a tradition of working with artists. Attracted to large-scale works, when Brychtová began working with Libenský she urged that they make monumental works that take advantage of factory resources. Her skill at being a factory liaison was critical to their production as a team. Only when they established their own glass studio in the early 1990s did they cease to work closely with factories.

Libenský and Brychtová were influenced by Cubism, the Surrealism of Constantin Brancusi, and the art of Africa and Oceania. The Cubism that is a cornerstone of their art was not the French Cubism of Picasso that focuses on a formalist sensibility, but rather the Czech version that treats Cubism as a philosophical approach to art-making. Libenský and Brychtová applied Cubist notions to their rendering of objects in which they "Projected both the real plane and the front plane, and the cubist principle of the frontal, two dimensional space was realized through light."[77] This approach led to their innovative use of internal space in their table-sized sculptures.

Head I (c. 1957–58) (ill. p. 14) is one of two known versions (its twin is at The Corning Museum of Glass, New York). Shown at Corning's "Glass 1959" exhibition, it was also the first team piece shown in the United States. Relying on African and Oceanic iconography, the face is elongated with a top knot of casually molded hair. In what would become their signature technique of glass-forming, Libenský and Brychtová modeled the piece to the interior of the glass rather than to the polished side. Called the "inner cavity principle" by Brychtová, this method led them to use glass thickness as a method of controlling color intensity and light.[78] The technique would allow them to transfer Libenský's paintings into paintings in glass. This piece represents a more personal expression than the larger monumental works that were to come.

In 1963 Libenský was appointed head of the Academy of Applied Arts in Prague following Professor Josef Kaplický's death. Renowned for his exacting standards, supportive teaching methods, and warmth, Libenský taught there until 1987, when he retired. For sixteen years Libenský and Brychtová worked together under successive Communist regimes that became increasingly more restrictive. Travel together outside their county was not allowed, salaries were paid in soft currency, and both had to contend respectively with restrictions on their teaching and on working with factories. These conditions changed after the 1989 Velvet Revolution that returned Czechoslovakia to a democratic government.

Head VI (1986), made during a dark period just before Libenský left the academy and before the Velvet Revolution, was formed by melting glass in a mold. The intensity of the vivid red glass is carefully modulated by skillful manipulation of the glass thickness. Feeling that the "Transparency of glass is the basis of the notion of the fourth dimension,"[79] Libenský and Brychtová hint at the spiritual content contained within their work. While the piece was cut and polished after it left the mold, the accretions at the top have been preserved as a counterpoint to the smooth body. Making "no distinction between aesthetics and technology"[80] and valuing them both, Libenský and Brychtová create studies in light and form that are unparalleled.

MARVIN LIPOFSKY

American, b. 1938

Marvin Lipofsky is the studio-glass movement's international ombudsman. An early student of Harvey Littleton (cats. 28 and 29), he came of age in glass as the movement was creating its own identity. He shares his knowledge with glass artists around the world, readily communicating the verve and spontaneity that marked the post-1962 American studio-glass movement.

Born in Barrington, Illinois, Lipofsky began his art education with industrial design and sculpture at the University of Illinois, Urbana-Champaign, where he also studied with ceramist David Shaner. At the suggestion of a professor, Lipofsky applied to the University of Wisconsin, Madison, where he took a few art-education classes along with his regular art curriculum, since art teachers generally were not drafted. Lipofsky remembers being inspired by the ceramic sculptures of Peter Voulkos and John Mason at The Art Institute of Chicago.[81] Lipofsky intended to follow their lead, but he met Harvey Littleton, who offered a class in glassblowing at the University of Wisconsin. Intrigued, Lipofsky stayed for two years.

In 1964 Littleton turned down a teaching position at the University of California at Berkeley and suggested Lipofsky instead.[82] Lipofsky moved to California to start the second glassblowing program in the United States. His first class consisted of six women; their initial task was to build the equipment necessary for the studio. Berkeley was an exciting place during the eight years of Lipofsky's stay: the free speech movement of Mario Savio, the fight for the People's Park, the Patty Hearst kidnaping, and the anti-Vietnam War protests were some of the highlights. The art world was also in turmoil. Art historian and curator Peter Selz mounted the influential "Funk" exhibition at the University Art Gallery, an exhibition that called attention to contemporary sculpture's decided break from traditional concerns of beauty and finished execution. All of this served as a volatile backdrop for the expanding glass program. Lipofsky had an impressive string of students with whom to work, including Paula Barton, Michael Cohn, John Lewis, Richard Marquis, Richard Meitner, and Alan Rice.[83]

But after eight years Berkeley ended the glass program and Lipofsky went to work for the College of Arts and Crafts in nearby Oakland, where in 1967 Trudi Guermonprez had invited him to teach a summer workshop, which spurred the establishment of a glassblowing facility. Lipofsky

Marvin Lipofsky
Assisted by Gianni Toso

Venini Series — Split Piece, 1975
Blown glass with canes, cut and polished
TWO PARTS
A: $3\frac{1}{2}$ x 10 x $8\frac{1}{2}$ inches (8.9 x 25.4 x 21.6 cm)
B: 9 x 15 x 10 inches (22.9 x 38.1 x 25.4 cm)
cat. 25

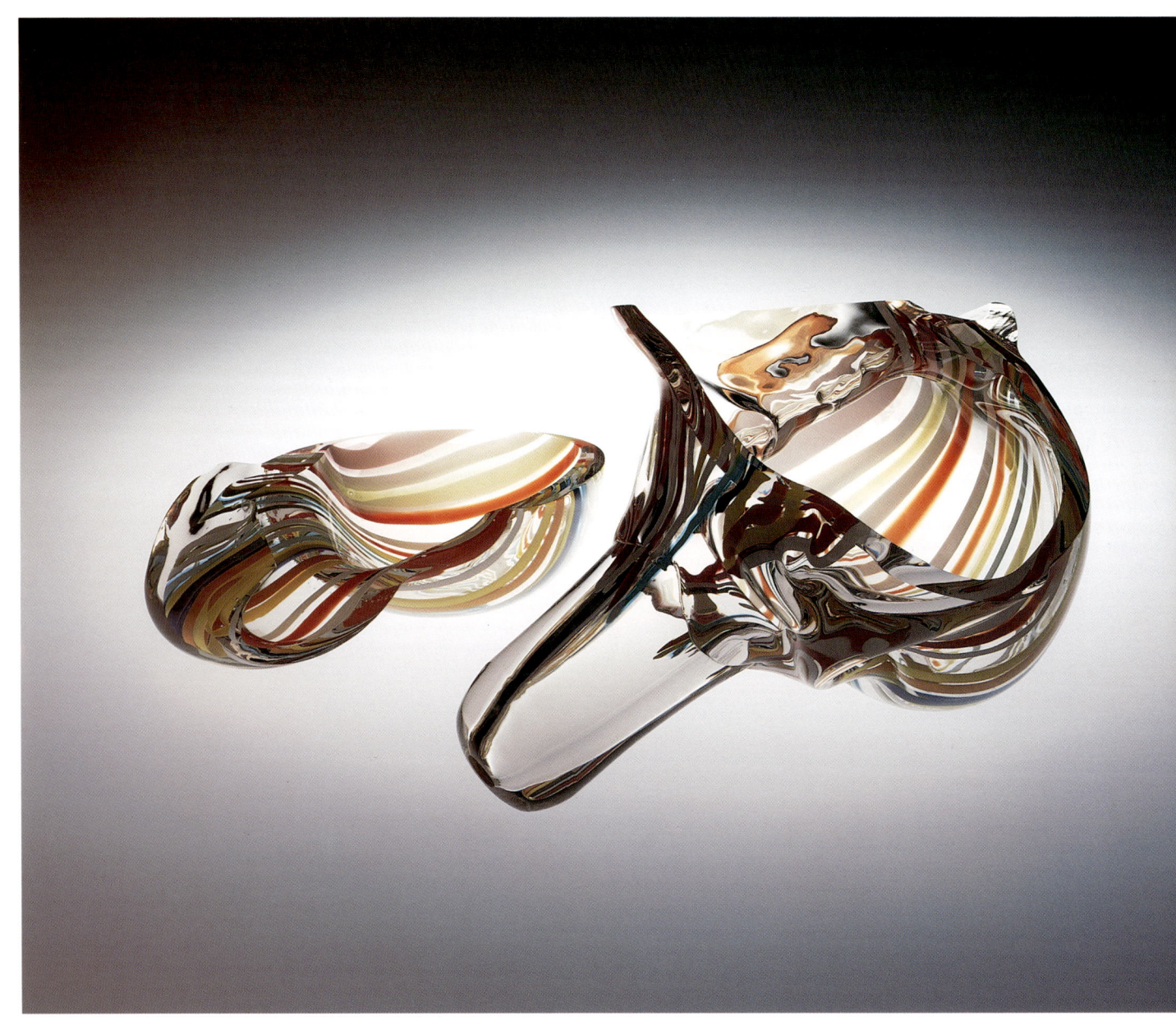

Marvin Lipofsky

Flowers/Mountains/Hana/Yama
(from the "Otaru" series), 1987–88
Blown glass, cut, sandblasted, and acid-etched
9$\frac{1}{2}$ x 12$\frac{1}{2}$ x 12 inches (24.1 x 31.8 x 30.5 cm)
cat. 27

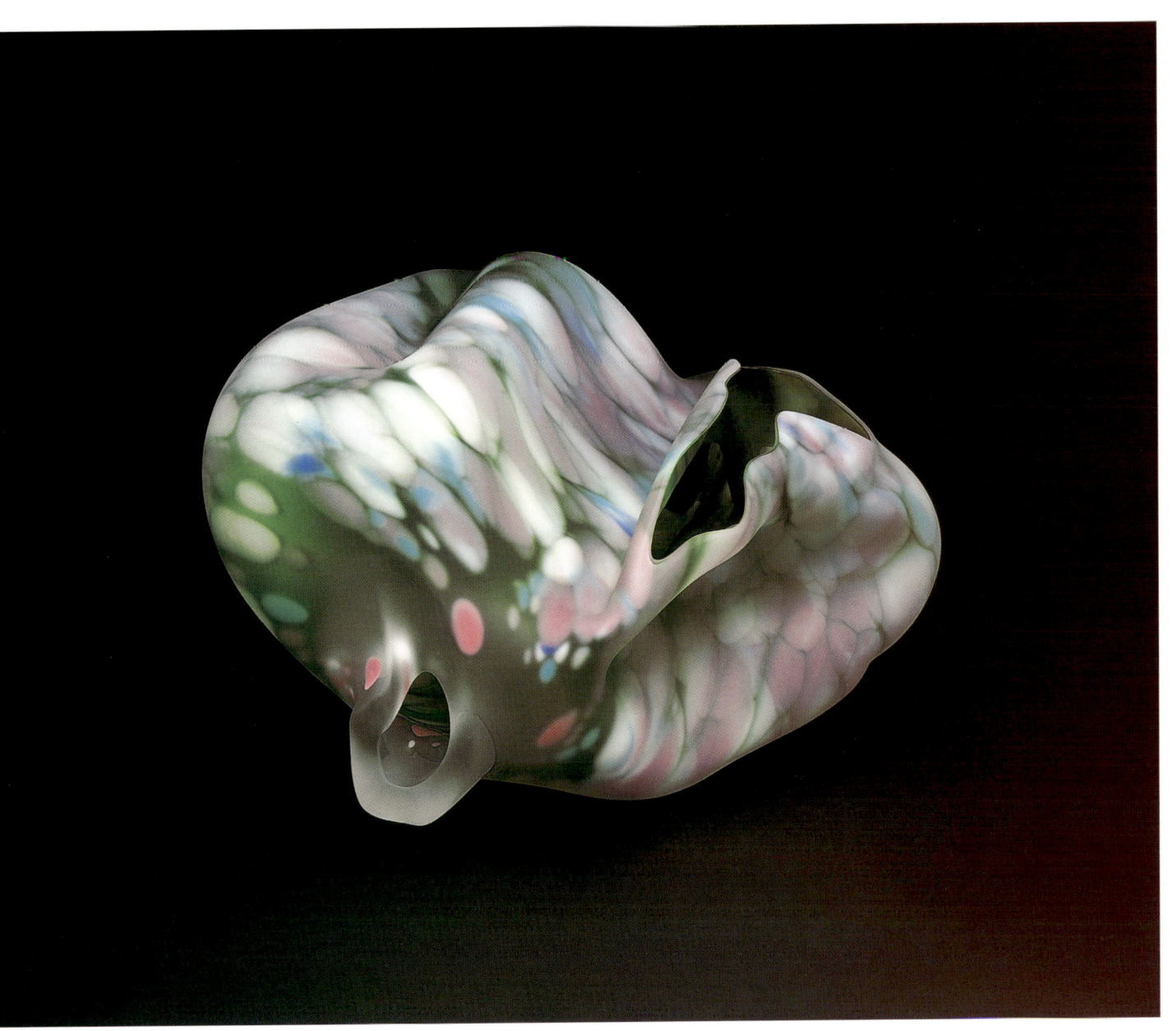

began to expand the glass program. Eager to explore the Funk sensibility, he experimented with electroplating on glass and flocking blown-glass objects. Perennially fascinated by hot glass, Lipofsky sought to capture its spontaneity.

While maintaining a full teaching load, Lipofsky took extended tours around the world. After visiting the Blenko Glass Factory, in Milton, West Virginia, to see the work of Joel Philip Myers (cats. 39–49), Lipofsky took a sabbatical in 1970 to travel for the first time to Europe. He was invited to the Rietveld Academie by glass artist Sybren Valkema as their first visiting artist.[84] He also worked at the Leerdam Factory, in Holland, and with factory master Van Der Linden. In Finland he worked at the invitation of designer Kai Frank and gained exposure to the northern European factory system, in which he could not handle the pieces himself, but could only direct their creation. Adapting to each factory's work situation became integral to Lipofsky's art and provided him with new artistic elements.

In 1972 Lipofsky traveled to Italy. He worked at a small factory outside of Milan owned by Roberto Niederer and also at the Venini Glass Factory (Venini e C.) in Murano. At the 1972 First International Glass Conference, at the Museum Bellerive, in Zurich, he met the Italian master glassblower Gianni Toso.[85] On a return visit in 1975, Lipofsky created his "Venini Series."

Venini Series—Split Piece (1975) was inspired by the similarity between brightly colored Italian canes of glass and the tiny, beguiling bikini beachwear. Lipofsky made this two-part piece using clear glass punctuated by white, orange, yellow, and blue stripes. Impressed by the Italian gift for color and spontaneous work, Lipofsky sought to capture the same qualities. In this work he shaped the glass through the manipulation of wooden molds into which glass was blown by Toso. Because in this method the wooden forms can catch on fire, an intriguing element of risk is added.[86] Lipofsky retains the taffylike consistency of the liquid glass in the gentle, organic curves of the finished work. After Lipofsky has blown and annealed his works, he ships the unfinished pieces home to cold-work them by cutting, grinding, and in some cases on later works, sandblasting the forms. This form was an innovation for him: his similar pieces had always been closed, but here he spilt open the object and exposed the interior space. This interest in the inside and the outside continues to this day in his work. Lipofsky again returned to Italy and worked at the Fratelli Toso Factory where he made *Serie Fratelli Toso—Split Piece* (1977–78) (ill. p. 16). He returned to the striped-bikini inspiration, but this time large red passages serve as contrast to the patterned sections.

The effects of a different working environment can be seen in *Flowers/Mountains/Hana/Yama* (from the "Otaru" series) (1987–88). Here Lipofsky was assisted by Mitsunobo Sagawa and this work was executed at the glass studio in Otaru in Hokkaido, in northern Japan. The colored chips that form the inside pattern are picked up from the marver and then cased inside a sheath of glass. In this example the configurations are reminiscent of traditional decorative patterns in Japanese design: the colors and forms are usually associated with the flowers and mountains of the title. This piece was finished in Lipofsky's studio, where he sandblasted the exterior to soften the sheen and create a contrast with the shiny interior.

HARVEY LITTLETON

American, b. 1922

Harvey Littleton was the catalyst for the mid-century American studio-glass movement: his work as a teacher and artist attracted adherents to the field. Born in Corning, New York, the site of Corning Glass Works and later The Corning Museum of Glass, Littleton was literally born into glass. His father, Jesse Littleton, was a physicist and the first PhD to be hired by Corning to aid in product development. Dr. Littleton is credited with discovering the temperature at which glass melts, known as the Littleton Point, which led to Corning's subsequent invention of Pyrex glassware.

At an extension class at nearby Elmira College, Harvey Littleton learned the rudiments of figure drawing and modeling.[87] Because of his family's wishes, in 1939 he enrolled at the University of Michigan, Ann Arbor, to study physics. After a two-year stint, he transferred to Cranbrook Academy of Art in Bloomfield Hills, Michigan, where he pursued his artistic interest while working as an assistant to sculptor Carl Milles. But Milles was not encouraging and Littleton returned to the university to study industrial design in the fall of 1941. Next came a three-year period in the Army Signal Corps, which concluded with a few months studying at the Brighton School of Art in England.

Littleton's early development interwove working in glass and clay. He also held a number of jobs relating to glassmaking, including serving as an inspector of blown-glass cookware and as a mold-maker at Corning for the fused-glass product called Vycor Multiform. At this time he made his first clay sculpture, a female torso which he later had copied in glass. Although he showed at the "Michigan Artists Exhibition" in Detroit in 1946, he did not show glass again until 1962.

In 1947 Littleton married and opened a design studio in Ann Arbor. A commission to build several potter's wheels moved Littleton into clay and he started the cooperative Ann Arbor Potter's Guild. In 1949 he reconnected with glass and took a teaching position at the museum school of The Toledo Museum of Art in Ohio. Toledo is an industrial glass town, which is celebrated in the museum's collection of historical glass. Littleton studied their collections and came to know the director, Otto Wittmann. Littleton continued to study clay under Maija Grotell at Cranbrook, receiving his Master of Fine Arts degree in 1951.

Next Littleton began teaching at the University of Wisconsin, Madison. He moved his family to a dairy farm and opened up a pottery studio, producing vessels of stoneware and porcelain. To further his understanding of ceramics, he traveled to Spain, France, and Italy. At the suggestion of Arthur Houghton of the Steuben Glass Works (part of the Corning Glass Works) and Thomas Beuchner, then director at the new Corning Museum, he visited glassmaker Jean Sala, an expatriate Spaniard living in Paris. Eager to see how Sala made glass in his small studio, Littleton arrived only to find the studio closed. But photographs were helpful and later visits to the factories of Murano, Italy, convinced him that glassmaking was possible outside a large factory setting.

As Littleton already had a pottery studio, it was just a matter of sorting out how to achieve the high temperatures necessary for working glass. Otto Wittmann agreed to sponsor two glass seminars, in March and June 1962. During these sessions some issues surrounding furnace design and melting glass were solved in a rudimentary manner with the help of Dominick Labino (cats. 21 and 22). Glassblowing outside a factory setting was seen to be possible.

Encouraged, Littleton gathered a group of fellow enthusiasts and sought to create glass programs at a number of universities. Wanting to push the limits of glass as an art medium, by the 1970s Littleton moved into making works that are sculptural. He also discovered his métier: the creation of cased and pulled linear forms. His book, *Glassblowing: a Search for Form* (1971), contains the then-radical statement that studio glass was an appropriate medium for artistic expression.[88]

During his travels in the late 1950s, Littleton had met Erwin Eisch (cat. 12). Eisch's work affected Littleton deeply and in 1967, after a visit from Eisch, Littleton's work began to change. The expressionistic and personal forms that Eisch made led to Littleton's "Loop" series. *Green Loop* (1978) (ill. p. 19) is from this series. As with most of Littleton's forms, layers of cased glass have been pulled to create a trumpet form at both ends. The latter has an added detail of an agitated line that articulates the larger end piece. Both top and bottom come to rest on a glass base that holds both pieces in balanced equilibrium. Much of Littleton's work manifests a Euclidean geometry that expresses his technical background.

By this time Littleton was entranced with color and glass' ability to lend luminescence to oxide-induced hues. During the middle of the 1970s, he began a second artistic exploration of glass as a intaglio print medium. Believing that he was on to a new technique, Littleton attempted to conquer the obstacles: he created a studio devoted to the process and invited a series of glass and print artists to work with him.[89] Only later did he learn that glass intaglio had been used in nineteenth-century Vienna and was displayed prominently at the international Great Exhibition of 1851 in London.

During the 1980s Littleton made color compositions with cased and drawn glass. *Blue Crown* (1988), a fine example of this group, has six major and six minor elements. Their arrangement is left to the owner, but the conceptual framework is for the larger elements to be placed in a crownlike form with the smaller pieces punctuating the spaces in between. This dramatic and beautiful work captures Littleton's dual interests in sculpture and in the technical ability to form such large glass pieces. In 1990 Littleton stopped making hot-glass pieces, but he still works on his intaglio glass printing.

arvey Littleton

ue Crown, 1988

lled and cased glass

t. 29

TWELVE PARTS

A: 20 x 10½ x 3 inches (50.8 x 26.7 x 7.6 cm)
B: 15 x 14 x 3 inches (38.1 x 35.6 x 7.6 cm)
C: 14½ x 12 x 3 inches (36.8 x 30.5 x 7.6 cm)
D: 20 x 16 x 3 inches (50.8 x 40.6 x 7.6 cm)
E: 16 x 12 x 3 inches (40.6 x 30.5 x 7.6 cm)
F: 20 x 12 x 3 inches (50.8 x 30.5 x 7.6 cm)
G–L: each 7 x 6 x 3 inches (17.8 x 15.2 x 7.6 cm)

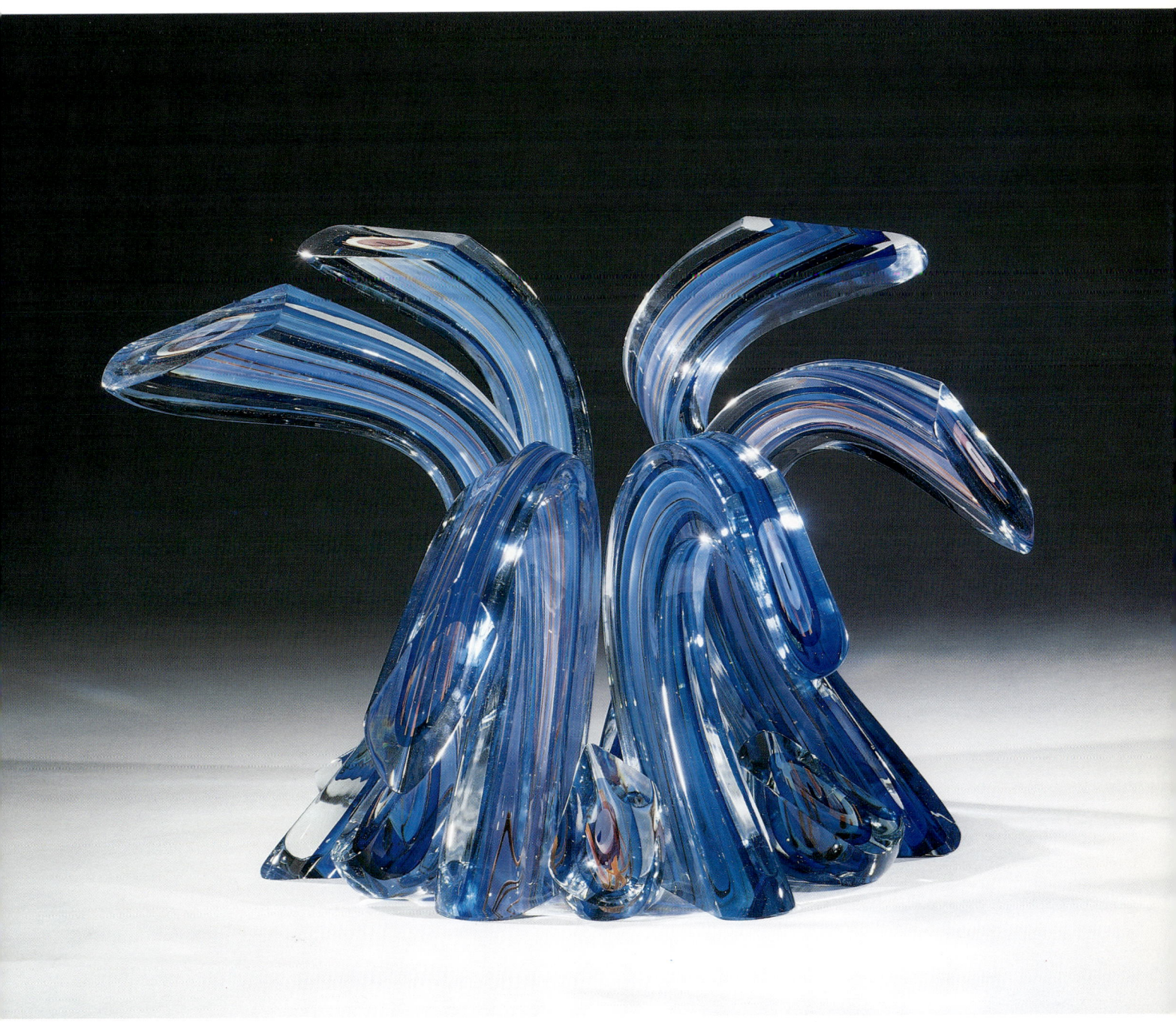

Richard Marquis

Murrine Teapot, 1984 (right)
Blown glass with *murrine* canes
6 x 6 dia. inches (15.2 x 15.2 cm)
cat. 30

Wizard Teapot, 1985 (left)
Blown glass with *murrine* canes
12 x 6¼ dia. inches (30.5 x 15.9 cm)
cat. 31

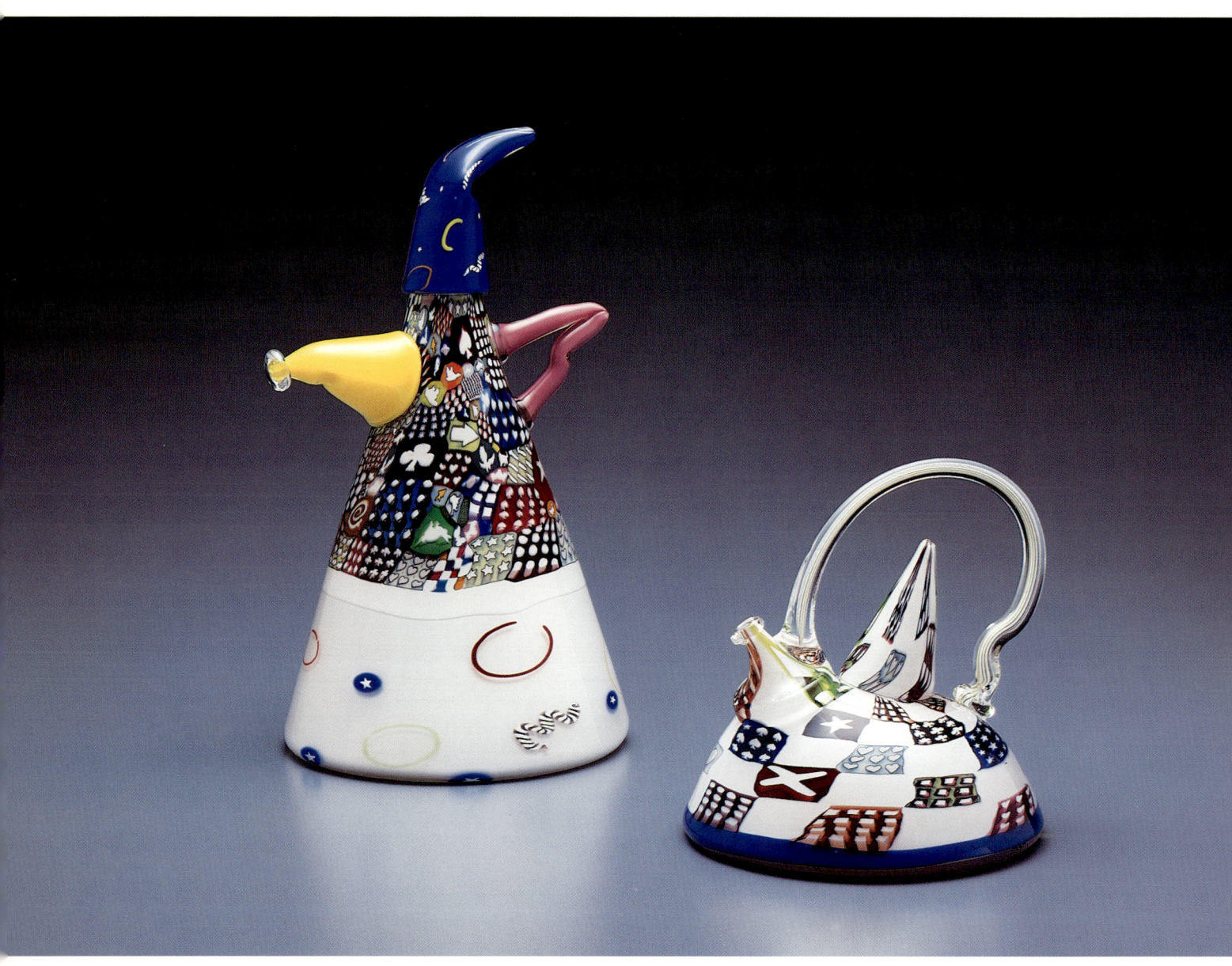

RICHARD MARQUIS

American, b. 1945

Richard Marquis makes colorful, whimsical glass sculptures of high technical virtuosity. Although he is serious about his art, he deflects self-importance though cheerful colors and amusing forms, which his skill allows to flow effortlessly. Born in Phoenix, Marquis attended the University of California, Berkeley (1963–69), where he worked as a teaching assistant for glassblowing under Marvin Lipofsky (cats. 25–27). Marquis then received a Fulbright-Hays Fellowship to study traditional techniques; initially he worked for Salviati & Compagnia, and then as a guest designer at the Venini Glass Factory in Murano (Venini e C.). Marquis studied Venetian glass-forming techniques and invited fellow student Robert Naess to assist him.[90] Marquis worked at any task from the lowest to the highest: he also designed lighting fixtures, but they were not put into production.

The technique that fascinated Marquis was the making of *murrine*. Known from ancient Roman glass, *murrine* are made of colored glass cane, drawn (pulled) after several casings, into sticks about a quarter-inch in diameter. After they are cool these rods are cut into discs, placed side by side on a steel plate *ferro*, and returned to the furnace for fusing into a sheet. The *murrine* sheet is then cased using the *pastorale* (a long-handled tool used to transfer the sheet of *murrine*) into the fusing oven, dubbed by Marquis as the "*pastorale* pick-up." In the final step the patterned glass is reheated and blown, distorting and expanding the *murrine* pattern. Traditionally, *murrine* are seen in vessel forms or as the central decorative passage in paperweights. In Marquis's hands they are used to make everything from teapots to written texts, in work laced with wit and whimsy.

Upon his return to the United States, Marquis went to the Penland School of Handicrafts, near Asheville, North Carolina, where he worked with Mark Peiser (cats. 52–54) and Richard Ritter. Next he went to California, where he worked at California State College, Chico, with Robert Naess. There Marquis made his famous *murrine* representation of the American flag and his inscription of the Lord's Prayer inside a single *murrina*. By linking the ancient technique of *murrine* and the then-current interest in appropriation of cultural icons into the service of larger art statements, Marquis moved this decorative technique into a content-driven application. During the 1970s and 1980s, Marquis traveled and

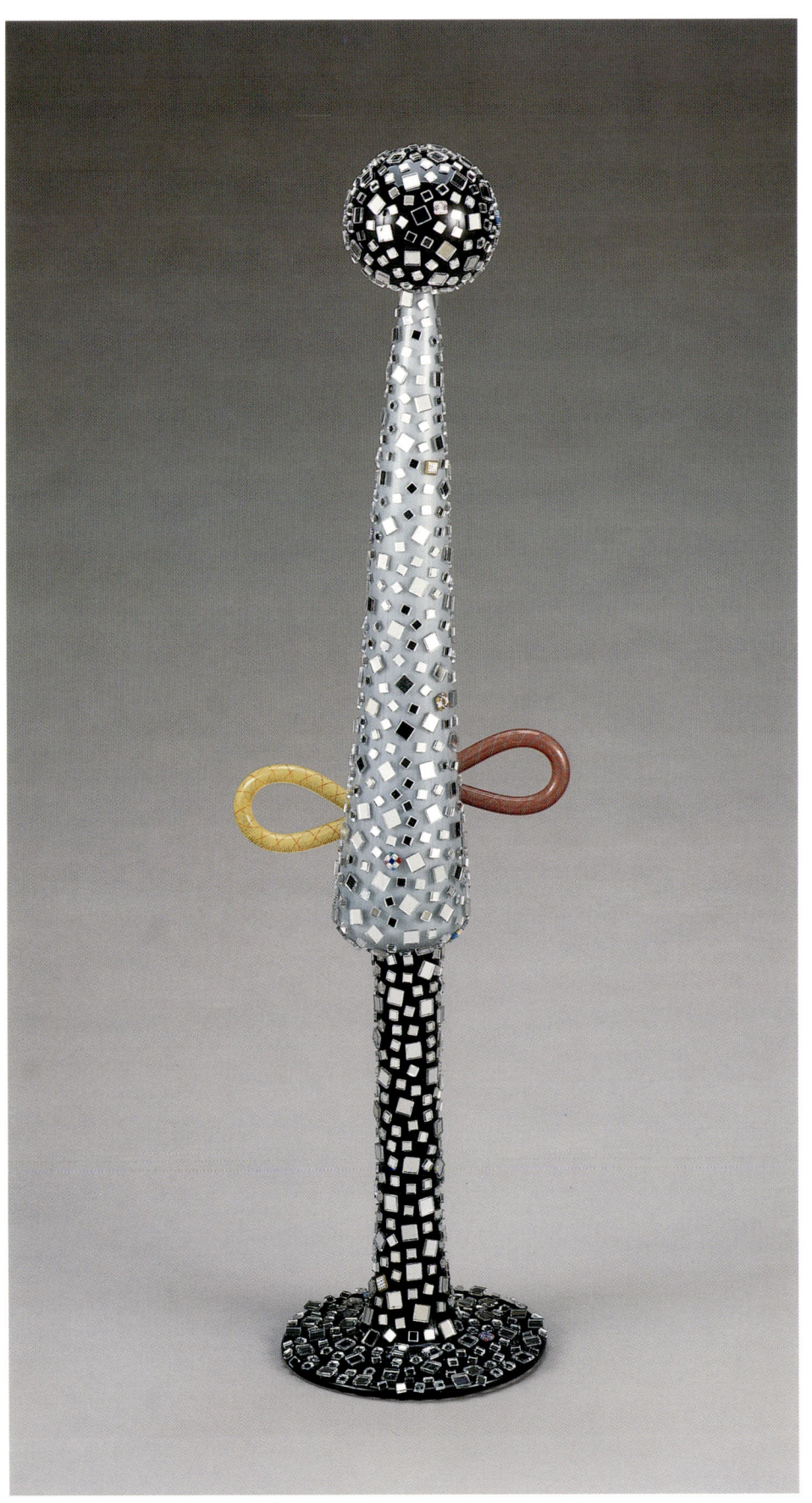

Richard Marquis

Mirrored Ball Trophy, 1988
Blown glass, mirror squares, and can
43 × 10 dia. inches (109.2 × 25.4 cm
cat. 32

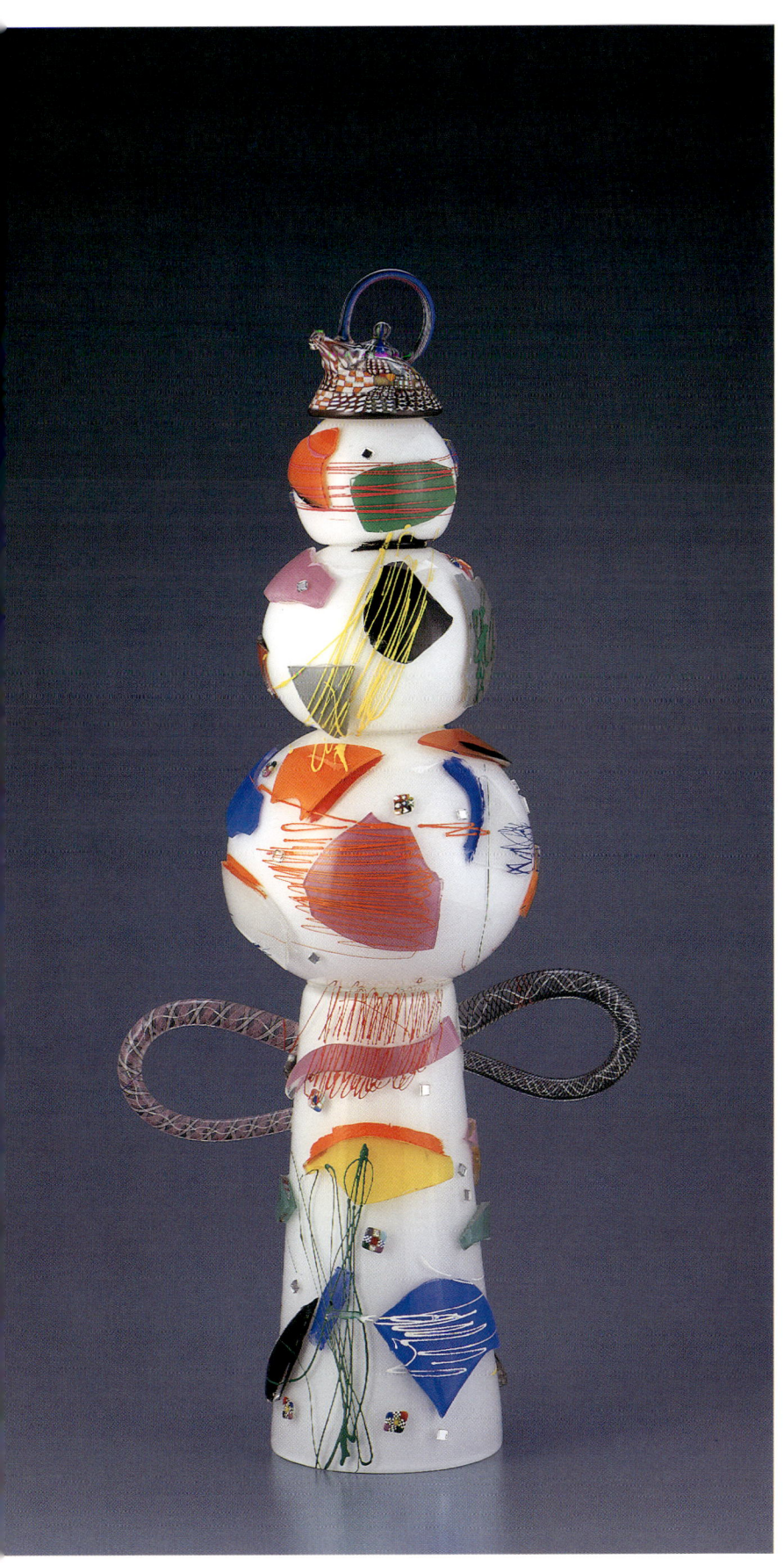

Richard Marquis

Bubble Boy, 1988
Blown and fabricated glass, *murrine* canes, paint, mirror, and glass shards
30 x 14 dia. inches (76.2 x 35.6 cm)
cat. 33

Richard Marquis

Marquiscarpa #23, 1992
Glass (*murrine* and *battulo* techniques), blown, fused,
slumped, fabricated, and wheel-ground, with gold leaf
5 x 8 x 3½ inches (12.7 x 20.3 x 8.9 cm)
cat. 34

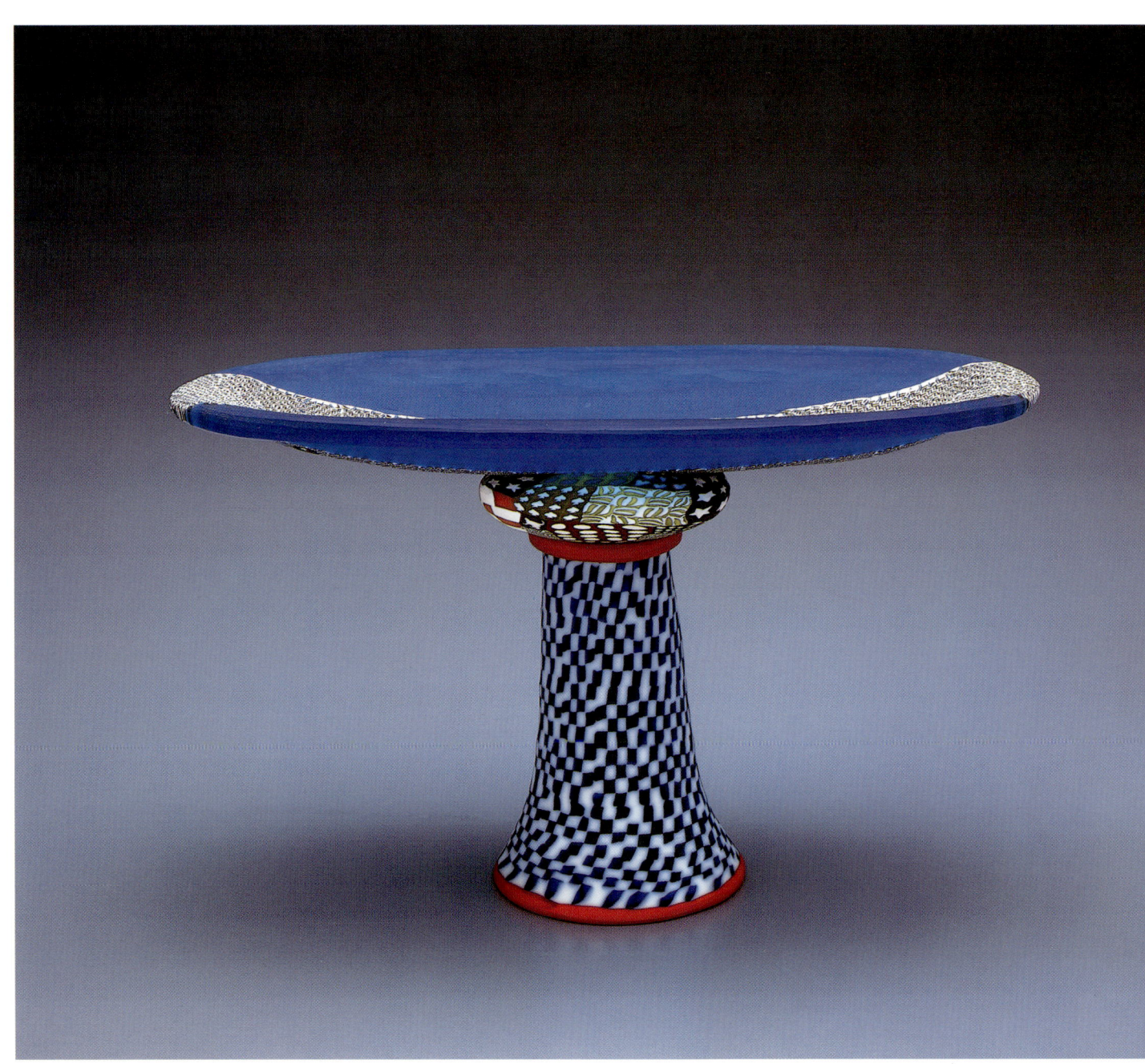

taught in the United States and Australia. He finally settled on Whitby Island, outside of Seattle, where he maintains a studio.

The Glick collection has five pieces by Marquis. *The Murrine Teapot* (1984) has a white body that is decorated with stars and geometric patterns placed in checkerboard fashion on the surface. Although nonfunctional, this work explores "teapotness" and elaborates on it through the whimsical handle and stubby spout. This series of teapot forms was begun in the 1970s, and reflects the influence of ceramist Ron Nagle's beaded checkerboard moccasins, which Marquis saw in 1965.[91] The early iterations of this form came with beaded tea cozies. *Wizard Teapot* (1985) expands Marquis's investigation of teapots, incorporating an anthropomorphic form topped with a wizard's hat. This time the *murrine* "dress" the wizard, and the stars and other decorative elements evoke the zodiac or cosmos.

Mirrored Ball Trophy (1988), a tall work constructed of blown-glass sections embellished with shards of colored glass and mirror squares, relates to the trophy objects explored by ceramist Robert Arneson during the mid-1960s. Without the sexual references of Arneson's works, this object features a similar casual structure. As a gesture of self-reference, Marquis topped the work with a miniature *murrine* teapot. *Bubble Boy* (1988) features both mirror and *murrine*, arrayed over a tall spare form. Again anthropomorphic, the piece features an unusually restrained palette for Marquis. The title, lightly tripping off of the tongue, refers to the glass bubble on top.

The final work is a tribute to the Italian designer and architect Carlo Scarpa (1901–1967). Scarpa was known for his innovative, Modernist 1950s reinterpretation of *murrine*, for Venini e C. In the title, *Marquiscarpa #23*, Marquis linked his name to Scarpa's and thereby attached himself to the tradition that Scarpa began. This petite *tazza* form (compote) is executed in three parts. Incorporating slumping (the top section), blown-glass *murrine*, and gold leaf, this work contrasts colorful glass elements with the crisp white armature. It expresses all of Marquis's skills and his sense of connection to the long tradition of Italian glassmaking.

Klaus Moje

Untitled ("Songlines"), 1989
Kiln-formed mosaic glass, slumped, with
wheel-ground surface
2 x 20 x 20 inches (5.1 x 50.8 x 50.8 cm)
cat. 35

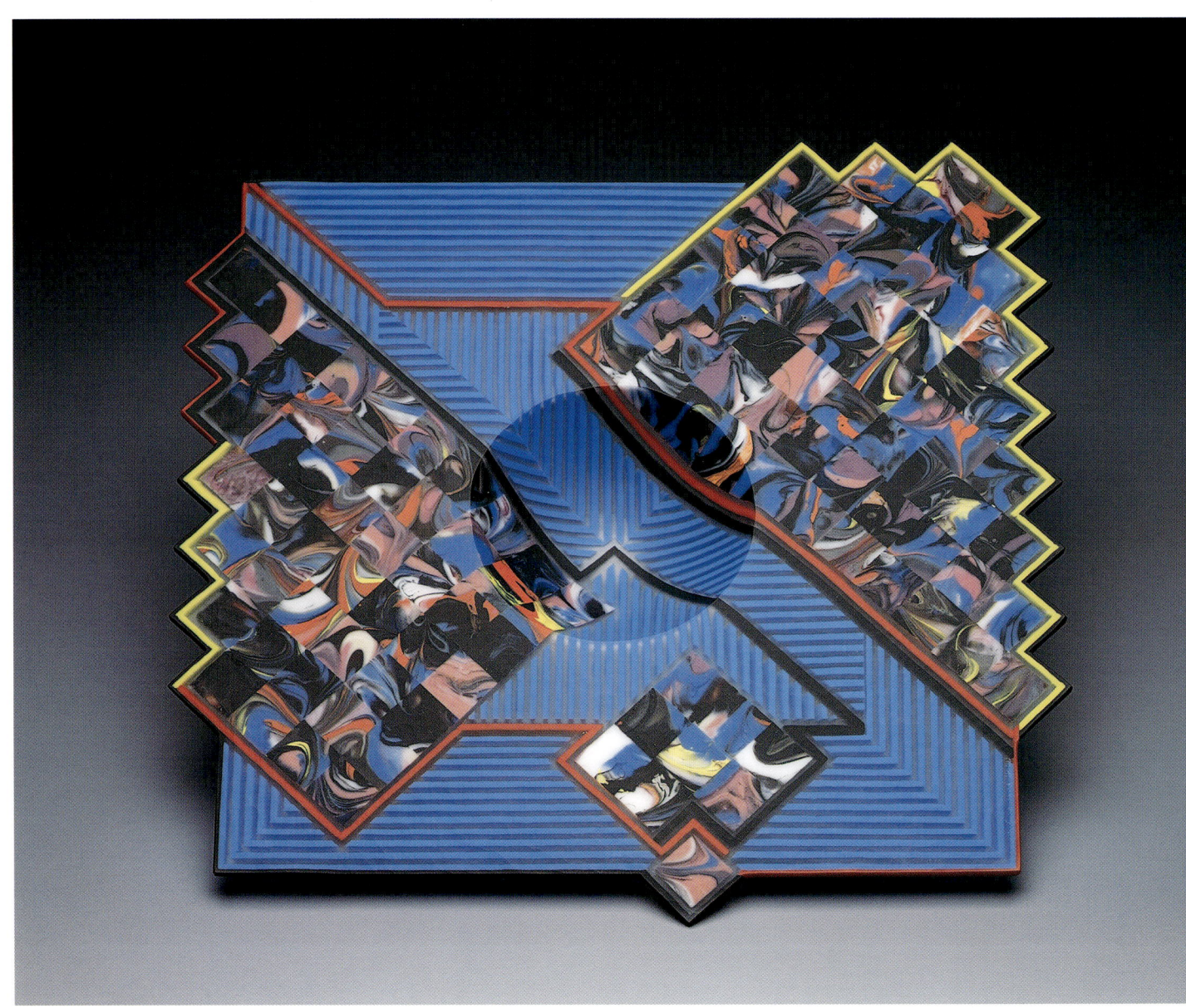

KLAUS MOJE

German, b. 1936

Klaus Moje treats his simple vessel-based forms as canvases for riotous color explosions or investigations of subtle tonalities: his work is both artistically and technically innovative. Born in Hamburg, Germany, in 1936, Moje learned the cold-working skills of cutting, grinding, and beveling glass from his father, Hugo Moje. Moje then attended trade school and by 1956 he had won the top prize in his journeyman's competition. To complete his education he set out to study at the Staatliche Glasfachschule Rheinbach and then at the Staatliche Glasfachschule Hadamar. Here he saw firsthand the potential that glass had as an art medium.[92] While still working in the historical styles favored by many European glasshouses, Moje experienced the attraction of breaking free from factory limitations and using glass for art expression.

In 1962 Moje and his then-wife Isgard Moje-Wohlgemuth took over his father's glass studio. There they fabricated numerous stained-glass window commissions out of luster glass, specially blown for them at the Hessenglas manufactory near Frankfurt. During this period Moje worked with Lothar Schreyer, who had been one of the nine "masters of form" at the Bauhaus. He also saw the work of Bauhaus silversmith Wolfgang Tuempel. This experience left the stamp of the Bauhaus aesthetic and its designer sensibility on Moje's work.

During this period Moje also made carved-glass vessels. In 1966 Moje and Moje-Wohlgemuth exhibited these vessels and stained-glass cabinet panels at the Christmas fair sponsored by the Museum für Kunst und Gewerbe in Hamburg. In 1971 they received the Hessischer Staatspreis für das deutsche Kunsthandwerk (Hesse State Award for Applied Art) for their painted hollow-glass vessels. Their studio became a meeting place for other craft artists and in 1976 they opened a gallery to serve as a retail outlet for their production.[93] Moje also shared his knowledge and enthusiasm freely at craft conferences and meetings.

Up to this time Moje had used strictly cold-working techniques, but in 1967 at the World Craft Conference in Dublin, he met Marvin Lipofsky (cats. 25–27) and tried his hand at glassblowing. He found that he was not a naturally skilled blower and produced only "misshapen bubbles."[94] Later, in 1979 at Pilchuck Glass School, Stanwood, Washington, Moje again attempted the blowpipe, but finally chose to hone the skills he already had.

Moje's first visit to the United States was in 1971. At the American Craft Museum in New York he saw works by Joel Philip Myers (cats. 39–49) and Dale Chihuly (cats. 7 and 8) that demonstrated the free methods of working glass that the Americans originated. While clearly infused with enthusiasm, these methods were actually the result of incomplete technical knowledge, compensated for by creative energy and artistic inquiry. This spontaneity intrigued Moje.[95]

In the mid-1970s Moje began making his hallmark mosaic glass. Mosaic has been known since Roman times, but the specifics of how it was done had been lost. *Terrerae glass* uses glass's capacity to become progressively more liquid. In a 900-degrees-centigrade firing furnace, it becomes soft enough to attach but not melt and intermingle. Small strips placed side-by-side on a flat surface can be fused in a kiln to make a sheet. This sheet can then be set into a clay mold and reheated in an annealing oven until it slumps into the form of the underlying plaster firing mold. The forms are then cold-worked (often sanded) to develop a muted, textured surface rather than the uniform, shiny whole usually associated with glass. It is this aspect of kiln-forming that Moje has most enjoyed.

Initially working with canes made by Hessenglas, Moje had to invent his own methods of working the tiny glass fragments.[96] Unsure about the viability of this technique, he was delighted to receive support from noted German glass scholar Axel von Saldern.[97] Further recognition came in 1979 in the exhibition "New Glass: A Worldwide Survey," organized by The Corning Museum of Glass, New York. Two of his mosaic vessels were included and from that time on it was his technique of choice.

In 1982 Moje was invited by Professor Udo Sellbach to establish a course in glass at the Canberra School of Art in Australia. Moje brought with him his guild training. Breaking the pattern of American glass programs, he placed kiln-forming on a par with glassblowing. Moje also insisted that his students define what they wanted to achieve and then determine the correct methodology for creating it.[98] In this way they focused on artistic intent first and skill acquisition second.

All three works by Moje in the Glick collection were made in Australia, during the mature period of his work. *Untitled* (1990) (ill. p. 32) represents the subtle side of Moje's work and relies on the beauty inherent in the striations natural to mosaic glass. The reductive vessel form features a small indentation surrounded by a wide rim. Pared down to its basic elements, a similar form is seen in *Untitled* (1989), where the passionate palette expresses the impact of Australia on Moje. Blasts of yellow and red stream across the blue surface, evoking that continent's bright sun. Moje's familiarity with the works of American artists Kenneth Noland and Frank Stella, and Op and Pop art movements can also be seen in works of this period.

In *Untitled* ("Songlines") (1989), a different format is used. The title is taken from a book by Bruce Chatwin that evokes the complexity of Australian culture with its overlay of British institutions on its aboriginal ancestry. Moje's piece is structured using a grid system, clearly architectonic in nature, and linked to his earlier stained-glass works. It balances passages of nuanced tonalities to an explosion of marbleized patterning. Graphically set off by the black and red line linking the disparate fields, the work sends the eye skipping from section to section, edge to edge. Part of a series that melds the two key aspects of his work, this piece illustrates Moje's technical virtuosity and artistic sophistication.

Klaus Moje

Untitled, 1989
Fused and slumped glass with wheel-ground surface
2½ x 20½ dia. inches (6.4 x 52.1 cm)
cat. 36

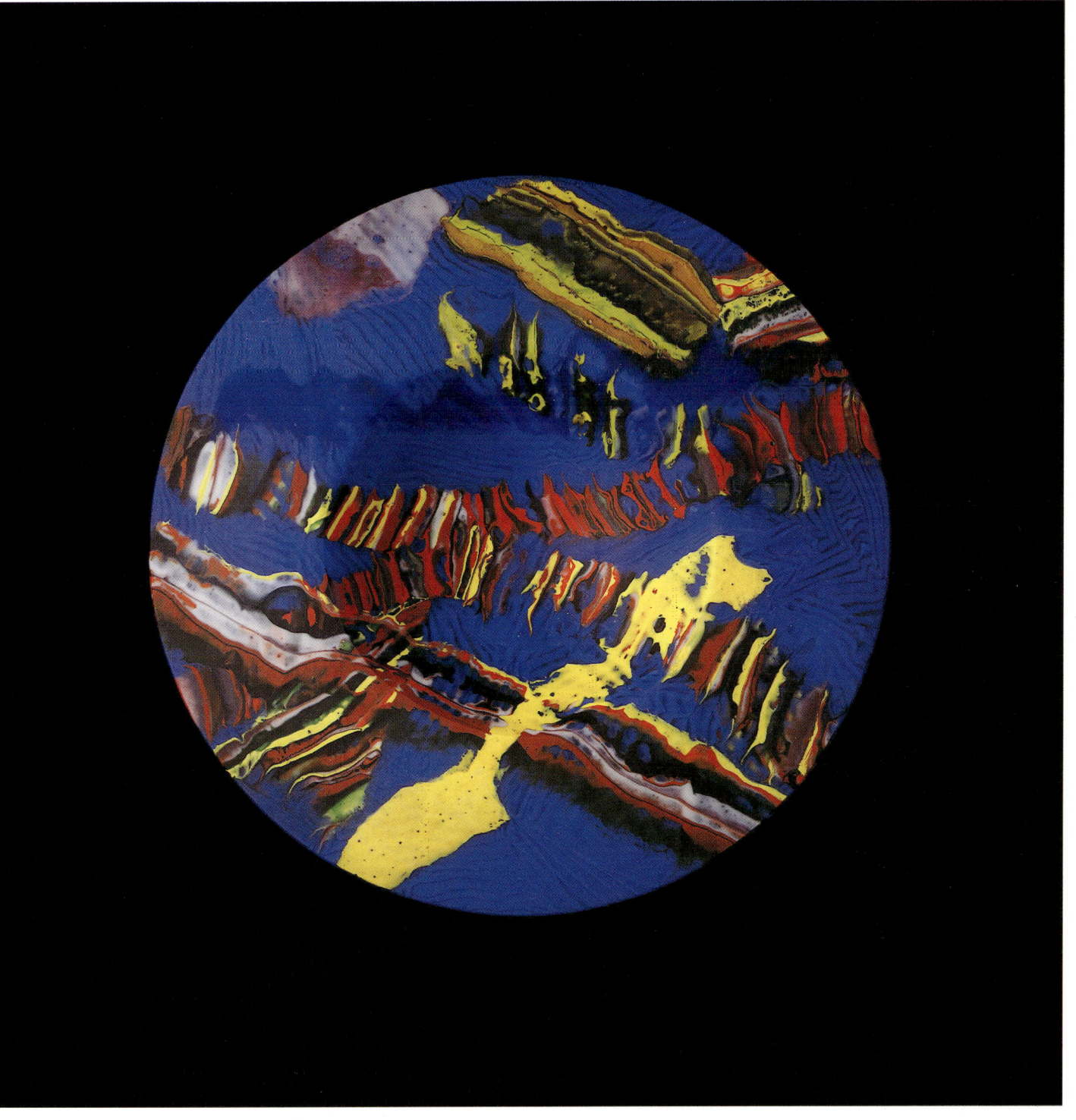

JAY MUSLER

American, b. 1949

Jay Musler's disquieting pieces shroud the beauty of glass behind a veil of paint. Musler was born in Sacramento, California to an Irish Catholic family. As a boy he explored the brown grassy Sacramento delta inlets and waterways, imprinting on his sensibility an affection for murky, evocative places and colors.

In high school Musler took a ceramics class from Larry Foster, who encouraged him to seek an education in the arts. Having been told that the California College of Arts and Crafts (CCAC) in Oakland was a good school, Musler applied and was accepted. He studied glassblowing under Marvin Lipofsky (cats. 25–27). The year 1968 was the height of the anti-Vietnam War movement and the school was located near one of the centers of that revolt, Berkeley. Using a student deferment to avoid being drafted, Musler was part of an experimental program that allowed students considerable leeway in their studies. So much leeway, in fact, that Musler was asked to leave because he was making no progress towards his degree.

In 1971 Musler was working for Steve Maslach in his small production-glass studio in Greenbrae, across the bay from Oakland. He spent the next eight years learning the skills of goblet-blowing, batch-melting, and everything else necessary to make "very crafty"[99] items. By 1978 Musler he wished to return to more serious art-making, and the next year Lipofsky invited him to be an artist-in-residence at CCAC. This opportunity allowed Musler to wrestle with issues concerning the "fossil fuel society"[100] and the lack of progress made after the years of hope in the mid-1960s. It was also during this period that he experienced his "fantasy-of-being-a-designer period."[101] He made conventionally shaped bowls engraved with geometric patterns, one of which was included in The Corning Museum of Glass' 1979 show "New Glass: A Worldwide Survey." Musler proceeded to make evocative vessels that deconstruct the gritty urban scene. The commercially blown glass vessels have edges that are tortured, cut, and burnt to express the sinister nature of the contemporary urban landscape; soft colors belie the menacing edges. In 1982 Musler was awarded a National Endowment of the Arts Craft Fellowship grant for this series.

Using blanks blown by his friend Therman Statom (cats. 60 and 61). Musler constructed boat forms from cut, sandblasted, and painted glass fragments. Airbrushed to a timberlike paint hue, the

Jay Musler

Untitled, 1991
Sheet glass elements, sandblasted, with oil paint
4 x 56½ x 10½ inches (10.2 x 143.5 x 26.7 cm)
cat. 38

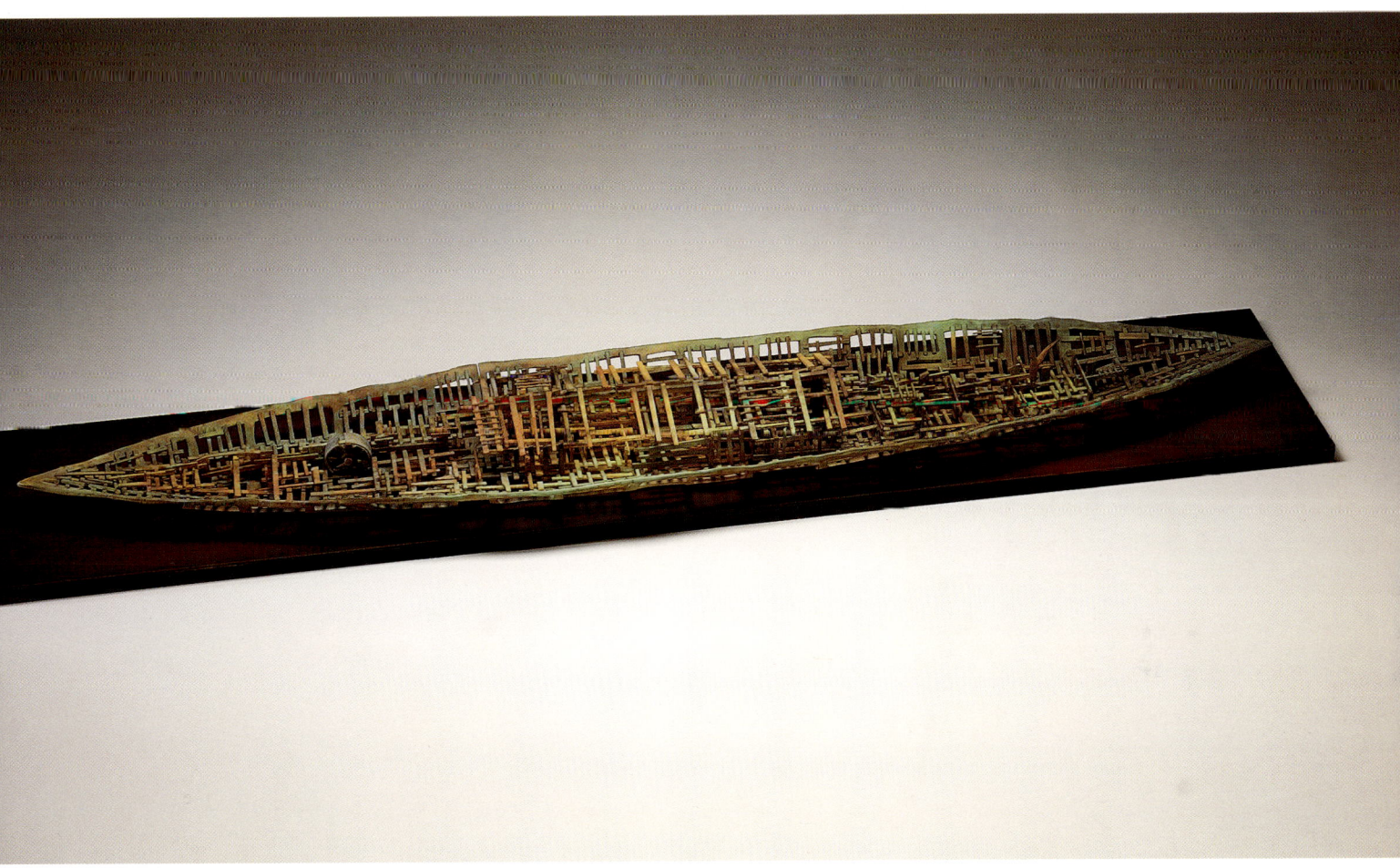

forms evoke decayed and deserted urban detritus. Musler's next series involved wall-mounted mask forms that are similar to the boat forms; they continue his evocation of a ghostly, postindustrial reality. Naturally attracted to dark subject matter, Musler was influenced by the work of German Neo-Expressionists Walter Dahn and Georg Baselitz. Uneasy content is not usually associated with the clean, clear beauty of translucent glass. By deliberately negating that characteristic through the application of paint, Musler transcends the limitations of glass as a seductive medium.

Untitled (1991), made of assembled bits of glass, colored like aged wood, focuses on the morbid connotations associated with boats: a derelict vessel that perhaps once was beautiful, is presented as old and worn. While decrepit, it is heroic in its mere existence.

Joel Philip Myers

Dr. Zarkhov's Tower
(from the "Dr. Zarkhov" series), 1971
Blown glass with gold luster, glued, and
gilded metal base (replacement)
26½ inches (67.3 cm)
BASE: 7 x 11½ dia. inches (17.8 x 29.2 cm)
cat. 39

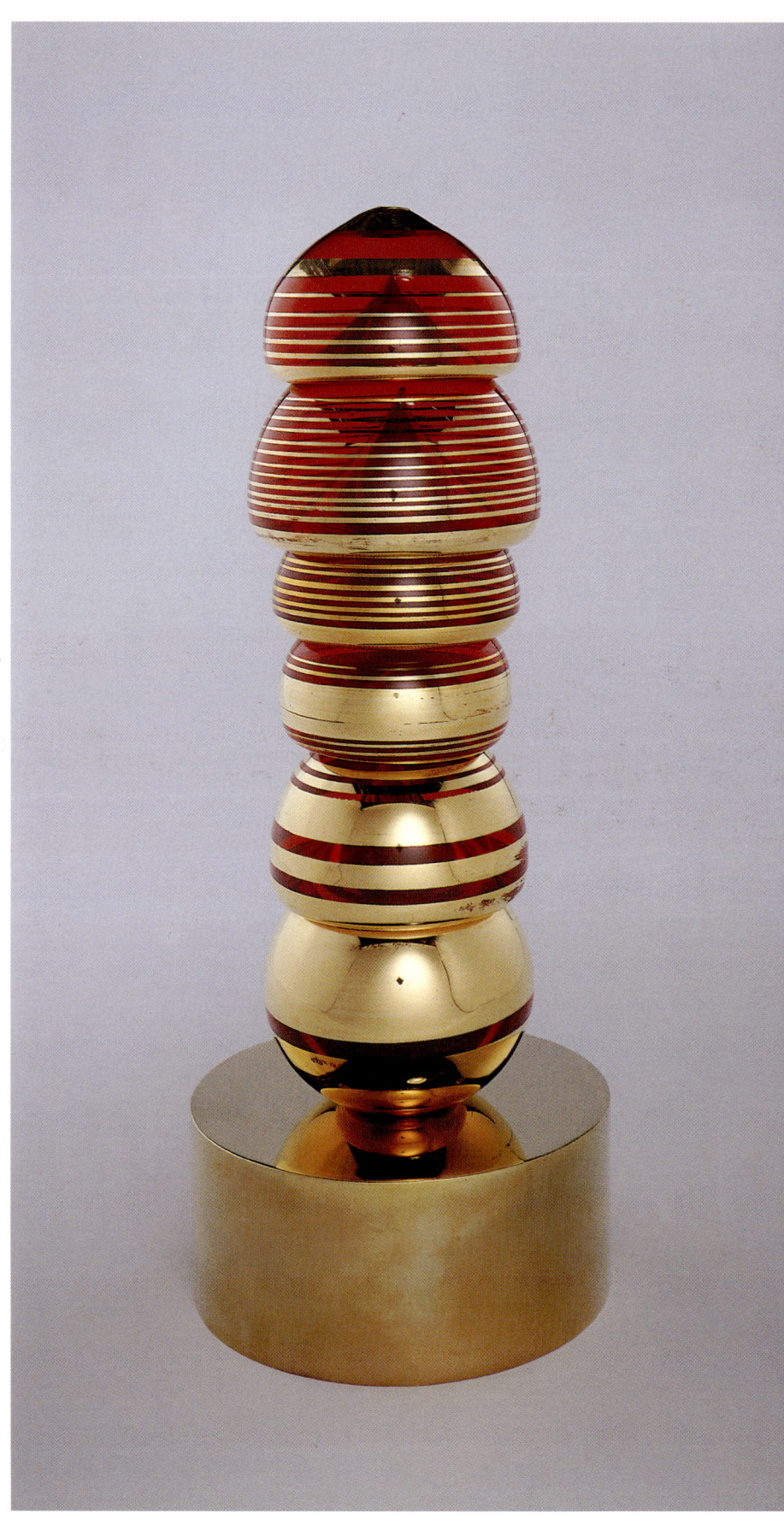

JOEL PHILIP MYERS

American, b. 1934

A rarity among glassmakers, Joel Philip Myers had no formal trianing in glass and did not come to glass until age twenty-nine. Trained as a graphic designer at Parsons School of Design, New York (1951–54), he was first hired as a package designer for the industrial-design firm Donald Deskey Associates in New York. Myers subsequently took an extended trip to Denmark. Danish design was in its heyday and Myers was attracted to its blend of design and craft. He studied ceramics with the noted production ceramist Richard Kjaergaard at the Kunstthaandvaerkerskolen in Copenhagen. Intending to stay one year, he remained eighteen months, returning home with a wife. He enrolled at Alfred University, New York State College of Ceramics at Alfred, to study ceramics for industry.

After graduation, Myers became director of design at Blenko Glass Factory in Milton, West Virginia. He applied what he knew about designing ceramics to glass and learned the new craft from the glassmakers at Blenko. Experimenting after regular hours, Myers was permitted to design pieces for his own pleasure, and while compatriots "never held [his works] in much regard,"[102] the unparalleled opportunity allowed him to learn the methodology and to appreciate glass as an art medium.

The year 1964 was a lucky one for Myers. The American Craft Council in New York sponsored the exhibition "Design for Production: A Craftsman's Approach." As one of the few craftsmen working in a factory setting, Myers attracted the attention of the exhibition organizer, Paul Smith, who selected Myers to participate. In another piece of good fortune, several pieces of his Blenko glass were featured on the cover of The American Craft Council's magazine, *Craft Horizons*. Finally, during the first World Congress of Craftsmen at Columbia University in New York, which Myers attended, the window of the America House shop on 53rd Street across from the conference was filled with Myers's one-off works fabricated at Blenko.[103]

The Glick collection has a number of important early pieces by Myers. Chief among them are the two works from the "Dr. Zarkhov" series, named for science-fiction hero Flash Gordon's brainy scientist friend.[104] Made by Myers at Blenko during his off hours, these imposing works capture the science-fiction aesthetic of 1950s popular culture. Myers sought to explore how scale could be altered through modular additions. Enlivening the transparency of the

Joel Philip Myers

Dr. Zarkhov's Tower
(from the "Dr. Zarkhov" series), 1972
Blown glass with platinum luster, glued, and chromed metal base
27 1/2 inches (69.8 cm)
BASE: 7 x 11 1/2 dia. inches (17.8 x 29.2 cm)
cat. 40

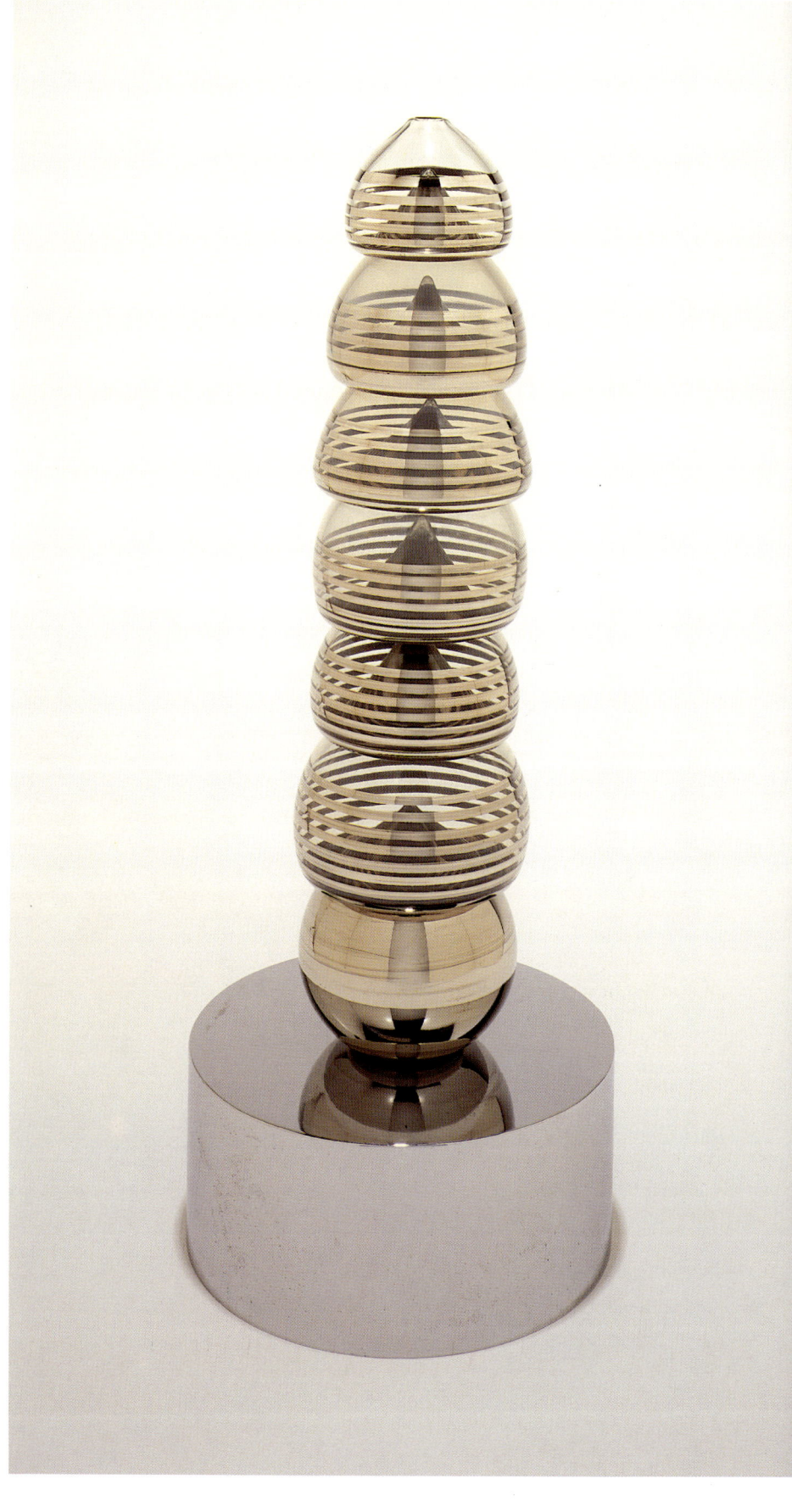

glass with lusters and mirroring, Myers created forms with clear passages balanced by lustered sections. The modular design allowed him easily to modify the size by adding preassembled elements. Myers continues today to use this postfabrication strategy for enhancing the final product.

Dr. Zarkhov's Tower (1971) features a series of blown sections of red glass ringed with bands of gold luster. With an overall appearance of a space-age housing development, the work is constructed from standard double-walled form sections, modified to have pointed tops and held in place by glue. *Dr. Zarkhov's Tower* (1972) is blown from clear glass and decorated with bands of platinum. The differing effect of these similar works illustrates how subtle modification can shift the essential sensibility of an artwork. This series consists of fewer than a dozen; four are in American museums and two are in European ones.

In 1970 Myers decided to leave the noisy, hectic Blenko factory.[105] He began teaching at Illinois State University at Normal. Hired as an art professor to found their glass program, Myers discovered that no provision had been made for setting up his teaching facility. Scrounging supplies and studio space, he solved the practical problems and attracted undergraduate and graduate students to his program. Because Myers uses the studio for his own work, students get to see works made in real time and to appreciate the complexity of working in glass. Graduates of Myers's program include Stephen Dee Edwards, Jim Harmon, David Huchthausen (cats. 17 and 18), David Schwartz, and Jack Schmidt.

During the 1970s Myers made a series of glass hands that dance on their fingertips on puddles of glass. Made in response to the anatomical bubbles that were flooding the field at the time,

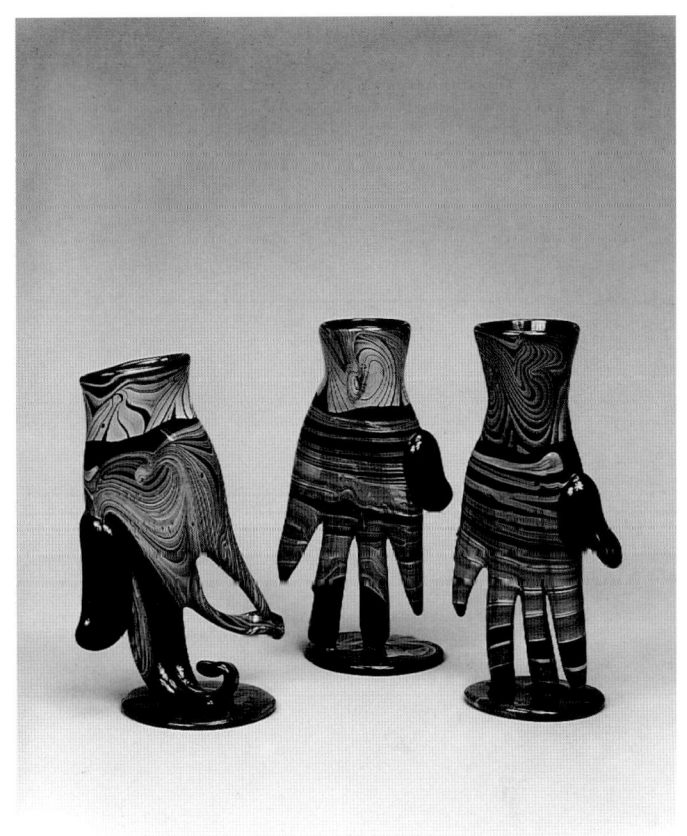

FIG. 8

Joel Philip Myers
American, b. 1934

Hand Forms, 1972
Blown and manipulated glass
LEFT: 8 5/16 x 3 3/4 dia. inches (22.1 x 9.3 cm)
CENTER: 9 5/8 x 3 3/4 dia. inches (24.5 x 9.3 cm)
RIGHT: 10 x 3 3/4 dia. inches (25.4 x 9.3 cm)
The Corning Museum of Glass, New York

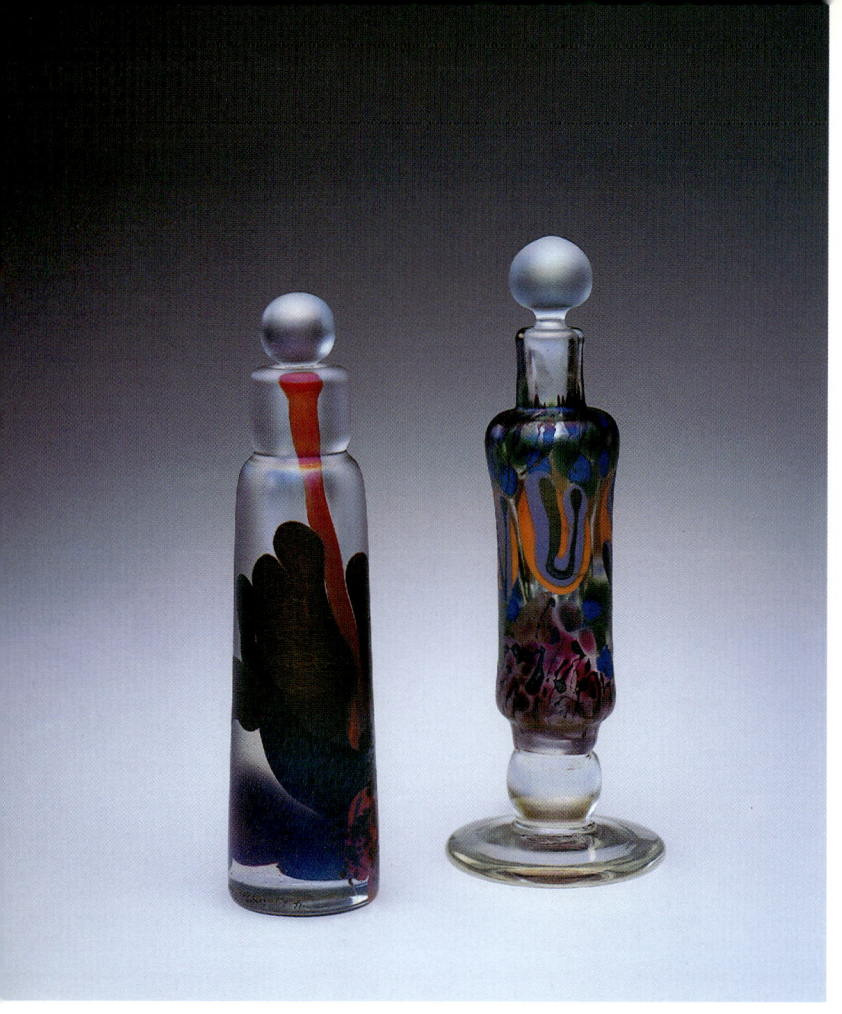

Joel Philip Myers

Knus (Hug), 1975 (right)
Blown glass with additions, acid-etched
9 1/2 x 3 1/4 dia. inches (24.1 x 8.3 cm)
cat. 41

Stoppered Form, 1976 (left)
Blown glass with colored shards
8 3/4 x 2 1/4 dia. inches (22.2 x 5.7 cm)
cat. 42

these forms have a disciplined composition and lively sensibility (see fig. 8). Next Myers tackled scent bottles, a favorite of the hippie culture. *Knus* (1975) is an example of Myers's petite scent bottles, emblazoned with the Danish word for hug and decorated with cold-worked and acid-etched colored-glass pieces. Fascinated by the richness of layered glass, Myers began a lifelong exploration of blown vessels that are then cold-worked with inlaid colors and pattern blocks. *Stoppered Form* (1976) is a further refinement of this intimate object created for personal use. Using a fumed-glass technique seen in Louis Comfort Tiffany's work, Myers offset the sparkle inherent in glass and softened the texture. As a response to the large-scale Blenko works, these small works manifest an accessibility that marks many of the early studio-glass movement pieces.

Two cylindrical works, *Untitled* (1976) and *White on White II* (1976), evidence the influence of Emil Nolde, Henri Matisse, and Paul Klee. Intrigued by the transition between the adjoining edges of the applied glass and the lozenge of the basic glass foundation, Myers articulated this juncture by placing each color panel by hand and carving a reveal. In *White on White II*, he attempted the difficult task of rendering a layered form without the benefit of color for articulation. When the cylinder series was displayed in Europe, it caught the eye and approval of German glass scholars Dr. Analisa Ohm and Dr. Helmut Ricke, and glass artist Klaus Moje (cats. 35–37).

Myers turned next to working in black glass. Elegant in their simplicity, three pieces from this "Contiguous Fragment" series are in the Glick collection. The first, from 1979, is actually white glass cased in black glass, with colored-glass shards placed on the body. Each piece was then cold-worked to reveal the underlying layers and "break to the transparency"[106] of the shards.

el Philip Myers

ntitled, 1976

own white opal glass with additions

x 4 1/2 x 4 1/2 inches (25.4 x 11.4 x 11.4 cm)

t. 43

Joel Philip Myers

White on White II, 1976

Blown white opal glass

10 1/4 x 3 3/4 x 3 3/4 inches (26 x 9.5 x 9.5 cm)

cat. 44

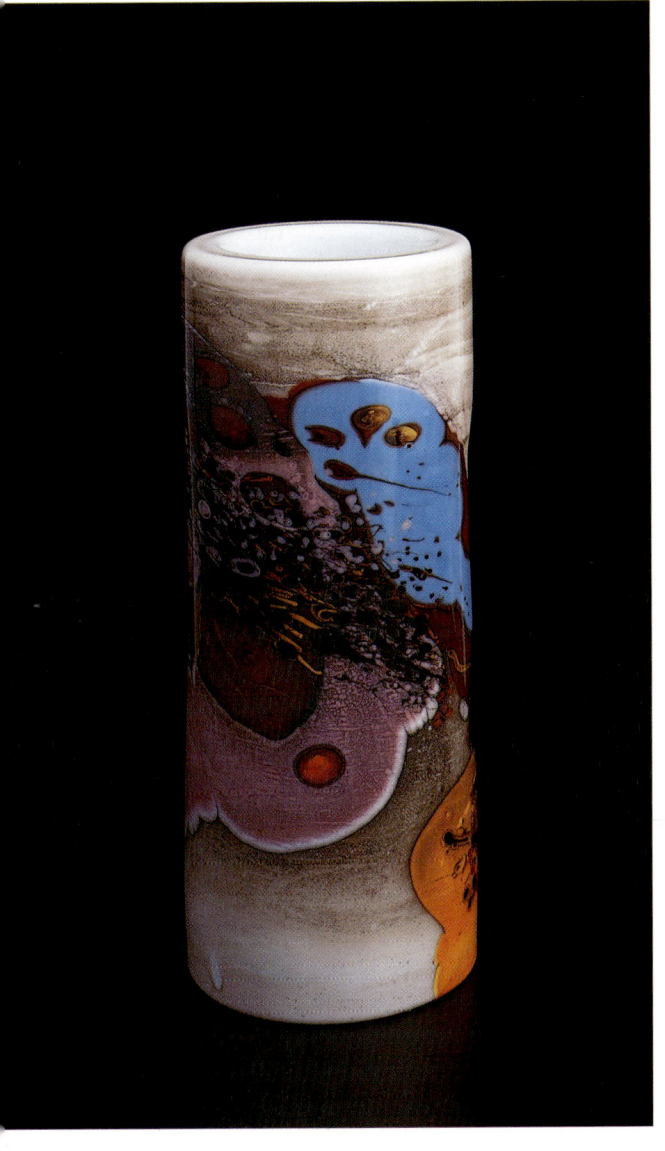

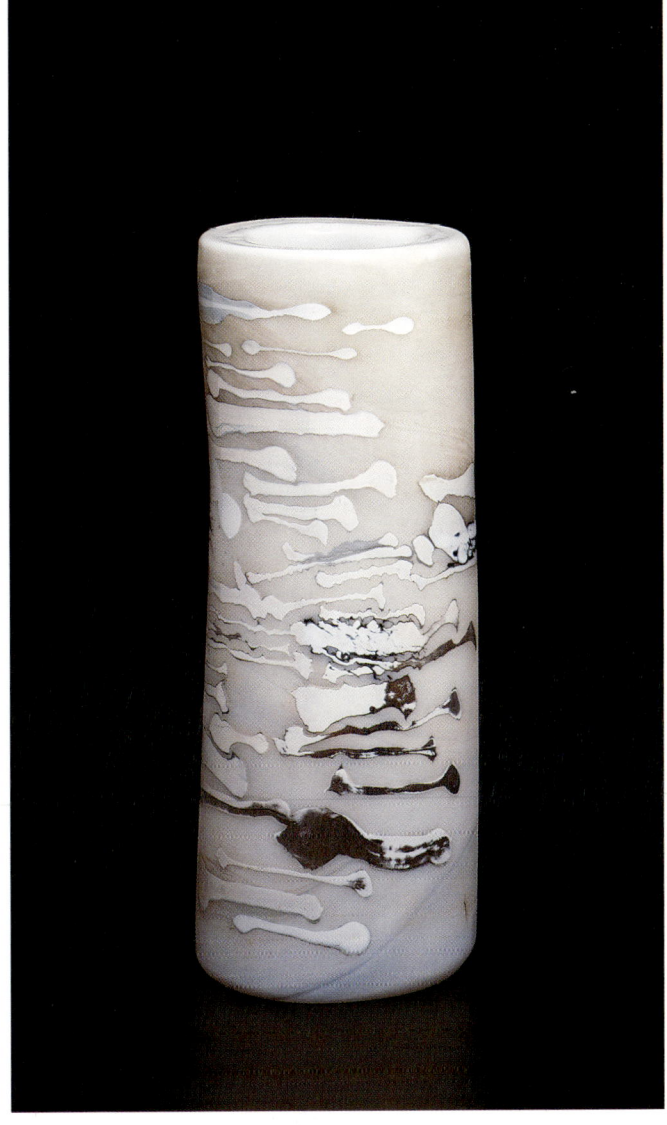

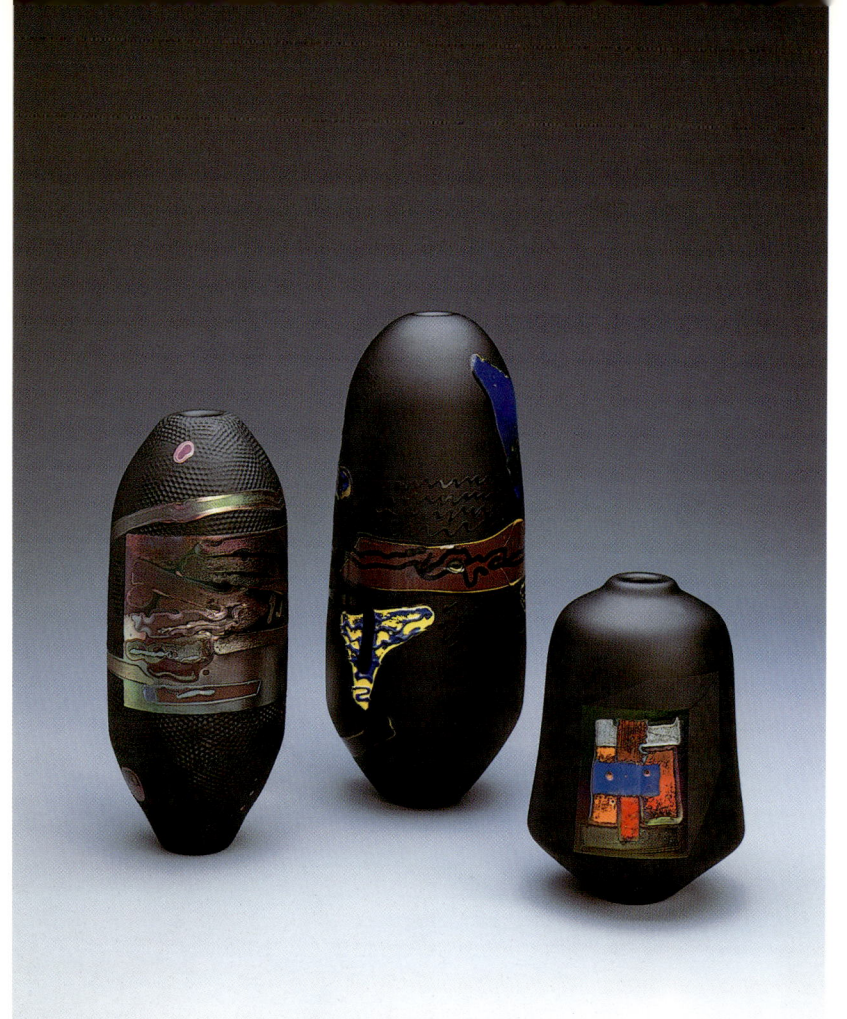

Joel Philip Myers

Untitled (from the "Contiguous Fragment" series), 1979 (ri
Blown glass, iridized, sandblasted, and acid-etched,
with additions
7³⁄₄ x 5 dia. inches (19.7 x 12.7 cm)
cat. 45

Untitled (from the "Contiguous Fragment" series), 1981 (l
Blown glass, iridized, sandblasted, and acid-etched,
with additions
10¹¹⁄₁₆ x 4¹⁄₈ dia. inches (27.1 x 10.5 cm)
cat. 46

Untitled (from the "Contiguous Fragment" series), 1981 (cen
Blown glass with additions, cane drawing, sandblasted, a
acid-etched
12³⁄₄ x 5 dia. inches (32.4 x 12.7 cm)
cat. 47

The other two pieces date from 1981 and feature sandblasting to reveal the edge of the shards. They take advantage of the play of matte versus shiny and the addition of textured glass to the body. A summer working at Pilchuck Glass School in Stanwood, Washington, in 1982 ended the black glass series because Pilchuck only had clear glass.

The final two pieces in the Glick collection are *Untitled* (1988) (ill. p. 28) and *Red Fish III* (1991). Larger in scale than the previous works, these pieces are sculptures in a vessel format. Relying on his superb sense of color, Myers presented solid vessels enlivened by applied gestural patterns. In the former piece, the clear, blown-glass vessel is a study in abstracted color and line. The two flat sides serve as a canvas for his "glass marquetry."¹⁰⁷ The thirty-five-pound piece was worked by a team of four glassworkers. Each shard was placed and modified by hand with a blowtorch. Resisting the temptation to reblow the work and further distort the applied patterns, Myers chose instead to maintain the intensity of the original color fragments without further modification.

Red Fish III was inspired by one of Myers's many fishing trips. In forms abstracted and obscured, his memories of water and fish were the source of decoration for this large blown vessel. The prismatic effect of the water (and its counterfeit, glass) is used to great advantage. After each element was applied, the piece was given its final form by swinging it from the end of the blowpipe. The centrifugal force affects the movement of the glass in a way reminiscent of how water moves. Myers's process takes split-second timing: at any point the work could be lost. Myers pushes both scale and skill to the limit.

Joel Philip Myers

Red Fish III, 1991
Blown glass, cased, with spiral cane drawing and inclusions
9 7/8 x 27 1/8 x 3 1/8 inches (25.1 x 68.9 x 7.9 cm)
cat. 49

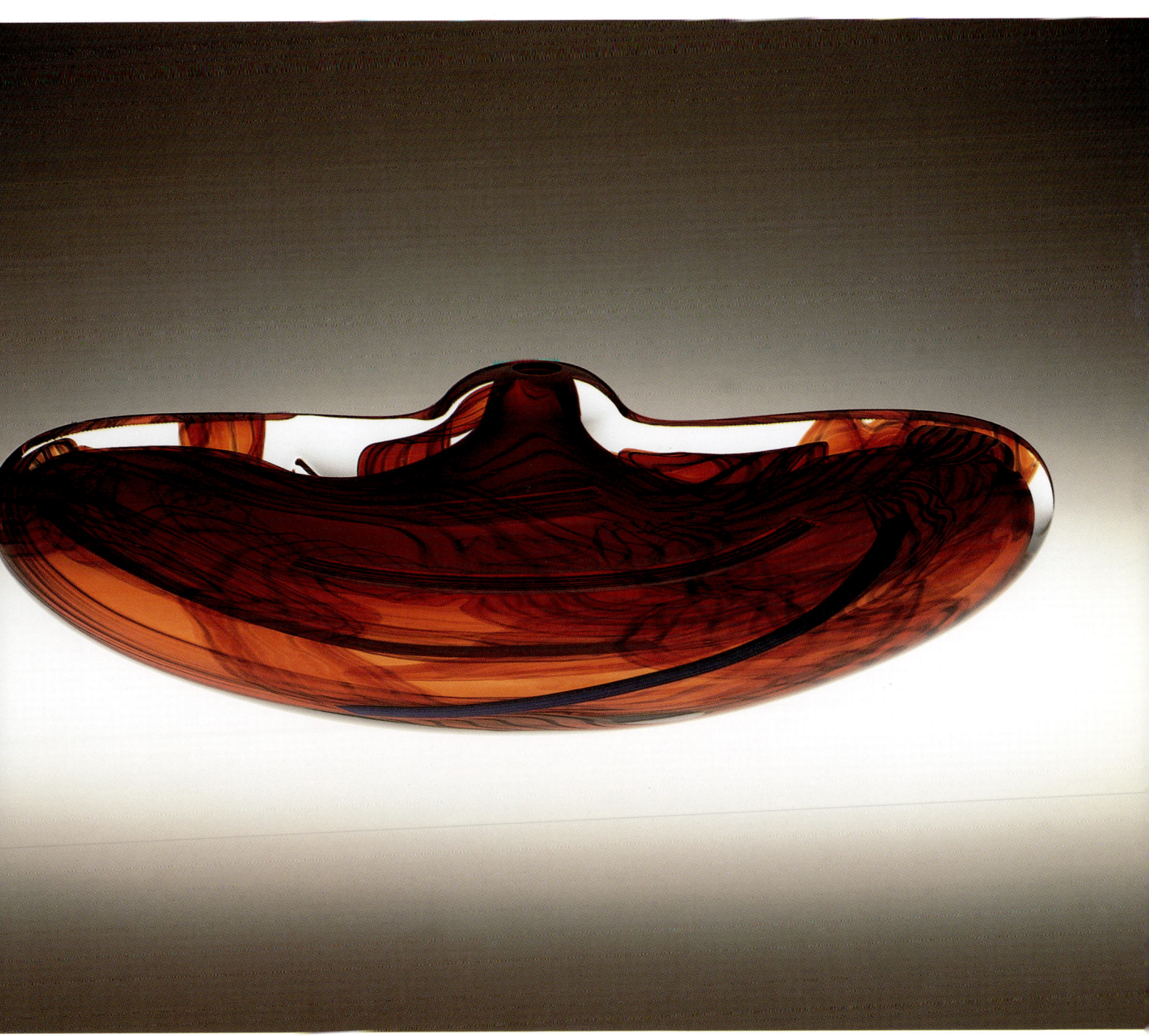

Tom Patti

Expanded Echo with Line (from the "Echo" series), 1989
Glass, fused, hand-shaped, ground and polished
3 7/16 x 6 3/8 x 4 9/16 inches (8.7 x 16.2 x 11.6 cm)
cat. 50

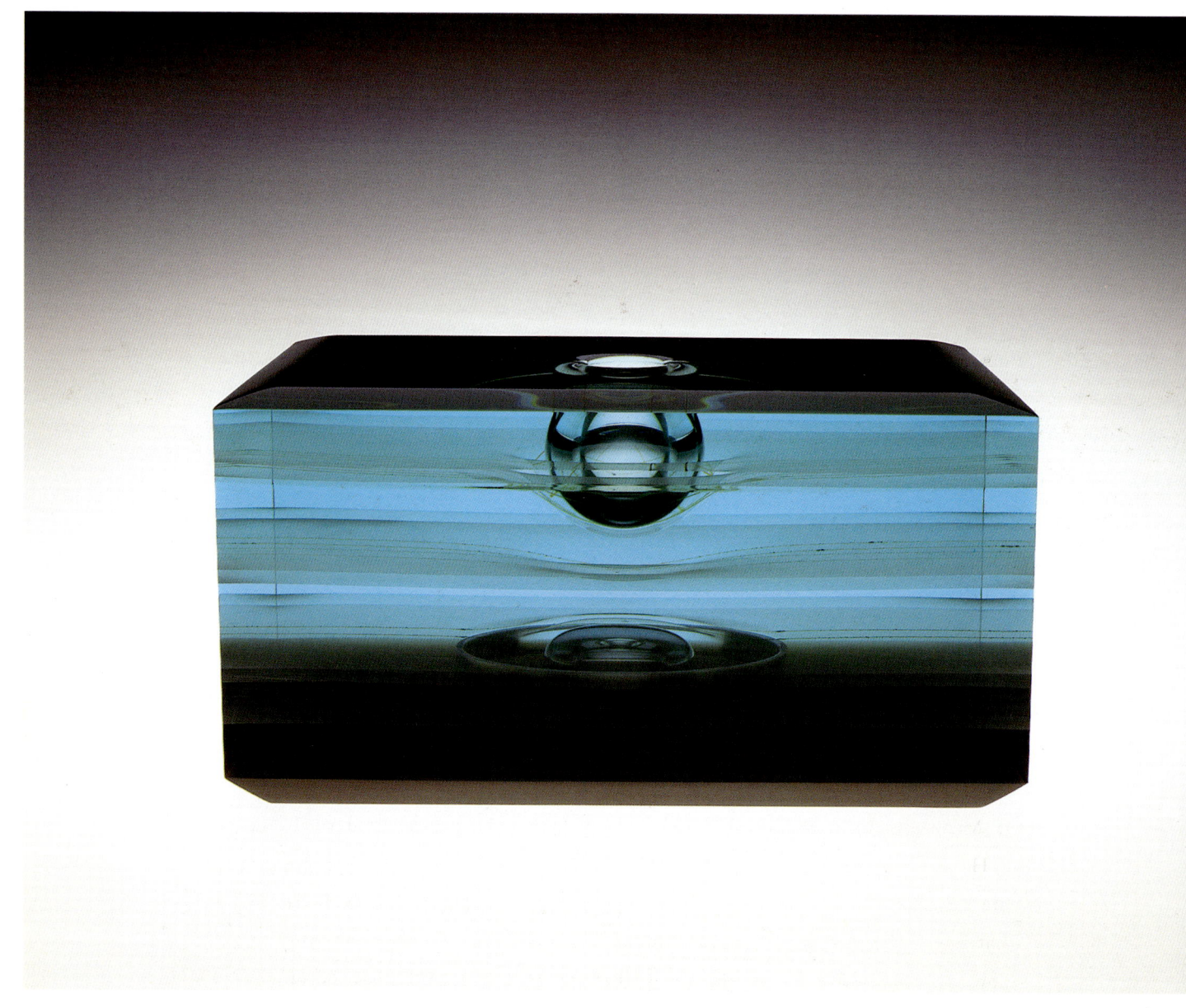

TOM PATTI

American, b. 1943

Mixing design, art, and science, Tom Patti makes monumental sculpture on an intimate scale. Born in Pittsfield, Massachusetts, Patti had a wide and varied education, with little of it focused on glass. After briefly attending Vesper George School of Art during the day and the Boston Museum School at night, Patti enrolled at the Pratt Institute in Brooklyn, New York, receiving a Bachelor of Fine Arts degree in industrial design (1967). He then studied perception theory with Rudolph Arnheim and architectural theory with Sybil Moholy-Nagy at The New School for Social Research, New York, which had been founded by Robert Rauschenberg to promote collaboration between artists and engineers. In 1969 he received his Master of Fine Arts degree from Pratt in industrial design.

As a student Patti worked with sheet glass, but concentrated mainly on creating art out of latex and other inflatable materials. In 1970, after attending a session at the Penland School of Handicrafts, near Asheville, North Carolina, he returned to Massachusetts and built himself a glass studio. Having little money, Patti used Vitrolite and plate glass that he scavenged from local buildings that were being razed. In 1976 he had his first show, at the Contemporary Art Glass Gallery, and in 1977 he exhibited at Heller Gallery, both in New York.

Patti's works fall into two categories: compact, free-standing glass forms (often only a few inches in size) and full-scale architectural commissions. An early example of the latter was the 1982 *Genic Doran Divider* for the General Electric Company's World Plastics Technology Center, Pittsfield, Massachusetts. The over-eight-foot-tall work was fashioned out of GE Lexan, aluminum, steel, and neon. Also in the 1980s Patti completed his twenty-four-foot-high *Survey-Slider*, a site-specific glass-and-water piece for the contemporary sculpture exhibition at Chesterwood, in Stockbridge, Massachusetts. Currently, Patti is collaborating with architect Cesar Pelli on a commission for Owens Corning World Headquarters in Toledo, Ohio.

Patti's compact, free-standing sculptures have shown a consistent development that can be traced back to his early work in latex. The early latex works incorporated steel rods that reveal Patti's industrial design background (see fig. 9). His glass output falls into discrete periods. From 1975 to 1977 he blew and laminated cubes into spherical forms. In his second phase he suspended

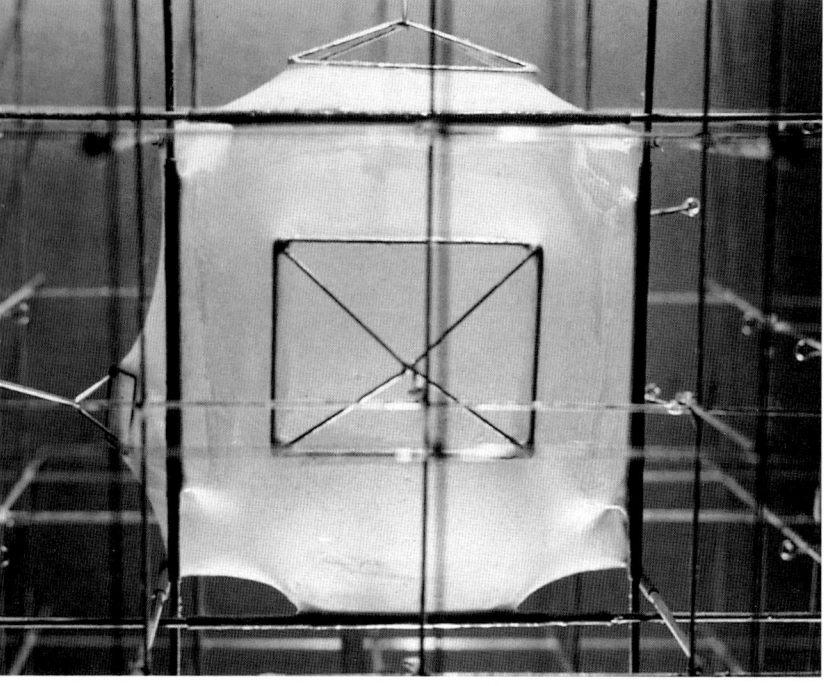

FIG. 9

Tom Patti
American, b. 1943

Untitled, 1966
Latex, steel, and wire
16 x 18½ inches (40 x 47 cm)
Courtesy the artist

bubbles within winglike frameworks. In 1980 the wings collapsed into two-dimensional vertical or horizontal extensions, with scientific names such as *Bi-axial Corded Optic*. These reflect the then-current Op art interest in the effects of artist-manipulated optical illusions. All of these early works are still related to the vessel form. Pieces from the early 1980s maintain their relationship to the vessel as they incorporate rectangular forms encasing a central blown chamber that opens at the top. From this investigation came the sharp-edged forms that led to Patti's next phase of laminated glass blocks. Throughout all his work issues of design (circles within squares), scientific investigations (the effect of an expanding element placed within the core of heated glass), and aesthetics have been the primary concerns. Patti makes no more than ten pieces a year; each object carries its own combination of design, scientific inquiry, and aesthetic statement.

The two Glick pieces are from Patti's latest series. *Expanded Echo with Line* (from the "Echo" series) (1989) appears to have a drop of liquid captured within the glass block. It emanates perfect concentric rings frozen in time. The liquid is actually an air bubble that has been trapped within the glass and allowed to expand naturally through the effect of heat. The inverted liquid/solid dichotomy is a leitmotif of Patti's work. The piece, laminated in green glass, and cut and polished to a petite six-by-four-inch size, manages nevertheless to be a forceful object that intrigues and engages. In the related *Solarized Red with Blue and Yellow* (from the "Lumina" series) (1992), the glass is brightly colored and punctuated with striations. An intriguing counterpoint is established between the gentle curve of the glass bubble and the hard-edged exterior. Again the combination of lamination and blowing captures Patti's spiritual and intellectual range.

Tom Patti

Solarized Red with Blue and Yellow (from the "Lumina" series), 1992
Glass, fused, hand-shaped, ground and polished
2 1/2 x 6 1/4 x 4 1/2 inches (6.4 x 15.9 x 11.6 cm)
cat. 51

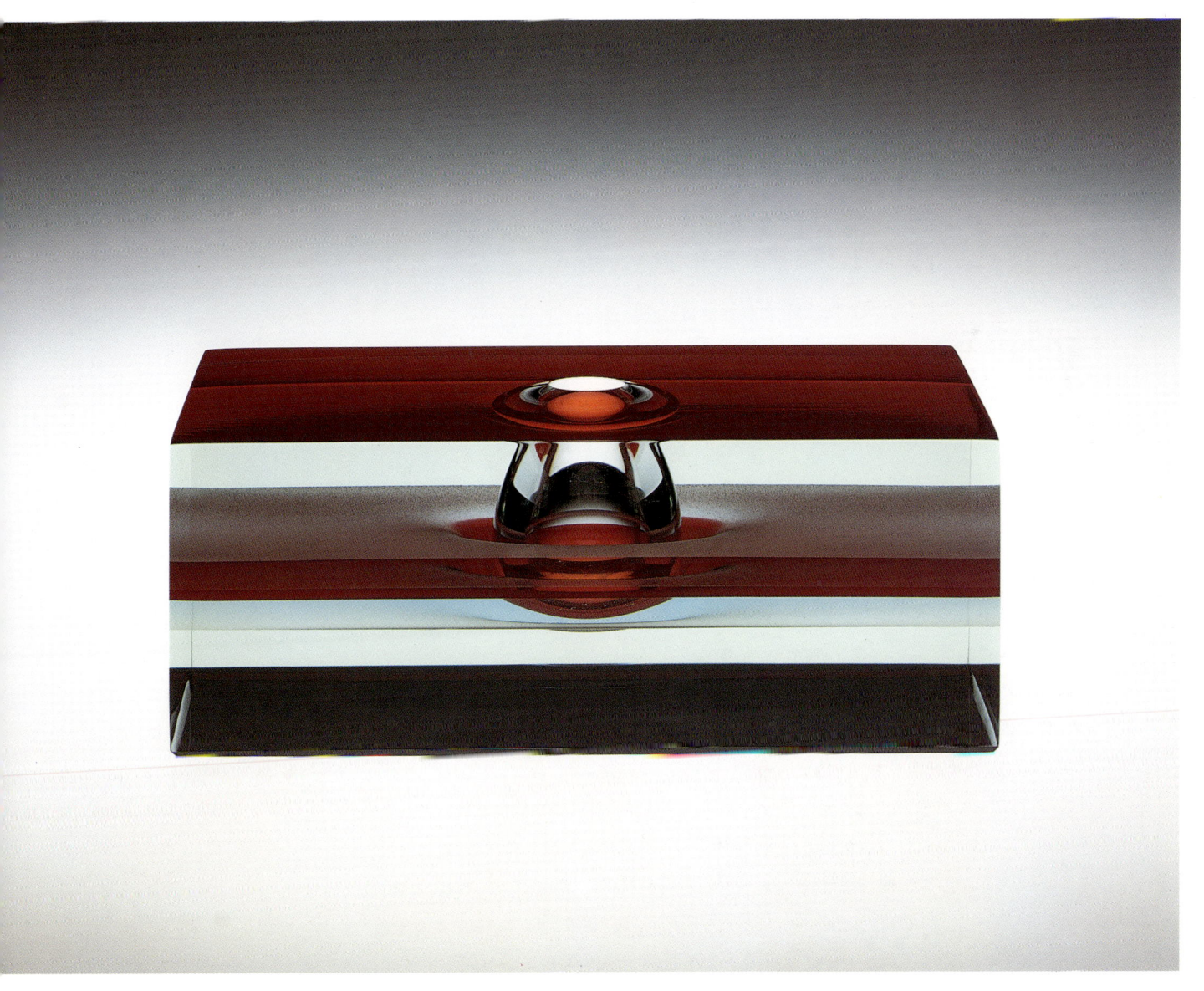

Mark Peiser

Lillies of the Valley (from the "Paperweight Vase" series), 1976
Blown glass with flamework
8½ x 5 dia. inches (21.6 x 12.7 cm)
cat. 52

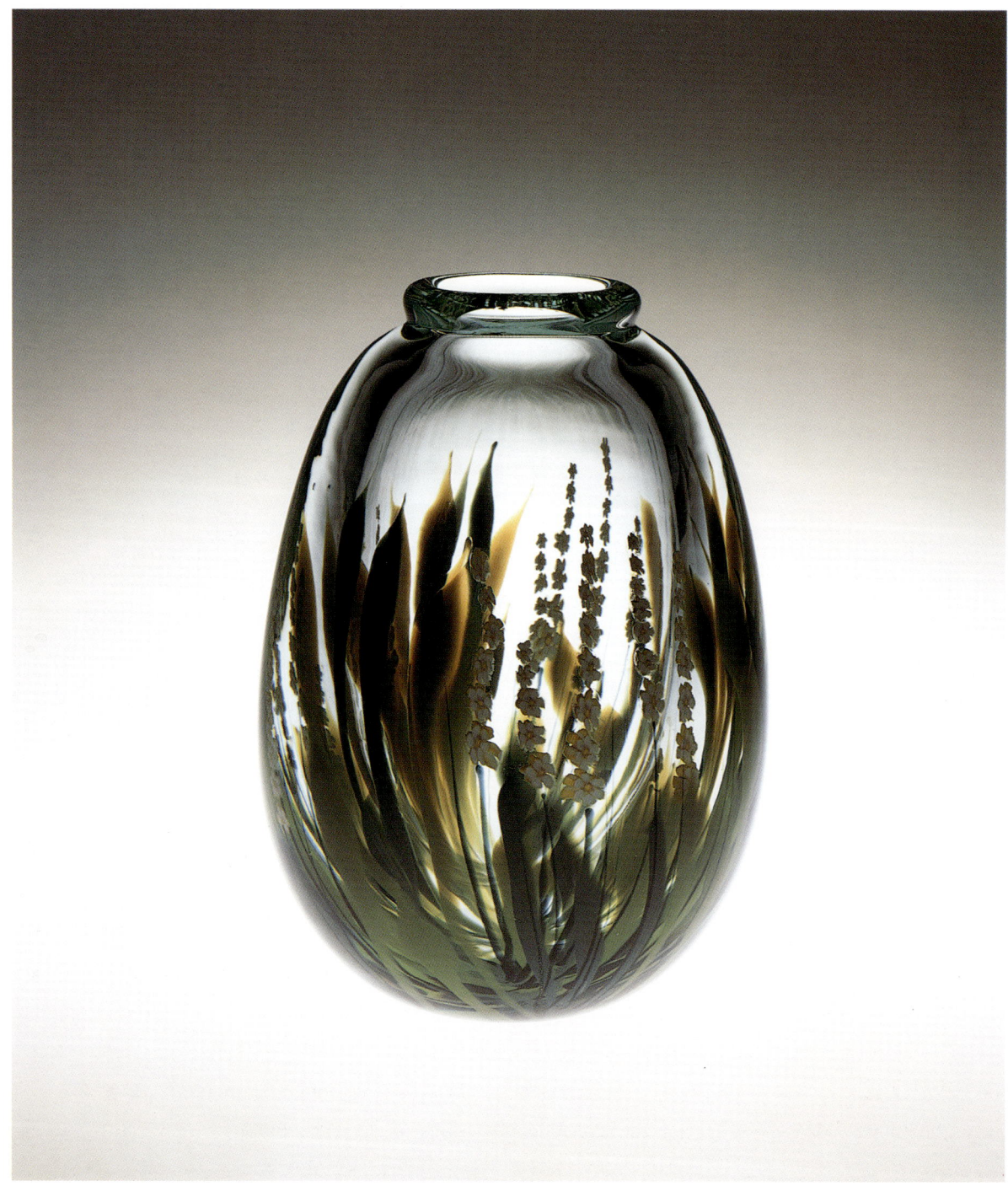

MARK PEISER

American, b. 1938

As a member of the first generation of glass artists, Mark Peiser balanced a passion for art with an enthusiasm for science. Although his education contained no formal fine-arts training, his unique background continues to inform his art. Inspired by his fourth-grade math teacher Lola May and watercolorist Ralph Rapien, Peiser, like many of the early glass artists, was intrigued by both the technology and art of glass. Trained as an electrical engineer at Purdue University, in Lafayette, Indiana, Peiser went on to receive a Bachelor of Science degree in product design from the Illinois Institute of Technology, Chicago, in 1961. But classical music was also a love, especially the wizardry of Vladimir Horowitz, so Peiser pursued a music degree at DePaul University, Chicago. Merging all of these disparate educational experiences, Peiser honed his glass aesthetic.

Finally in 1967 Peiser attended a glassblowing demonstration by Rodger Lang at the Penland School of the Handicrafts, near Asheville, North Carolina.[108] Attracted to the beauty of Penland, the integrity of the craftsman ethic, and the potential of glass, Peiser applied to be Penland's first resident glassblower. He remembers that the screening was casual and that when he asked if he could become a resident, Director Bill Brown "nonchalantly said 'Sure.'"[109] Starting with no knowledge about the technical aspects of glass-forming, Peiser began to explore creating a better glass batch material than the #475 fiberglass marbles from Johns-Mansville Fiber Glass Corporation that were currently used. This quest for a better metal placed him at the forefront of glass technology at the time. However, during this early period, it was difficult to earn a living from glass production. Peiser managed by selling his small blown vessels for $7.50 at local craft fairs. In 1971 Peiser and glass artist Fritz Dreisbach, with the support of Bill Brown, invited glassblowers from across the county to meet at Penland to share information and mutual support. This event became the founding meeting of the Glass Art Society.

Early on Peiser began to incorporate into his work imagery from nature. Because he used a relatively opaque metal and had limited forming skills, his early pieces were simple, vessel-based objects. Always interested in color and searching for a more translucent glass metal to work with, Peiser started batch melting any and all combinations of elements. By 1973 he began to incorporate flameworked fragments into his vessels,

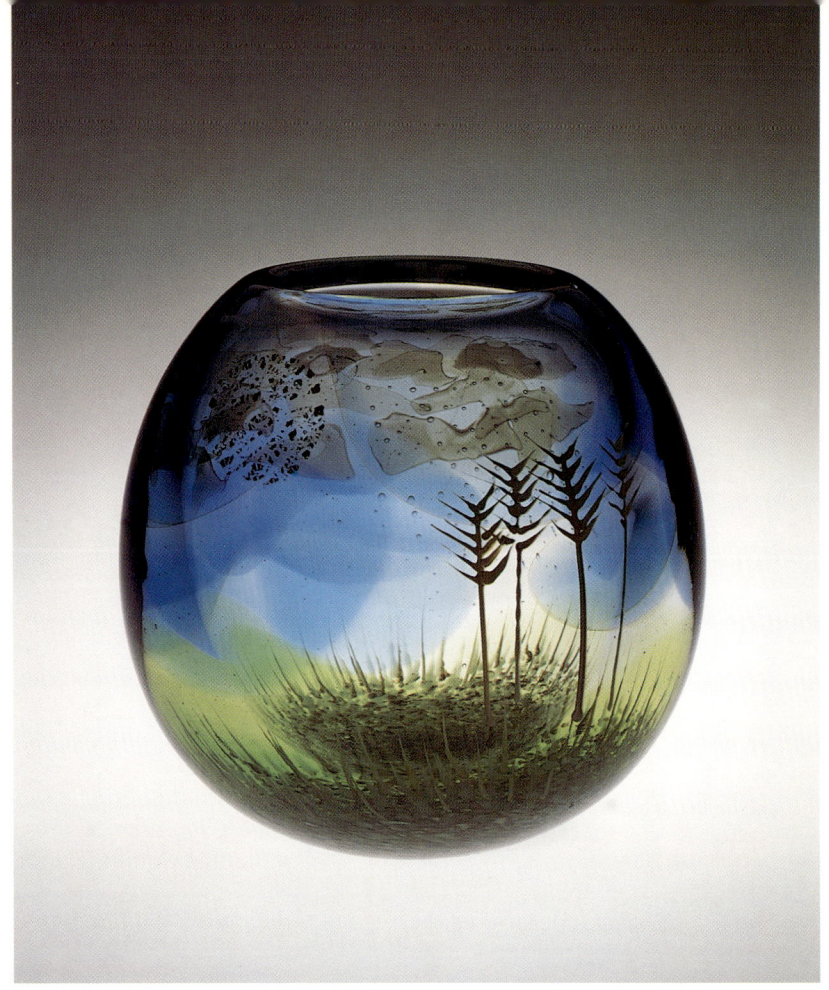

Mark Peiser

The Wheat Piece
(from the "Paperweight Vase" series), 19
Blown glass with flamework and gold foi
7 x 7 dia. inches (17.8 x 17.8 cm)
cat. 53

which added a liveliness to his decorative vocabulary. When he achieved a workable and beautiful crystal glass batch, Peiser began his "Paperweight" series of vessels. These progressions from opaque to clear glass and from decoration patterning to literal imagery allowed Peiser to create a visual haiku in glass.

Lilies of the Valley (1976) and *The Wheat Piece* (1978) date from this fruitful period. Each landscape element is painstakingly composed in successive layers of glass, adding a sense of space to the object and supporting Peiser's assertion that he is a "romantic Realist."[110] Each vessel functions in the round as a seamlessly constructed visual whole. Similar to the graal and ariel glass landscapes made at Orrefors Glasbruk, Sweden,[111] these pieces have a sensitivity and uniqueness not seen in their factory counterparts. Each vase is meticulously marked with numbers and letters that record exactly how it was fabricated.

Ever restless, Peiser wanted to move in a new direction. By 1981 he had left blown glass for casting and cold-working. For his next series, "Inner Space," he used a casting technique that combines several colors of glass added to the graphite mold in a single pour. Peiser was able to bring out the expressive potential of gently modulated colors. As with most glass techniques, casting is a risky activity: these "blanks" have a one-third defect rate.

In the Birth of Io (from the "Inner Space" series) (1988), the title refers to a moon of Jupiter that is known to have the only active volcanos in the solar system other than those on earth. Shaped in a vertical "V" form, the colored glass graduates from magenta to yellow to sky blue. Polished to a high sheen, the work has a glassy coolness. The prism effect caused by the faceted edge also modifies the colors and makes them appear to vibrate.

Mark Peiser

The Birth of Io (from the "Inner Space" series), 1988
Cast glass, cut and polished
14 1/2 x 9 1/2 x 3 inches (36.8 x 24.1 x 7.6 cm)
cat. 54

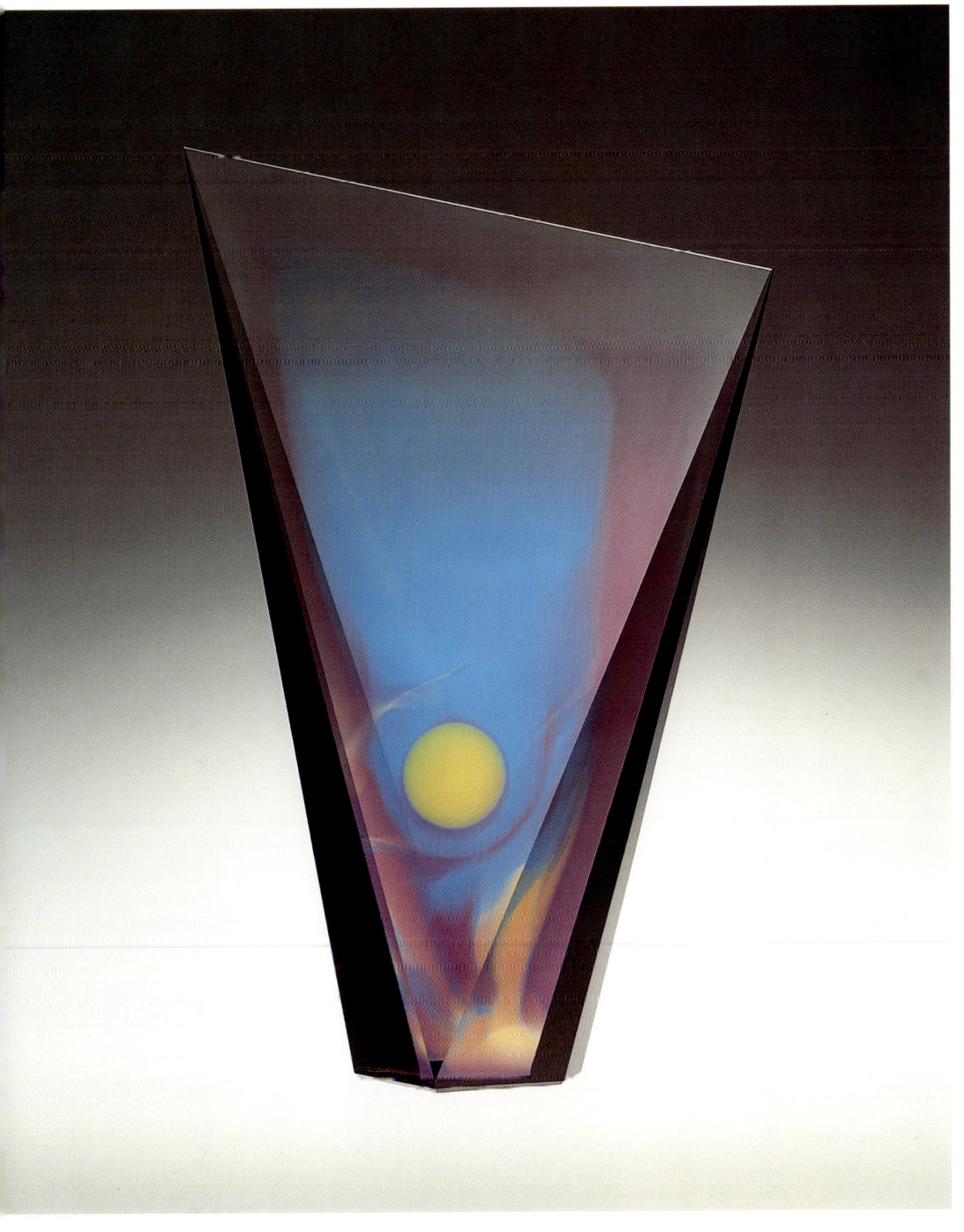

COLIN REID

English, b. 1953

Colin Reid's kiln-formed glass captures texture, movement, and the material's viscus flow in archetypal forms. Born in 1953, Reid attended art school in the 1970s with the intention of becoming a painter. But Conceptual Art was in its heyday, and its antiobject orientation was not for him. He spent two years in Israel setting up a spiritual community, then returned to London where he ran a playground. While perusing the government training courses listed at the Brixton Labor Exchange,[112] he saw a scientific glassblowing class. After completion (and another brief trip to Israel), he took a job at a factory forming glass vessels for industrial applications.

With the income derived from flameworked perfume bottles that he made on the side, Reid set up his own glass studio. His work received a commendation from the British Design Council. In 1978 Reid entered the Stourbridge College of Art, where he studied blowing with Keith Cummings. He then focused on the sculptural potential of kiln-formed glass.

Kiln-forming glass has a long history, dating from the eighth century B.C.E. In Reid's hands the technique is coupled with lost-wax forming and captures the texture and flow of glass. Although these techiques were usually employed for detailed forms, Reid modified this application to make large forms that can be cut and sanded to a smooth surface. Mold materials and colorants (crushed glass, ceramic stains, or oxides) also demanded attention, and carefully controlled heating and cooling required new equipment. The eventual adoption of microprocessor technology allowed for longer firings and consequently the creation of larger works. Rociprolaps (vibratory lapping and polishing machines) and diamond tools enabled Reid to achieve mirror surfaces.[113]

Double Arches (1986), a two-part sculpture that combines all of Reid's skills and vision, recalls architectural forms that both support and are self-supporting. Additionally, the arch by its nature moves through space and links "two points on the earth."[114] Reid included ordinary dirt to effect a rough texture that contrasts with the still sheen of the polished surfaces. Oxides are the colorant of the lead crystal. The tension and balance of these elements, coupled with the clarity of form, give Reid's work visual power and spiritual solidity—counterpointed by the delicate air-bubble veiling captured within. Arrangement of the pieces is up to the viewer; even minor adjustments modify the color, form, and textural interplay of the work. In this way the viewer becomes part of the creation of the work itself.

Colin Reid

Double Arches, 1986
Kiln-formed lead glass with oxides
TWO PARTS
A: 11 1/2 x 19 x 1 1/2 inches (29.2 x 48 x 3.8 cm)
B: 11 1/2 x 19 x 1 1/2 inches (29.2 x 48 x 3.8 cm)
cat. 55

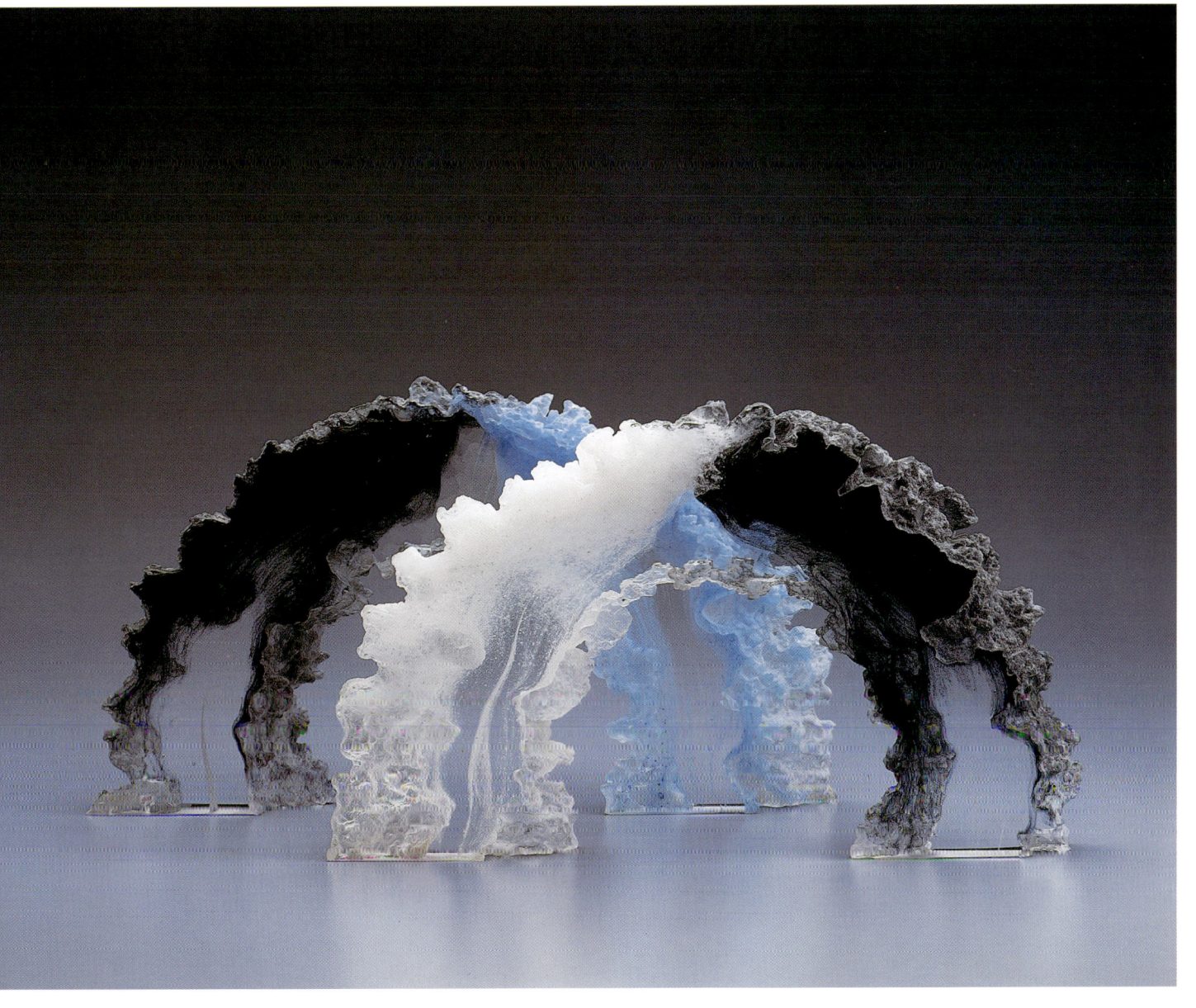

GINNY RUFFNER

American, b.1952

Ginny Ruffner's smart and beautiful artworks are made of flameworked and painted glass. Her pieces are vividly described by The Corning Museum of Glass' Curator of Contemporary Glass Susanne Frantz as "little bombs coated in M&M wrappers. They look easy, they slide down easily, but they're very serious."[115]

Ruffner attended the University of Georgia, Atlanta, where she studied painting and drawing with Bill Johanssen and Jim Herbert. She graduated in 1974, and received her Master of Fine Arts degree summa cum laude one year later. Next she taught at a community college and then opened her stained-glass studio. During this period she explored glass engraving and began flameworking.

Ruffner's early flamework is not painted, although she continued to paint and create other mixed-media sculptures. But in 1985 she decided to apply oil paints to the glass, thereby creating her signature style. During the 1980s Ruffner explored themes that have proved central to her work: issues surrounding the meaning and uses of beauty, pattern, fecundity, literature, language, and what it means to be a female artist. This last issue is particularly meaningful as studio glass has long been a male domain.[116]

During the 1980s Ruffner was also emerging as a leader in the glass community. From 1984 until 1991 she taught at Pilchuck Glass School in Stanwood, Washington, and was invited to join the board of trustees. She served on the Glass Art Society board from 1988 until 1990 and was only the third woman[117] to be president (1990–91). In 1991 she curated the insightful "Glass: Material in the Service of Meaning" for the Tacoma Art Museum, Washington. Her numerous architectural commissions led to her appointment as an honorary member of the American Institute of Architects. In among these activities Ruffner found time to have Tom Robbin's novel *Skinny Legs and All* (1990) dedicated to her.

Stella at the Louvre (1990) brings together many aspects of Ruffner's facile mind. Referring in her title to paintings by Frank Stella, Ruffner incorporated nude figures in a style similar to that of the Italian sixteenth-century Mannerist painter Jacopo Carucci da Pontormo. The figures are languid and sensual, but oddly separated; the female seems to be displaying herself to an indifferent viewer. Around this disconnected couple float Stella-esque three-dimensional forms (difficult to execute in warm glass). By juxtaposing the modern

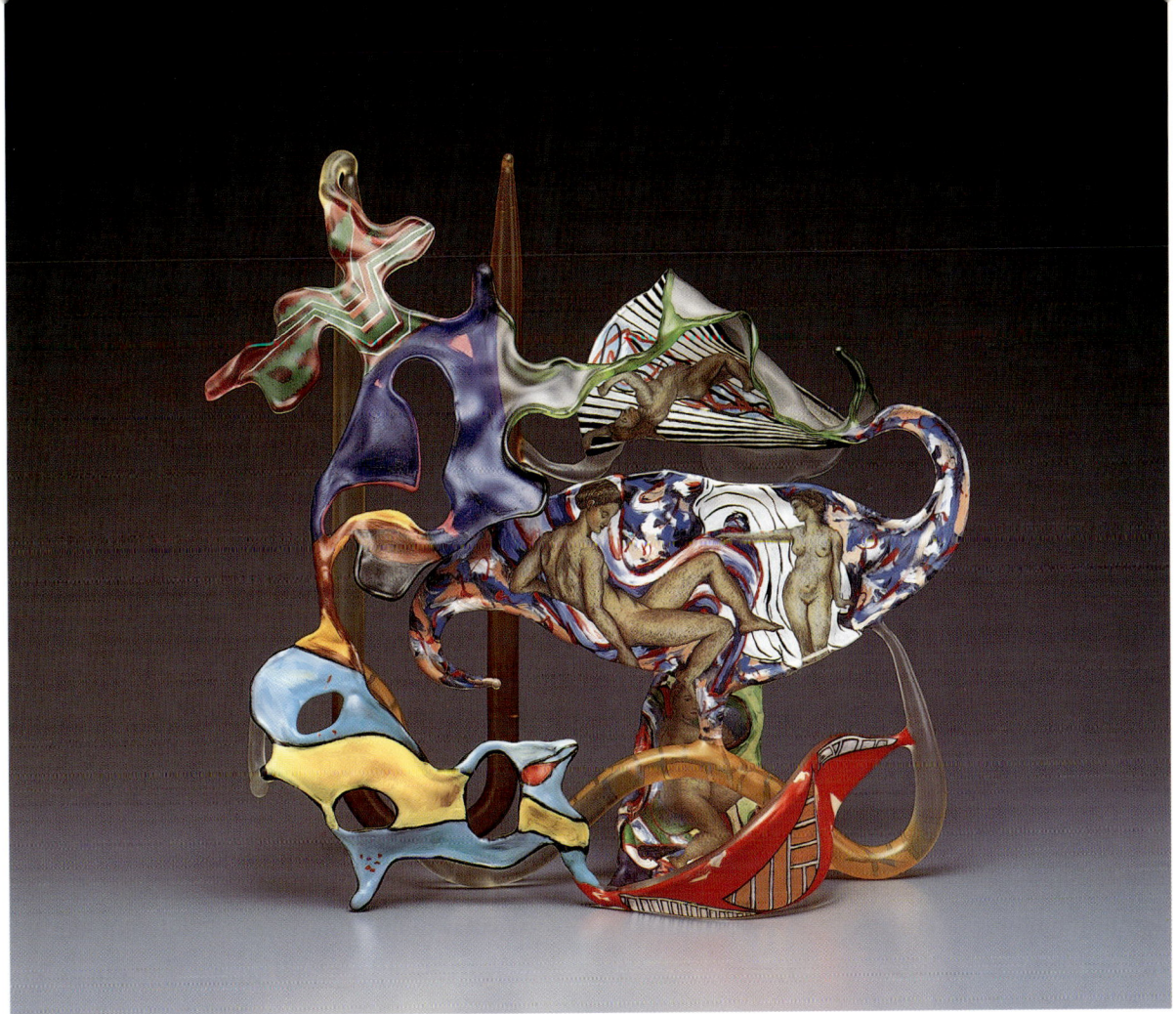

Ginny Ruffner

Stella at the Louvre, 1990
Flameworked glass, sandblasted and painted
17 x 17 x 9 inches (43.2 x 43.2 x 22.9 cm)
cat. 56

Stella and the late Renaissance humanistic figures, as such works place adjacent in museum settings, Ruffner asks her audience to ponder the effects of time on the uses of beauty, a query that runs through many of her figurative pieces.

A tragic automobile accident abruptly changed Ruffner's life in December 1991. In a coma for six weeks, with an uncertain prognosis, it was several months before she could again reconnect to her life. Later she described the accident as having "rearranged" the synapses in her brain, albeit leaving it still sprightly and well tuned. Her body needed therapy, but great progress has been made. During her recovery Ruffner has lived in New York for part of each year and worked with artist and friend Steve Kursh, while maintaining her studio in Seattle. Their collaborative work combines Ruffner's blown and painted glass bubbles within metal matrices fashioned by Kursh. Working now in Seattle with the aid of assistants, Ruffner continues to make her flamework pieces. As glass is usually a collaborative process, her voice comes through clearly in tight new works that contain the intelligence, wit, and informed observations that have always been the source of her artistic power.

MARY SHAFFER

American, b. 1947

Mary Shaffer's conceptual glass sculptures explore a dialogue between plate glass and metal and between liquid and solid states. Born in Walterboro, South Carolina, Shaffer began her art training by studying painting at the Rhode Island School of Design, Providence. When an official glass program was started, she had ready access to it through her then-husband, painting instructor Hardu Keck. After graduating in 1970, Shaffer turned her attention to her two children and traveled to Rome. She returned to her art in 1972.

Incorporating a variety of materials, including fabric, wind, fire, and light, Shaffer explored a range of formal issues. She became intrigued with the notion of the "window" as applied to artworks. Sometimes referred to as the Albertian Window after the Renaissance architect Leon Battista Alberti, who helped to formalize Western perspective methodology, this visual construct frames the subject and delimits the visual field available to the viewer. As Shaffer explored its implications, she came to see that it was a powerful tool that affects both the artists and objects they make.[118]

Meanwhile Shaffer continued to experiment with unusual media combinations. One such venture involved combining glass with an oven heating element. While the result was not an artwork, the attempt revealed the strength that glass had and its potential when paired with other materials. During the 1970s assemblage, found objects, and nontraditional materials became the rage in the larger art world. For Shaffer the next exploration involved a four-inch-high test kiln given to her by glass artist Therman Statom (cats. 60 and 61). Capable of reaching 1500 degrees Fahrenheit in twenty minutes, the tiny kiln permitted experimentation in heating nails, sand, hooks, chains, and rusted tools—all elements that would later appear in Shaffer's glass work. Over time she succeeded in modifying the petite kiln to accommodate pieces up to eight inches high.[119]

Shaffer's initial exposure to glass came from her using it to create a wavy substratum for painting.[120] But after she saw the glistening, undulating glass, she began to work with the glass itself. When her work was seen by glass artist Fritz Driesbach (who was living in her basement at the time and substituting at Rhode Island School of Design for department head Dale Chihuly), he suggested that she try investigating slumped glass. Slumping, a technique favored by the pioneer studio-glass artists, is easier to do in a small studio setting than other

Mary Shaffer

Off Ledge I (from the "Inversion" series), 1994
TWO PARTS
A: Slumped plate glass
32 x 20 x 20 inches (81.3 x 50.8 x 50.8 cm)
B: Cast bronze with furric-nitrate patina
32 x 20 x 20 inches (81.3 x 50.8 x 50.8 cm)
cat. 57

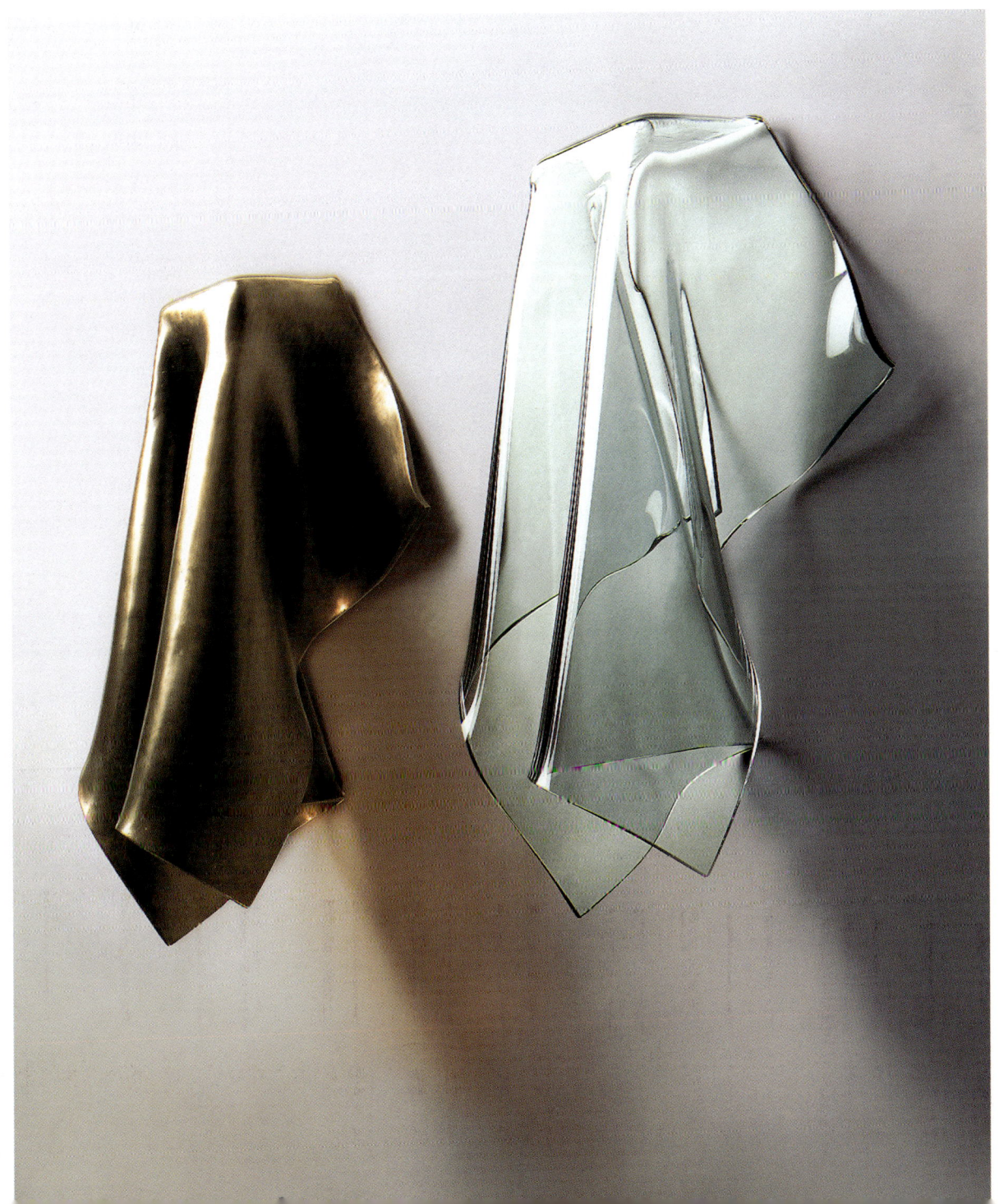

warm- or hot-glass forming methodologies. Familiar with the work of Glen Lukens and Maurice Heaton, Shaffer also took inspiration from the commercial applications of this technology to the forming of automobile windshields.

Taking a cue from this use, Shaffer wanted to make large-scale slumped works that encroach on sculpture. Still drawn to the window with its painting associations, and interested in light, Shaffer made her first slumped-glass "Hanging" series. She heated plate glass to its slumping point and then allowed it to deform against a matrix of wire mesh, creating a solid mass of glass. Light passing through the finished work has a quality similar to that seen in window panes. To finish these works, Shaffer would patinate the metal with a texture that complemented the transparent, shiny glass. She eventually pushed this idea further in her mid-air slump technique and her over-sized works.

In *Off Ledge I* (from the "Inversion" series) (1994), Shaffer paired the slumped glass with cast bronze that has been patinated with furric nitrate. After years of working with controlled glass melting, Shaffer has developed a full vocabulary of slumping "moments." In her current work she permits the glass to fall without manipulation.[121] In this case the glass melted and was caught at the right second, then frozen in place as it cooled. Formally the work mimics cloth or taffy folds and illustrates how metal, too, can mirror other substances. While Shaffer's works exploit the beauty of glass, they are also about movement and light. As with all of the pieces in this series, this work is about the play of polar opposites: glass/metal, transparency/opacity, light/dark, fragility/immutability.

PAUL STANKARD

American, b. 1943

Paul Stankard, a self-taught master of flameworking, has always derived great joy from nature and the beauty of plant forms. Growing up in Massachusetts, he was familiar with the Ware Collection of Glass Models of Plants (created by Leopold and Rudolph Blaschka), on display at the Botanical Museum of Harvard University, Cambridge. Fabulous in their detailed recording of botanical specimens, the models intrigued Stankard with their beauty and accuracy. While attending the Salem County Vocational and Technological Institute in Pennsgrove, New Jersey, Stankard turned to glasswork at the suggestion of a guidance counselor who told him about the profession of scientific glassblowing.[122] Supported by his father in his decision, Stankard studied blowing techniques and met skilled flameworker Francis Wittemore.

Flame- or lampworkers form the patterns and floral objects that serve as the center and decorative heart of paperweights. A nineteenth-century European and American art form, paperweights capture the enthusiasm for artisanal technique that was the hallmark of the early years of the industrial revolution. These works were made in large numbers as novelties and decorative objects for Victorian living rooms. To maintain the market, the technique used in making paperweights was shrouded in mystery. Secrecy was still the practice when Stankard met Wittemore, who chose not to enlighten the novice.[123] In 1986, after Stankard had taught himself the secrets of flameworking, he broke with paperweight traditions and held a workshop at Wheaton Village in Millville, New Jersey. In front of a fascinated audience, he revealed his hard-won knowledge. Later that year he offered a five-day workshop at the Penland School of Handicrafts, near Asheville, North Carolina. From then on the prized technology of paperweights was open for all to share.

In 1964, while working at Andrews Scientific Glass Co., Vineland, New Jersey, Stankard began making small, clear-glass animals — a success at thirty-five cents each. Still intrigued by the intricacies of paperweights, he next experimented with flame-formed flowers, eventually discovering how to case a simple glass flower in clear glass to form a marble. For the next five years he worked to refine his technique. By studying paperweights in museums and books, Stankard realized that the nineteenth-century paperweight factories used simplified flowers with interchangeable parts. Stankard soon learned which elements could be

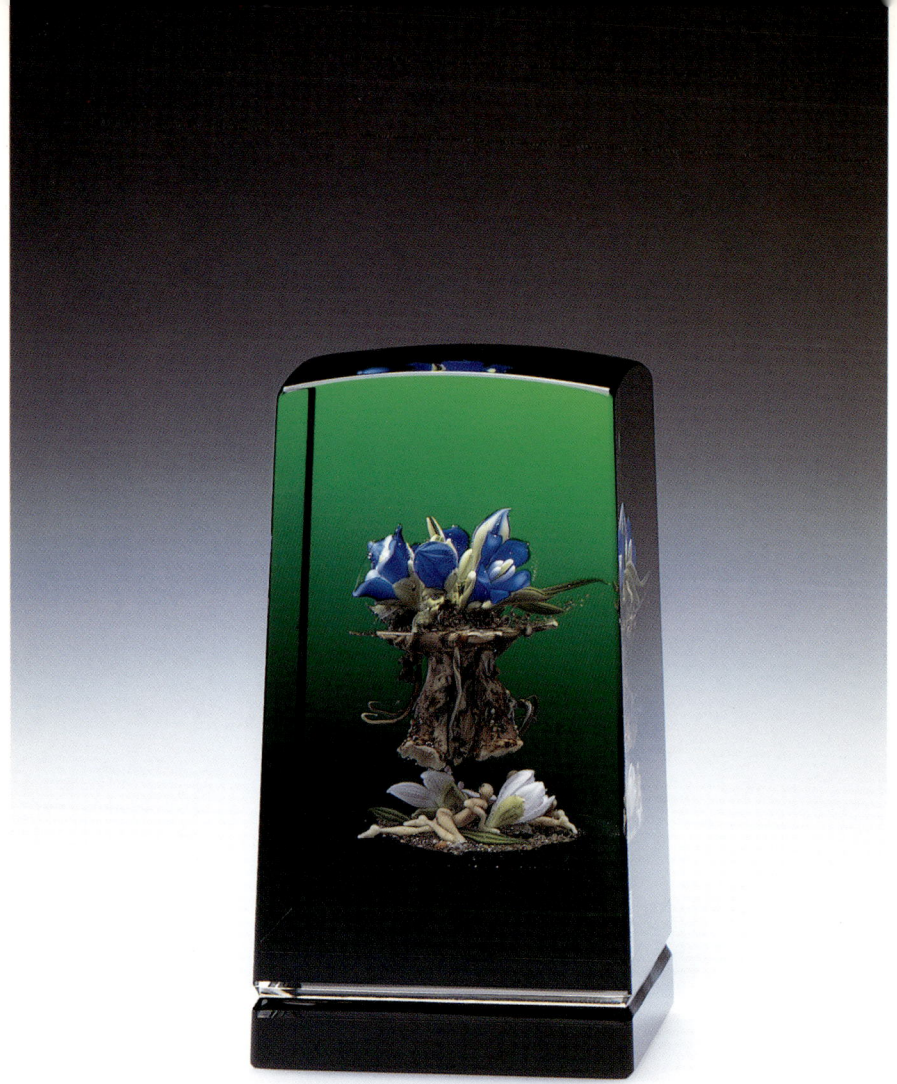

Paul Stankard

Cloistered Block with Cactus and Spirit, 1988
Flameworked glass flowers and figures in cryst
cut and polished
4³⁄₄ x 2¹⁄₂ x 3 inches (12.1 x 6.4 x 7.6 cm)
cat. 58

modified to withstand the stress of being cased in molten glass and still have some of the complexity and beauty found in nature.

In 1971 Stankard met Atlanta gallery owner Reese Palley, who offered to pay him $250 a week so that he could concentrate on making paperweights. In return Palley had the right of first refusal on the pieces produced.[124] This arrangement lasted for five years. By the late 1970s Stankard was successfully producing paperweights. Inspired by the dense woods around his studio, Stankard created works that "presented nature in a poetic way" rather than in a botanically correct manner.[125] To further under-

score the poetry of his interpretations, Stankard began to include "root people" in his creations made after the mid-1980s. Derived from medieval herbalist woodcuts, these figures are placed underneath the flowers, below the ground line, and among the root structure. This addition necessitated a new glass format to accommodate the elongated structure. Instead of continuing with the traditional paperweight domed form, Stankard designed columnar shapes, which he dubbed "botanicals," to suit the increasingly vertical compositions.[126]

Cloistered Block with Cactus and Spirit (1988) is an early "botanical." The green color is

126

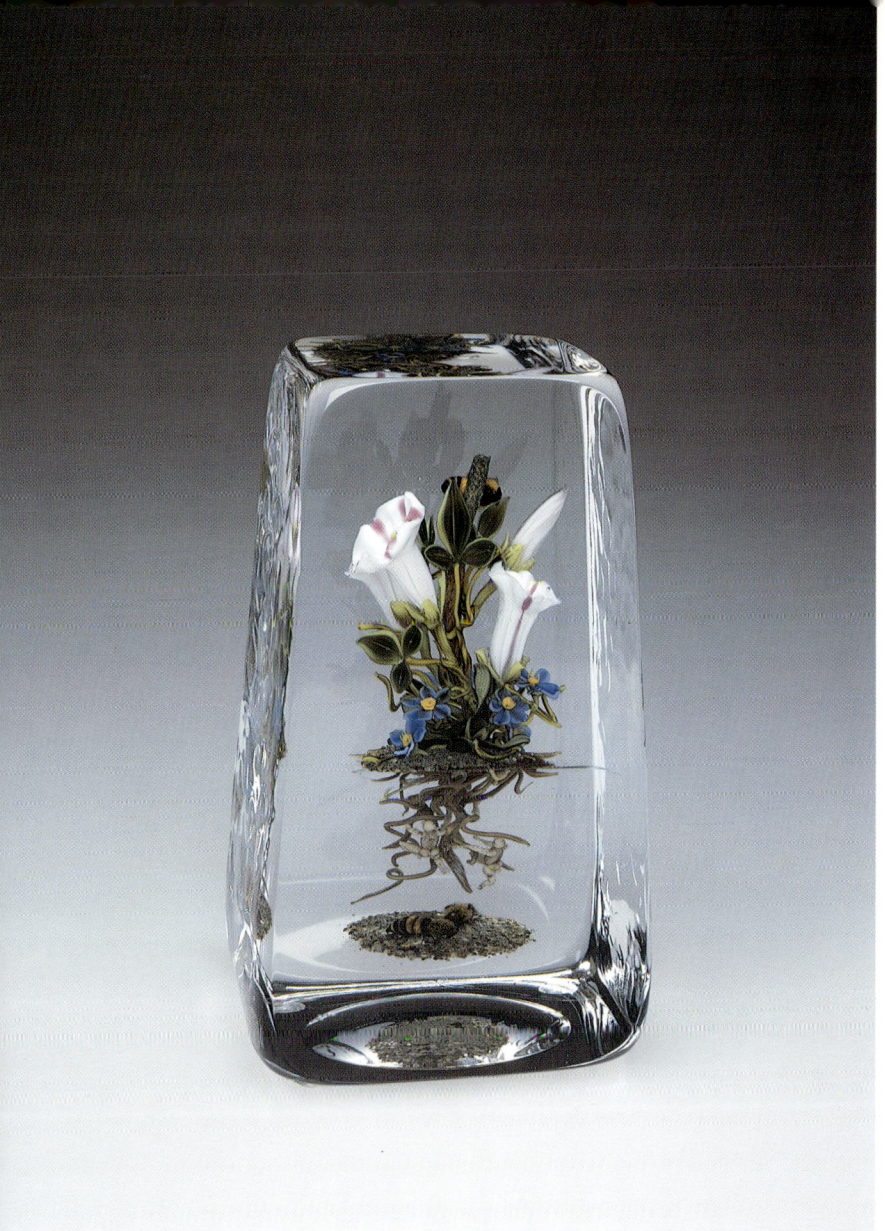

Paul Stankard

Morning Glory Bouquet Botanical, 1991
Flameworked glass elements in crystal, cut and polished
5¼ x 3 x 3 inches (13.3 x 7.6 x 7.6 cm)
cat. 59

achieved through the lamination of green glass to the back of the piece. The soda-lime, clear-glass vertical form is compositionally segmented into three sections: the flowering top, the root center, and a mystical base. The figuration is also threefold: a cactus plant, a root system, and a "root person" languishing underneath. In Stankard's lexicon these sections embody notions of both spirit and myth, with the figure underneath provoking speculation as to its meaning.

Morning Glory Bouquet Botanical (1991) exemplifies Stankard's next conceptual development. Instead of placing a root person under the plant, he incorporated a perfectly formed bumblebee into the overall composition. Stankard first became fascinated by bees as they visited his studio. He installed a beehive in his house in order to study them and to learn how best to render them in glass. For Stankard the bee symbolizes creative activity and the mutuality that allows nature to join plant and insect (and man by extension) in a productive system. All of Stankard's works require intricate flameworking before they are cased. After casing they then take up to thirty hours to anneal. Even with years of experience, failures due to technical errors occur about one third of the time.

THERMAN STATOM

American, b. 1953

Therman Statom's colorfully painted sculptural glass assemblages can be divided into two categories: discrete works in a range of scales, and large installations. Born in Winterhaven, Florida, but raised in Washington, DC, where his father was a lawyer and his mother a preschool teacher, Statom studied glass at the Pilchuck Glass School in Stanwood, Washington. He then attended the Rhode Island School of Design, Providence, receiving his Bachelor of Fine Arts degree in 1974. Statom studied with Fritz Dreisbach, and as a member of the generation of glass students that included James Carpenter, Bruce Chao, Richard Harned, Mary Shaffer (cat. 57), and Toots Zynsky (cats. 69 and 70), Statom joined a school overflowing with talent. In 1980 Statom was awarded a scholarship to continue his studies at the Pratt Institute in New York.

Statom has received an impressive number of awards for his art, including a Ford Foundation award (1977), a National Endowment for the Arts Fellowship (1982 and 1988), and a Brody Arts Foundation Fellowship (1985). In 1983 he was invited to head the now-defunct Glass Program at the University of California, Los Angeles — a two-year position that ended when the program closed.

Additional teaching has included time at Colorado Mountain College, near Vail; Pitzer College, Claremont, California; Pilchuck Glass School; and San Francisco State University. As with other glass artists, these activities led to a peripatetic lifestyle in which Statom's only constant was his art.

Statom's early works presage the pattern of production that has endured throughout his career. In 1974 he constructed a room installation of plate and blown glass elements that incorporated the corner of the gallery. The work was made of clear glass that relied on the sparkle and transparency of the material. But Statom has a talent for color and concurrently was making colored vessels that combine large blown forms within complex vessels-within-vessels. While these forms are related to early work by Dan Dailey (cats. 10 and 11), Statom was evolving his own form and color vocabulary, for example, the cones that soon became part of his more playful later style.

Statom also experimented with found objects. In 1977 he combined second-hand kitchen chairs with a piece of sheet glass by inserting the glass perpendicular to the chair back (see fig. 10). This multimedia approach was common at the time and illustrates Statom's ability to adopt new art concepts.

Therman Statom

Green Chair with Base, 1991
Sheet glass, blown elements, with painted decoration
45 x 25 x 36 inches (114.3 x 63.5 x 91.4 cm)
cat. 60

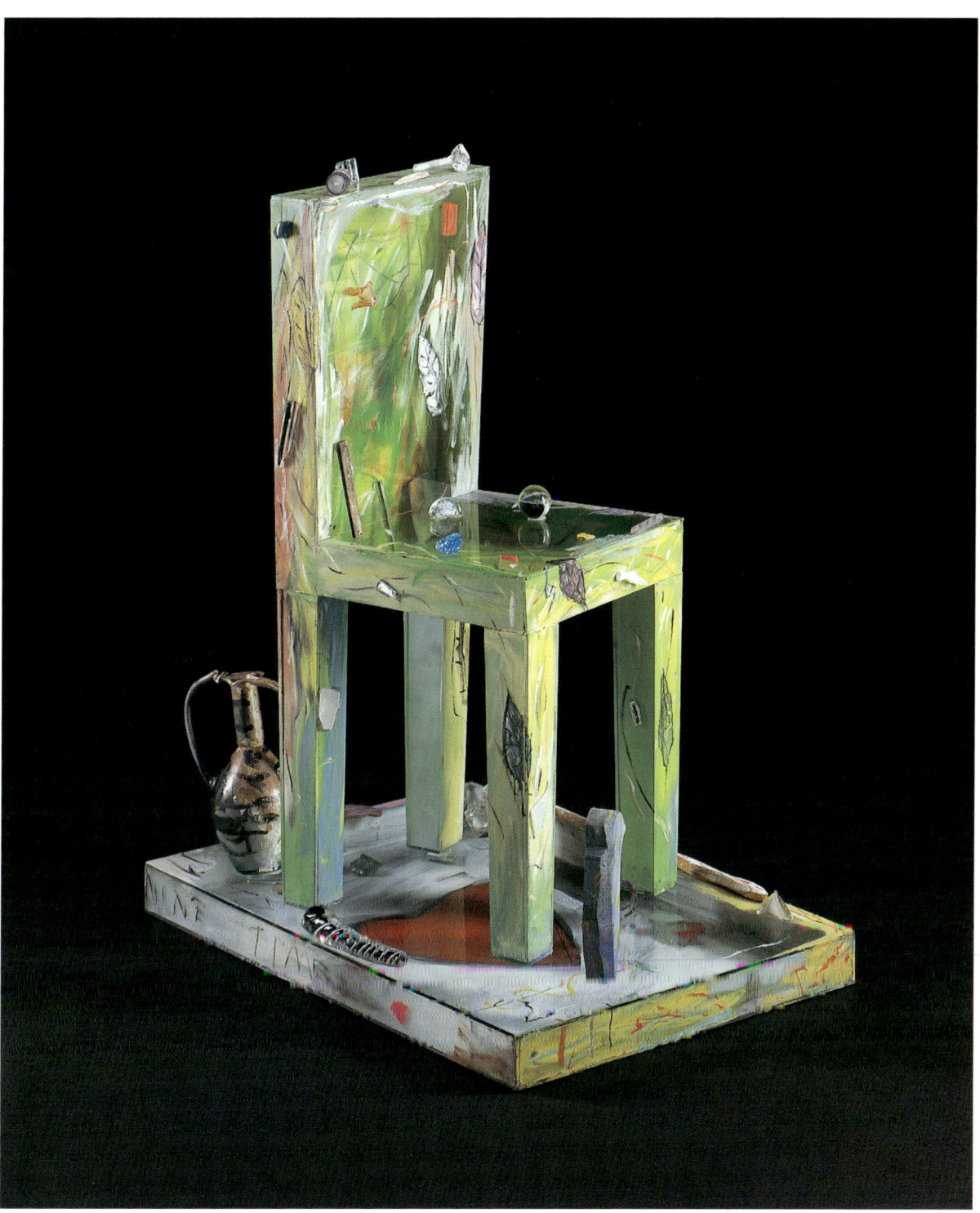

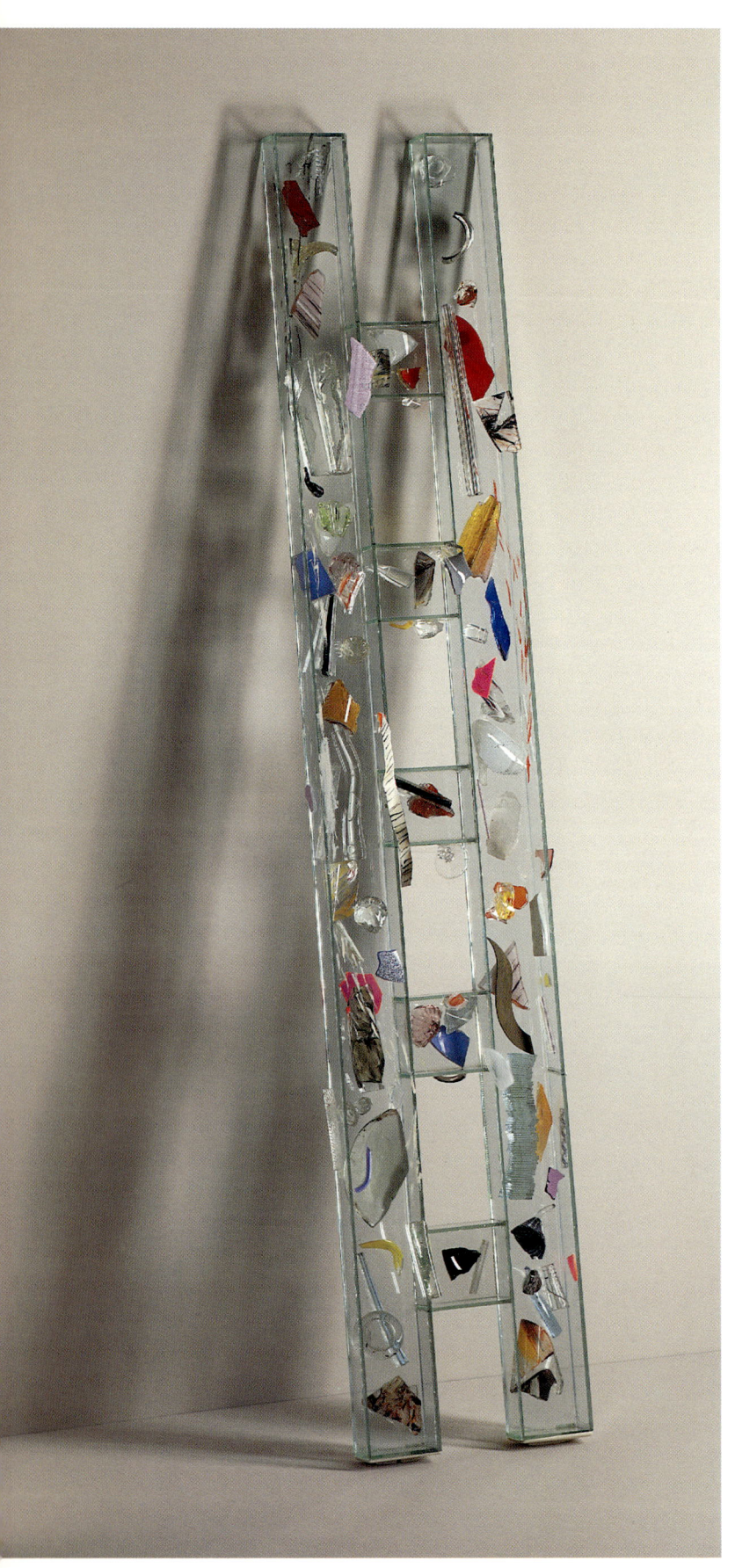

Therman Statom

Untitled, 1991
Sheet glass and paint, with glass shards by
Curtiss Brock, William Morris, Dick Weiss,
and others
83 1/2 x 15 1/2 x 2 3/4 inches (212.1 x 39.4 x 7 cm)
cat. 61

He also made tables, a series of colorful blown vases, and transparent glass screens. Statom then hit upon what became his signature form: the house. First executed in cast glass with paint or other colorful materials applied to the surface, the form had a resonance that was both whimsical and mystical. While retaining the directness of a child's rendering, Statom's houses have the solidity of sculptural forms. These works also signaled the emergence of his sunny pastels.

By the early 1980s Statom had established his formal vocabulary: the cone, house, ball, ladder, chair, table, and narrow box form—all became vehicles for his painted surfaces.[127] Statom also discovered sculptor Larry Bell's cubes and the assembly technique of siliconing together sheets of glass. First in installations and then in discrete forms, Statom's expressive color and the painting on glass became the focus of his work, becoming ever more assertive and denser. Critic Matthew Kangas noted that Statom "had imbibed at the well of the action painting school in his colorful and expressive…installation."[128] Using cheerful colors and casual craftsmanship, Statom incorporates Surrealist and randomly linked elements and takes an irreverent view of glass as a medium. Painting, gluing, covering up the glass, he manipulates

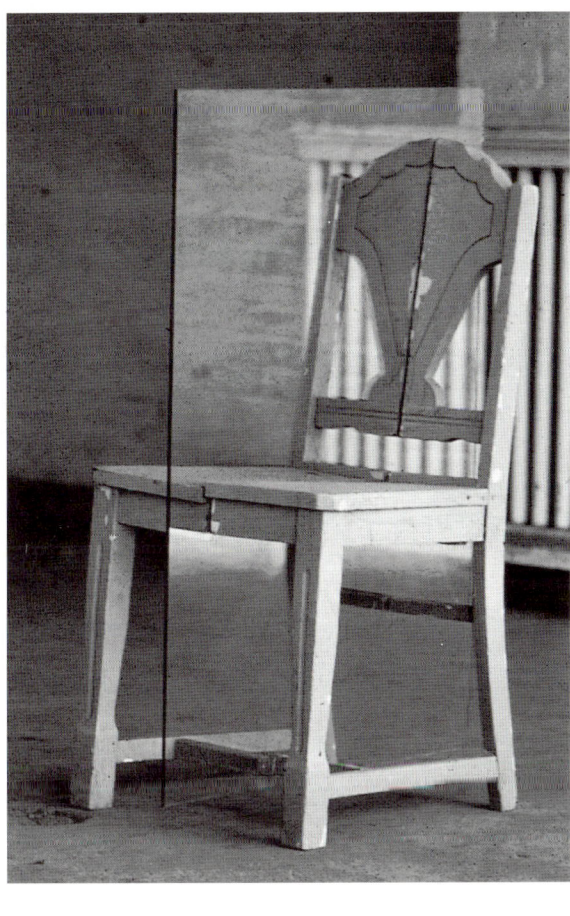

FIG. 10

Therman Statom
American, b. 1953

Untitled, 1977
Sheet glass and wood
42 x 26 x 28 inches (106 x 66 x 71 cm)
Courtesy the artist

the transparency of glass, its refractive ability, and its reflective nature to great advantage. For example, *Green Chair with Base* (1991), an assembled and painted, sheet-glass chair, is colored both inside and out. Painted with green foliage punctuated by attached glass shards and ball forms, it is formally set on a low, boxed plinth that contains a large, throbbing red heart. Statom has explained that glass serves him "like a canvas...except it's got more sensibility."[129] As with other artists who have accessed commonplace forms, Statom's piece invites us to contemplate "chairness."[130]

Untitled (1991) is a transparent ladder form densely decorated with glass shards, canes, and geometric forms. The ladder became part of Statom's vocabulary during one of his installations, when the real ladder used in putting up the work seemed to fill a necessary compositional role. The glass versions came to symbolize travel and pathways between physical reality and the spiritual world.[131] This 1991 piece incorporates glass shards blown by Curtiss Brock, William Morris, and Dick Weiss, among others.

In the late 1980s and early 1990s, Statom received numerous important commissions for civic works in Los Angeles. In 1989 he was asked to make three massive chandeliers for the Los Angeles Central Library (working with Norman Pfeiffer of Hardy Holzman Pfeiffer Associates of New York). Statom was one of five artists[132] selected to work on the project.

KARLA TRINKLEY

American, b. 1956

Karla Trinkley's technically challenging *pâte de verre* forms trick the eye and delight the mind. In 1974 Trinkley began her formal study of art at Bucks County Community College, in Newtown, Pennsylvania. Then in 1976 she transferred to the Tyler School of Art in Elkins Park, Pennsylvania, where she studied ceramics with Rudolph Staffel, and learned how to work with porcelain. After completing her studies, she moved into glass. From 1979 to 1981 she attended the Rhode Island School of Design, Providence, receiving her Master of Fine Arts degree.

One of Trinkley's early slumped-glass works was acquired by The Corning Museum of Glass, New York. Building on this auspicious beginning, Trinkley tackled the challenge of *pâte de verre*. Tyler professor Jon Clark introduced Trinkley and her classmates to this historical technique by reading them an article about a gallery on Madison Avenue in New York that specialized in the medium. Known since Egyptian times, the technique was last in favor during the late nineteenth century, when French artists Henri and Jean Cros and François Décorchemont rediscovered the technology.

Information about how to create *pâte de verre* was not readily available. In broad outline, *pâte de verre* uses ground glass that has been made into a paste and mixed with oxides for color. The paste is placed inside a mold, then heated in a kiln, so that it melts and fuses. One of the technological challenges was to perfect a mold release. The objects produced are textured, and depending on the amount of finishing, they have either a subtle shine or are pitted and scarred. The process and visual character of the method has more in common with clay formation and aesthetics than with traditional glass-forming.

When she decided to adopt this technique, Trinkley took on the daunting task of rediscovering suitable materials for mold-making, chemicals that could serve as glass colorants, and compounds that would allow the mold to release the final formed object. Spurred by a remark that Dale Chihuly (cats. 7 and 8) made when he stated flatly that she would never produce successful *pâte de verre* work,[133] Trinkley built on what she knew from her ceramics training. Fortunately the material that she had used for her early slumping was workable as a mold medium for this new endeavor. Because the usual shiny surface produced by most glass-forming techniques did not interest her, *pâte de verre*'s imperfections were compelling for Trinkley.

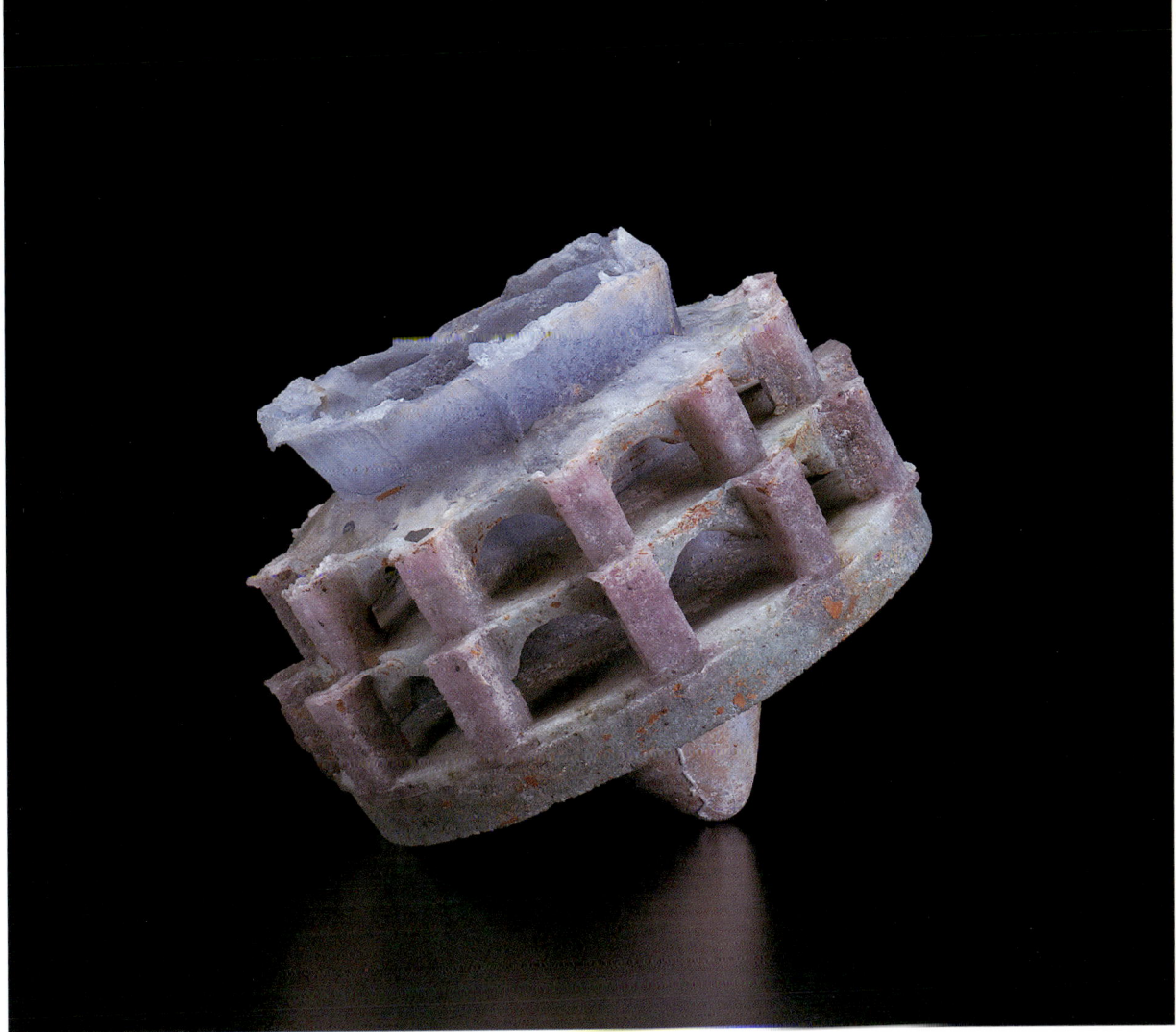

Karla Trinkley

Axis, 1985
Pâte de verre
7 x 9 dia. inches (17.8 x 22.9 cm)
cat. 62

Axis (1985), a table-sized *pâte de verre* piece, is one of an untitled series of similarly constructed works. Often erroneously described as a restatement of the famous cage cup (*vasa diatretum*) of Roman times, these works reflect Trinkley's avid interest in all forms of architecture and specifically the architecture of Japan, China, and ancient cultures. Here, the piece recalls a Japanese pagoda, albeit an inverted one. Its delicate palette is typical of Trinkley's mid-1980s production. The elements on the exterior relate to African scarification patterns.

Trinkley's works present an intriguing tug of perception versus reality. When the pieces are removed from the mold, natural accretions on the exterior mark where the glass melted and leaked out of the mold. Trinkley enhances these areas by sandblasting to augment the pitted and "weathered" texture. The fragile and enticing formations appear as delicate and innocuous as spun sugar, but in fact they are glass splinters. Trinkley delights in the seductive nature of her pieces as she laces them with sinister potential.

BERTIL VALLIEN

Swedish, b. 1938

Bertil Vallien makes unique glass sculptures and designs for industry. Born in Sollentuna, a northern suburb of Stockholm, Vallien was raised in a strict, religious household headed by his father, a painter-decorator. At age fifteen Vallien ran away from home. He met artist Bo Notini,[134] who became the first in a line of artists who encouraged the young man's art ambitions. In 1955 Vallien entered the Konstfack School of Arts, Crafts, and Design in Stockholm and later the School for Advanced Industrial Design, where he met ceramist Lis Husberg and sculptors Olle Adrin and Nisse Bruland. After a stint in the army, Vallien decided in 1959 to make art his life. He went to study with ceramist and designer Stig Lindberg, an association that exposed Vallien to the factory process. But at that time Vallien was more interested in a craft orientation: he concentrated on learning the skill of wheel-turning clay objects. In 1961 Vallien heard that HAL Fromholt Ceramics Company in Los Angeles was looking for a Swedish designer. Vallien's trip was supported by a grant funded by King Gustav Adolph VI of Sweden.[135] For the next twenty-five years, Vallien continued to design for industry and pursue his independent work as well.

In Los Angeles, Vallien saw the innovative Abstract Expressionist ceramics of Peter Voulkos and Jerry Rothman, and the Funk ceramics being made in the San Francisco Bay Area. As an artist resident in the United States, Vallien entered the biannual "Young American" competition at the Museum of Contemporary Crafts, New York (later the American Craft Museum), winning first place for his stoneware *Family on Whale*. Vallien also visited Mexico and saw Mayan artifacts. Although the American studio-glass movement was emerging, Vallien was not aware of its development.

In 1963 Vallien took a job at the Kosta-Boda glassworks in Åfors, Sweden. Swedish factories are organized with a master designer who works with a team of gaffers to create the master's designs. Vallien was to provide design concepts for industrial production, but was also permitted to work on his own artworks. Vallien faced the challenge of learning glass technology. Aided only by his background in clay and metal, he made several innovations, such as the technique of masking ultra-thin layers of colored glass with a plastic resin that allowed the artist to brush on a resist that defined the desired pattern. He also followed the work of Hungarian ceramist Imre Schrammel and the Swedish ceramist Anders Lijefors in production-ware glass that was blown into sand molds—the technique that became the hallmark of his production-glass vocabulary.

In the 1970s the Swedish glass industry was facing financial difficulties. The issue revolved around the place of craft in the factory. Vallien's response was to urge the Åfors factory to create a series of craft-based objects that could be marketed to fine-arts collectors—in the manner of the nineteenth-century French manufacturer Gallé. Dubbed the "Artists Collection," they had the appearance of unique pieces, but were in fact made in large numbers. Vallien stated that "machines to take over the heaviest labour is good—but to use them for more specialized types of work would soon mean enslavement!"[136] This passion for the crafted object stands in contrast to the attitude of other designers for industry, and marks Vallien as one of the leaders in the field.

The vessel *Untitled* (1985) is a signature production work. The blown form was altered into an imperfect shape and decorated with folkloric figures, sandwiched between layers of glass. The bowl represents an early example of Vallien's 1983 breakthrough technology, which allowed artistic expression to take precedence over technical concerns.[137] Vallien was particularly proud that these glowing works took advantage of "glass art's light."[138]

In the mid-1980s Vallien began exploring in glass the boat form that he had investigated in metal as a young man. Throughout history the boat has symbolized the journey; in Vallien's hands it is both a comforting structure and a container of archetypal and personal memories. Self-contained worlds, punctuated with Surrealist imagery, Vallien's boats tap into a universal human subconscious.

Calendarium (1990) (ill. p. 36) is from the final years of Vallien's initial boat series. The title, which means "calendar" in Latin, refers to the continuum of life. In the boat are objects symbolic of various aspects of that life: a mail pouch, a copper horse and man, a glass ball, a life preserver, a glass boat, ladders, and a glass mummy. Attached to the rough exterior are glass masks, a cross, and the ♂ symbol. These appear to be bits of wreckage and detritus that have attached themselves to the hull. The fragility of the boat and its cargo is enhanced by the slender wire girdle that suspends the sculpture in mid-air.

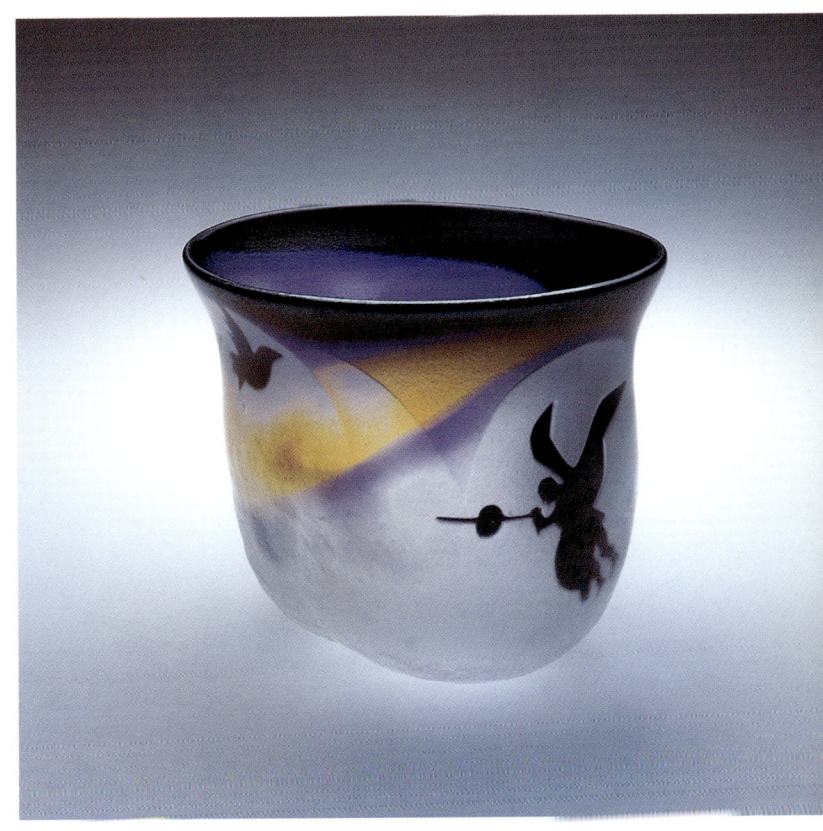

Bertil Vallien

Untitled, 1985
Blown glass
4¼ x 6 x 5 inches (10.8 x 15.2 x 12.7 cm)
cat. 63

František Vízner

Untitled, c. 1992
Cast glass, cut and polished
3³⁄₄ x 11¹⁄₂ dia. inches (9.5 x 29.2 cm)
cat. 65

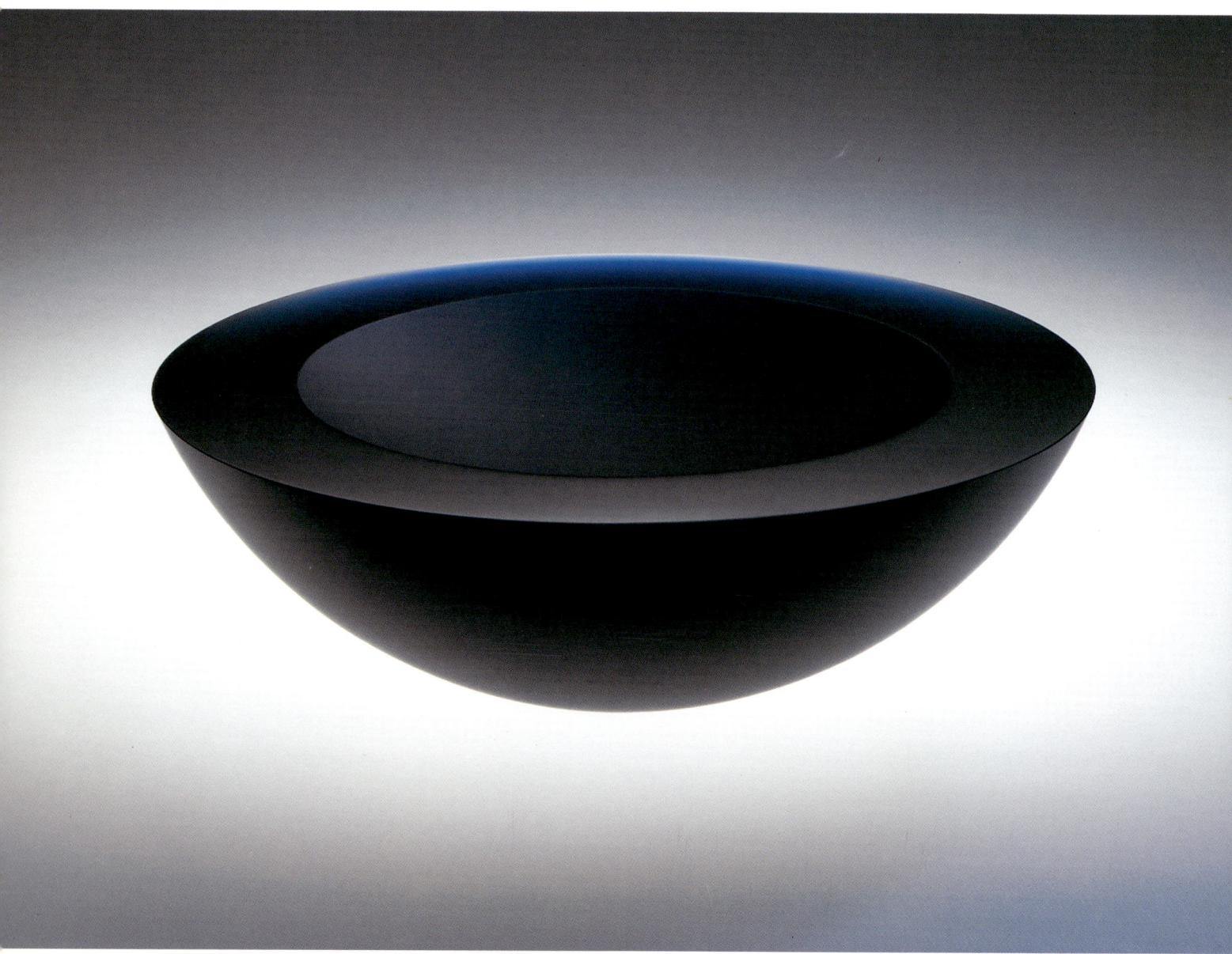

FRANTIŠEK VÍZNER

Czechoslovakian, b. 1936

Master glassmaker František Vízner's deceptively simple containers are both monolithic and subtle. The forms appear machine-made, but in fact are hand-hewn from solid blocks of cast glass.

Glass has been Vízner's life, beginning with, in traditional European style, an apprenticeship at Nový Bor, Czechosolvakia, in the early 1950s. Vízner then attended glass school in Železný Brod from 1953 to 1956. He completed his education at the Vysoká škola uměleckoprumyslová in Prague under Professor K. Štipl in 1962. Immediately after finishing his studies, Vízner went to work for industry, first at the Sklo-Union Corporation at Teplice, then at the Glassworks Škrdlovice. In 1976 Vízner left factory design work to be an independent artist.

All of Vízner's work has centered around the vessel form. In 1984 he stated, "The vase always was and still remains my positive destiny in glass…. I look upon the contemporary decline in interest in the functional value of glass and the preference for free creation as fashion."[139] Although Vízner is content to make vessels, the larger art world (with its disdain for utilitarian form) has preferred to assess his works as sculptural objects; they are successful in either category.

The Glick collection has two pieces by Vízner: *Untitled* (c. 1992) and *Untitled* (c. 1993) (ill. p. 10). Both works are hand-carved from cast factory glass. Following red pencil marks on the block, Vízner labors with intensity, eliminating all extraneous flourishes that might compromise the rationality and harmony of his works. While his simple shapes seem suited to machine production, Vízner prefers his handmade approach, thereby reinvigorating the argument about the use of machines versus the innate sensibility of the handmade object. Somewhat begging the question, Vízner's works are handmade to express a machine aesthetic.

Untitled (c. 1992) is polished to a flawless shine and *Untitled* (c. 1993) is sandblasted to a fine soft texture. Both works are essays on ideal proportion and the power of softly modulated color: they stand as functional form raised to sculptural statement.

DANA ZÁMEČNÍKOVÁ

Czechoslovakian, b. 1945

Dana Zámečníková uses glass as a structural canvas for her powerful painted images. Unlike most Czech glass artists, Zámečníková was not trained in glass, but first studied architecture at the Czech Technical University in Prague, then took a degree in theatrical design with Dr. Josef Svoboda at the Academy of Applied Art, Prague. Her first job after graduation was in stage design, and for a time she was the youngest stage designer working for the Prague National Theater.[140]

Zámečníková was introduced to glass in 1973 by her future husband, Marian Karel. A student of Stanislav Libenský (cats. 23 and 24) at the Academy of Applied Art, Karel acquainted Zámečníková with the potential of glass as an expressive medium, and provided the technical information she needed to work in her new medium. Ironically, Zámečníková's lack of formal glass training gives her work a freshness and original sensibility not always seen in Czech studio glass.

Zámečníková works in a painterly, theatrical style. Her early works involved painting on cubes or spheres of glass cased within larger glass constructions, but by the late 1970s she had adopted her signature technique of painting on layers of window glass. This notion may have been the result of a Baroque-style set design that she made for Molière's *Amphytrion*.[141] Baroque painters and sculptors explored layering as a way to augment visual and dramatic effects. Their heavily embellished works communicate expanded meanings and visual delights through their skillful manipulation of light and dark passages. Zámečníková translated these concepts to her glass art. Interestingly, Czech glass has a long tradition of using layers of glass as an expressive and technical element, evidenced in Bohemian double-walled beakers of the nineteenth century and the experiments of the Czech painter Vladimír Kopecký (b. 1931).

Zámečníková's uses her layered formats to house narratives, noting, "The layers of glass I use are layers of events I experience."[142] The layers add both actual and metaphorical depth, and permit a play of images that allows their meaning to deepen in intensity. With figures in various stages of dematerialization, depicted alternately with scratchy outlines and dense passages of color, Zámečníková can "record mutually incongruous stories, a summary of history and contemporary time, confusion of symbols."[143] Breaking from traditions, she works with oil paints rather than the more traditional, and slower, enamels.

The title of *Pepik/Joe* (1989) refers to Zámečníková's dog who had died at the age of fifteen. The work captures some of her sadness and affection for this beloved pet, but as with all of Zámečníková's work, the personal is transformed into the universal. Seeing herself as an artist who is not confined by her choice of medium, Zámečníková states, "My idea was to use glass simply as one of the many materials available because it offered the best possible way for expressing my ideas — not to use glass because I am a glass artist."[144]

Dana Zámečníková

Pepik/Joe, 1989
Sheet glass, sandblasted, engraved, and painted
8 3/4 x 8 3/4 x 4 inches (22.2 x 22.2 x 10.2 cm)
cat. 67

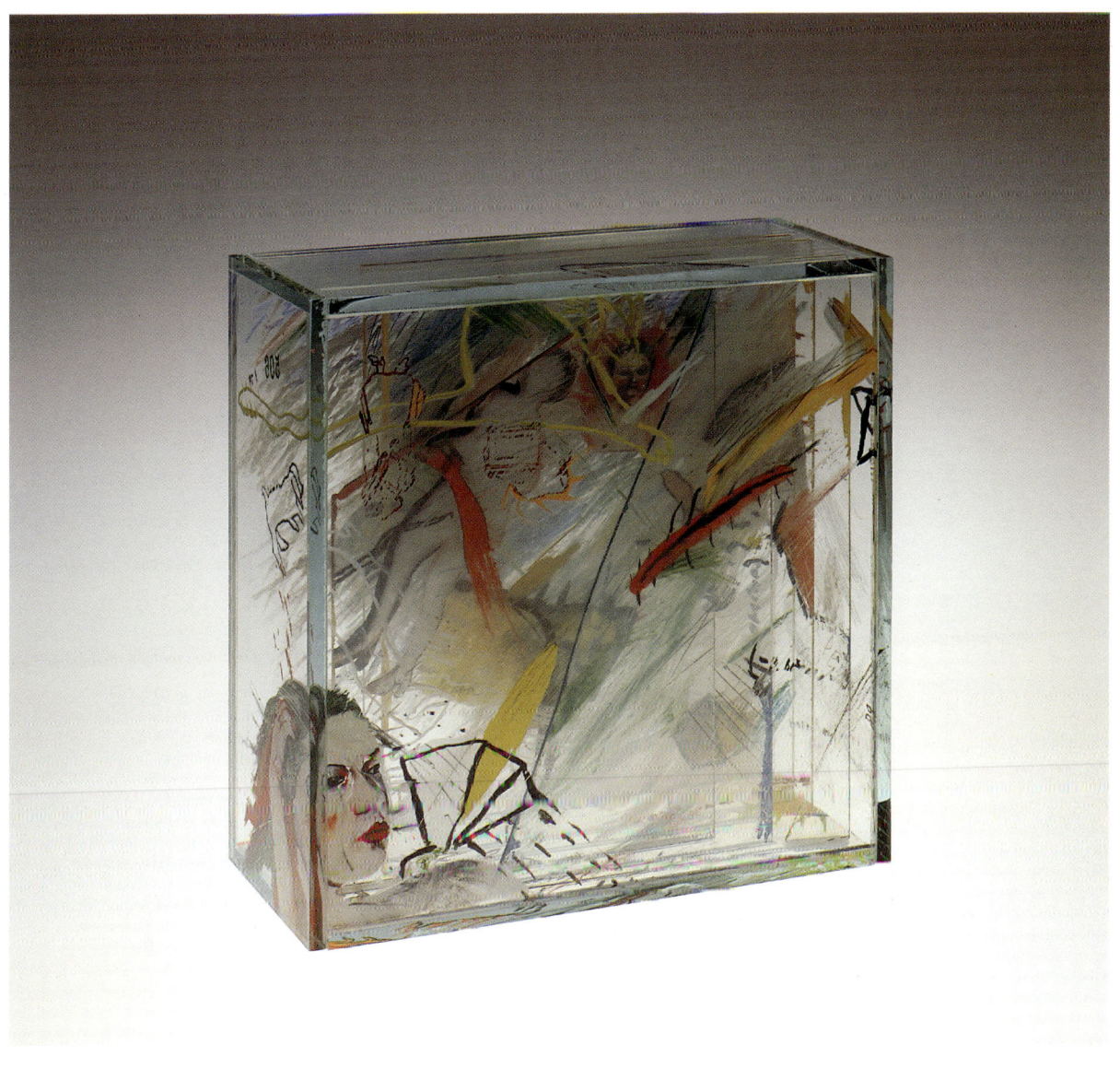

YAN ZORITCHAK

Czechoslovakian, b. 1944

Yan Zoritchak's cast-glass sculptures seek metaphorically to conquer the universe. Born in the Slovakian village of Zdiar, in the Carpathian Mountains, Zoritchak has always been intrigued by space travel and the quest to know what lies outside our universe. He studied glassmaking at the High School of Applied Arts in Železný Brod (1959–63), then attended the Academy of Applied Art in Prague under Stanislav Libenský (cats. 23 and 24), receiving his diploma in 1969. Although trained as a master glassblower, Zoritchak demonstrated his versatility in 1968 by working with Louis Franchéo on stained-glass windows for the church in Lot-et-Garonne, France, but soon was drawn to shaping solid blocks of crystal with a diamond-toothed saw. This difficult, premeditated, and mathematically precise technique of cold-forming glass would become his métier.

During his time at the Academy of Applied Art, Zoritchak had met his future wife, Catherine, who was studying animation. Catherine is French and in 1969 they moved to live there permanently.[145] There was no active studio-glass movement when the Zoritchaks arrived in France. They settled in Annecy, in the French Alps, and built their home and studios.

Zoritchak begins his glass sculptures with studies on paper that then are turned into three-dimensional geometric drawings, consisting of precise cubes, pyramids, and tetrahedrons. He chooses these forms for their mystical and metaphysical potential to express his passion for the cosmos. He works in a range of sizes, from table-sized to monumental outdoor sculptures.

Zoritchak's fascination with space began in 1957 when as a thirteen-year-old, he dreamt of Sputnik's achievements and intergalactic space flight. Neil Armstrong's walk on the moon struck a deep resonance in him.[146] Zoritchak states, "My passion for the cosmos started when I was a small child, when I spent my evenings watching the pure and vast star-studded dome blanketing the night of my home in the Carpathian Mountains. This passion fed on many discoveries, conquests, and progress made by Man during the years and centuries towards this knowledge in Infinite Space."[147] Zoritchak now creates sculptures titled variously, "Cosmic Signals," "Space Messengers," "Space Birds," and "Heaven Flowers,"[148] in an effort to contact other universes.

Untitled (1989) is from Zoritchak's "Heaven Flowers" series. The work features a dominant

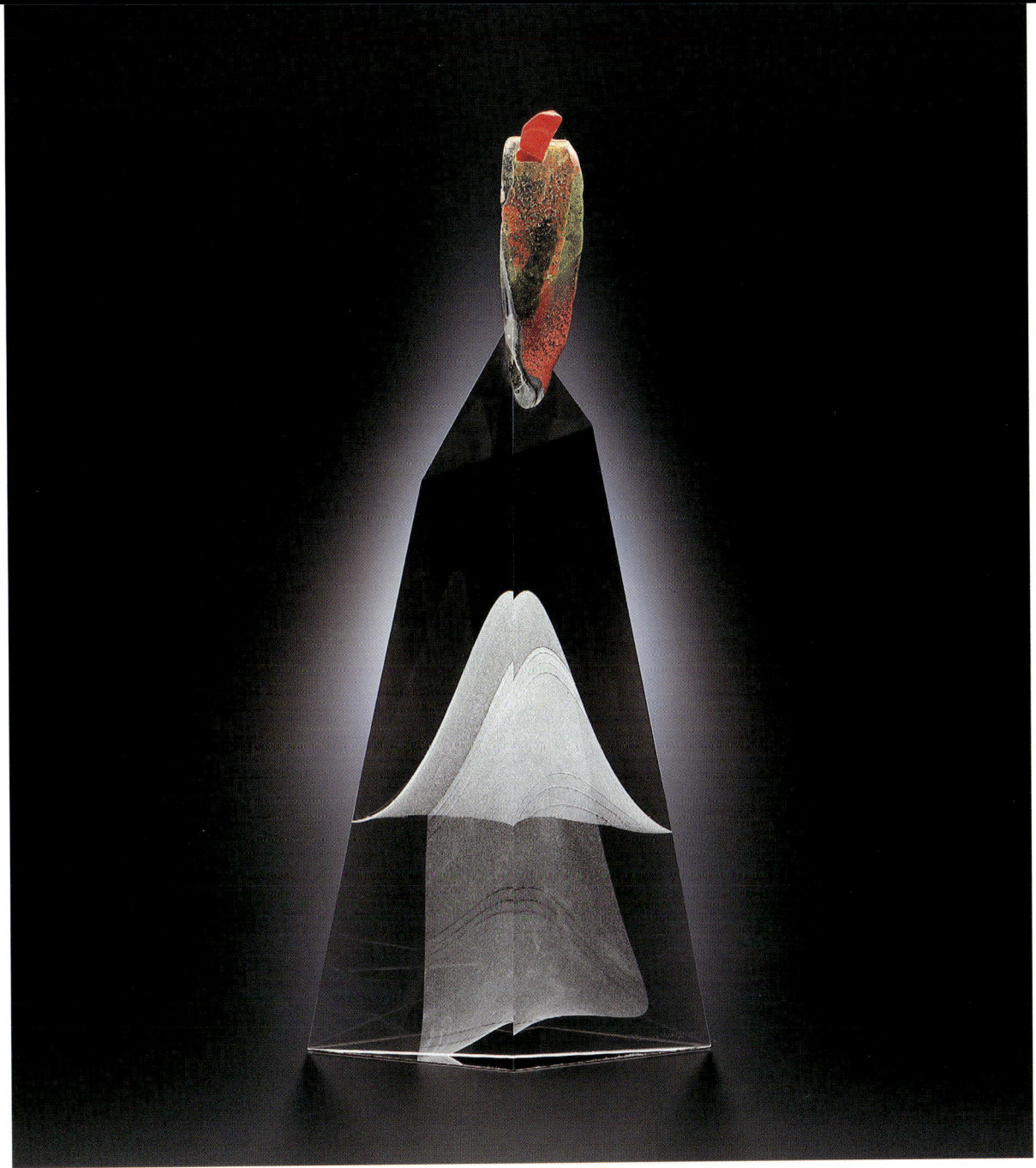

Yan Zoritchak

Untitled (from the "Heaven Flowers" series), 1989
Lead glass with additions, cut and polished
23 x 9 ¾ x 1 ¾ inches (58.4 x 24.8 x 4.4 cm)
cat. 68

pyramidal form, topped with a "flower" of ruby-red achromatic glass cullet. Simple in design, form, and construction, the piece has a rough-cut top carefully balanced with the architectonic and disciplined base. As the viewer moves around the piece, the vivid colors of the cullet and the nuances of the cast-crystal base appear to vibrate. On April 26, 1993, Zoritchak, traveling with the first Slovakian polar expedition, placed a similar piece at the North Pole. His goal is to have the work "send and receive its line of force while drifting [on the] polar cap in the immensity of Space and Time."[149]

TOOTS ZYNSKY

American, b. 1951

Mary Ann (Toots) Zynsky celebrates the exuberance of color in the form of brilliantly hued vessels made of fused glass threads. Born in Boston, Zynsky went to the Rhode Island School of Design, Providence, to study painting. Feeling discouraged during her freshman year, she was contemplating withdrawing when she saw students in the glass studio dressed in odd costumes in preparation for the making of a film. Zynsky recalls that she "saw them and all this hot glass swirling through the air. It was nuts."[150] She completed her Bachelor of Arts degree, studying with Dale Chihuly (cats. 7 and 8) and Buster Simpson, who taught her how to slump large glass sheets. The rest of her work involved fusing, casting, and breaking glass. For the next six years, Zynsky abandoned glass and focused instead on making "ephemeral, temporary sculptural installations" out of impermanent materials.[151]

In 1984 Zynsky was invited by the Ghanaian Ministry of Culture, at the Institute of African Studies at Legon, Ghana, and the Klankschap Foundation of Holland to serve as a special researcher to record the contemporary music of Ghana. During the six months she lived there, Zynsky collaborated with Kente weaver Samuel Agbanu on a large textile. After completing both projects, Zynsky moved to Amsterdam, where she lives today.

Through her experiments with slumping and fusing glass, Zynsky invented a new technique for forming glass filaments by applying to her art fiber-optic filaments technology gleaned from the Corning Glass Works.[152] Eventually she invented what she jokingly calls the "*filet de verre*" technique, which uses threadlike fibers drawn from colored glass rods of ten to fourteen millimeters thick, and fuses them into a variety of shapes; the forming process involves laying out the filaments on a bed of compressed plaster. Zynsky credits her friend and colleague Albinas Elskus with the ideas for this approach.[153]

In 1982 Zynsky premiered her "*filet de verre*" vessels at the Theo Portnoy Gallery in New York. Her friend Mathijs Teunissen Van Manen saw her work and made a visit to her studio. When he discovered that Zynsky pulled her glass strands laboriously by hand, he worked with her to jerry-rig a machine for the continuous pulling of glass filaments. Zynsky still uses the machine that Van Manen helped design.

The Glick collection contains two pieces by Zynsky. *Untitled* (1986) (ill. p. 23) is part of her

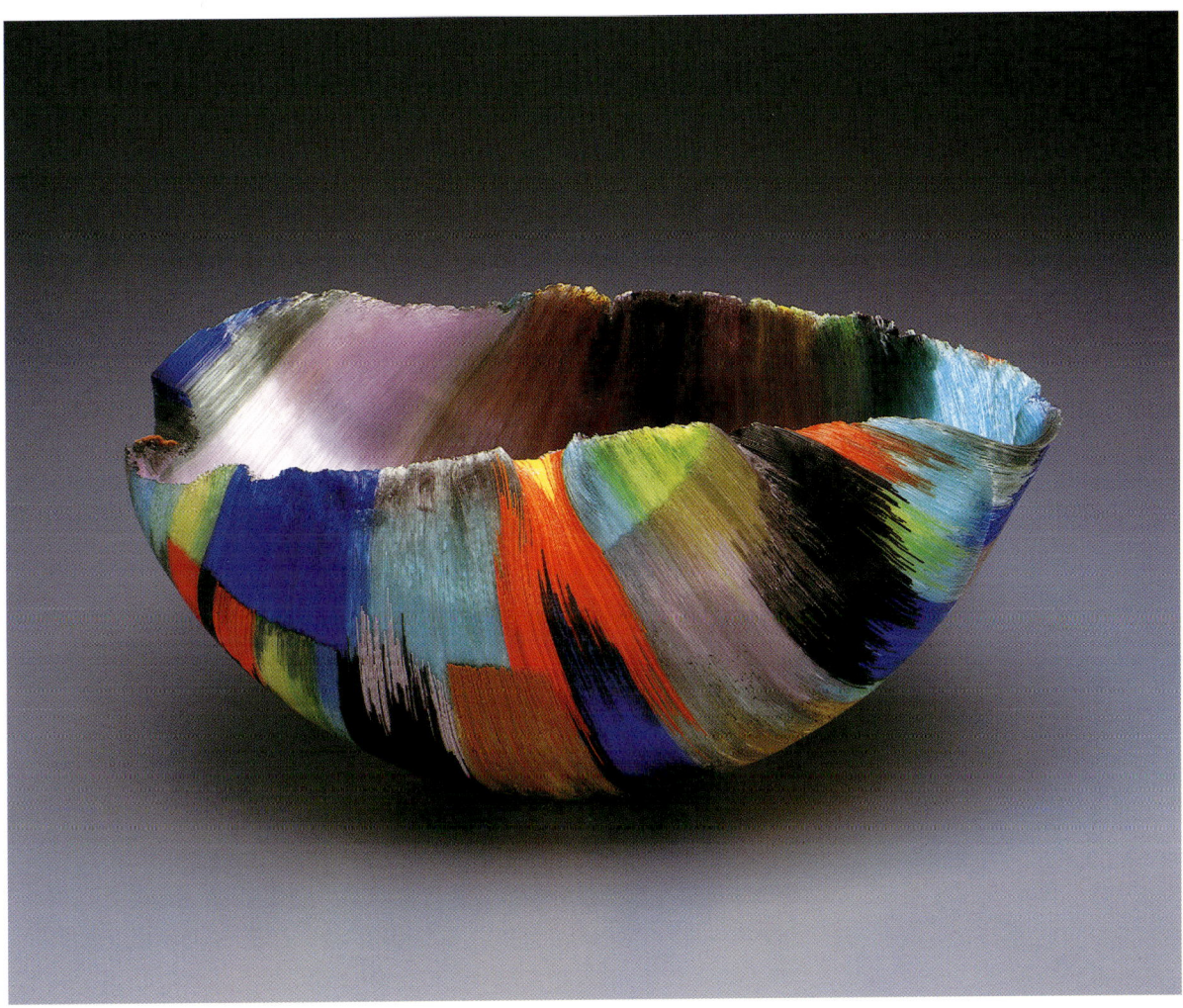

Toots Zynsky

Cityscape, 1992
Glass threads, fused and kiln-formed
6½ x 13 x 9 inches (16.5 x 33 x 22.9 cm)
cat. 70

"Exotic Bird" series. The *"filet de verre"* vessel form features a bright red interior with a black and bright yellow exterior. Vividly colored to mimic a tropical bird, the captivating piece is daring in its color combination. The second piece, *Cityscape*, was made between June and September 1992 as part of a transition group between the "Terra del Fuego" and the "Chaos" series. Zynsky deftly placed each color in precise proximity to allow them to spark one another. She also took advantage of the filament nature of the construction process by placing slender wisps of glass color so that they penetrate the contrasting sections and make stepped junctures between color passages. No glass artist working today can equal Zynsky's bravery and finesse as a colorist. In 1988 Zynsky was honored with the Third Annual Rakow Commission from The Corning Museum of Glass, New York.

NOTES

1. Quoted in Susanne Frantz, *Contemporary Glass: A World Wide Survey from The Corning Museum of Glass* (New York: Harry N. Abrams, 1989), p. 43.

2. Hot-glass techniques include blowing and casting. Warm-glass techniques include slumping, fusing, *pâte de verre*, *filet de verre*, and drawing with canes of glass. Cold-working techniques encompass cutting, polishing, engraving, painting (before firing), fabricating, and assembly.

3. Stained glass was also capable of being made outside the industrial setting, but as an art form that operates on a flat plane and has existed in varying levels of intensity since its invention during the Middles Ages, it has a separate tradition. Although contemporary American studio-glass artists do make stained glass, they have more in common with painters than with the glass artists who make three-dimensional works.

4. Paul Hollister, "Studio Glass Before 1962: Maurice Heaton, Frances and Michael Higgins and Edris Eckhardt," *Neues Glas* 4 (1985), pp. 232-40.

5. See Frantz (note 1), pp. 32-39.

6. Earl McCutchen, "Glass Molding: Experimenting on a Budget," *Craft Horizons* 15, 3 (May/June 1955), pp. 38-39.

7. The attendees for the first workshop were Clayton Bailey, Edith Franklin, Karl Martz, Tom McGlauchlin, William Pitney, Dora Reynolds, and John Stephenson. The second was attended by Erik Erickson, Robert Floian, Rosemary Gulassa, Sister Jeannine (O.P. Siena Heights College, Toledo), John Karrasch, Howard Kottler, Elaine Lukasik, Octavio Medelin, Diane Powell, June Wilson, and Stanley Zielinski; Clayton Bailey also returned.

8. Robert Arneson, "Six Glassblowers," *Craft Horizons* 27, 5 (Sept./Oct. 1967), pp. 39-40.

9. By the early 1960s, due to the work of Peter Voulkos and Robert Arneson, clay had become a sculptural medium. Glass would not make that shift until the late 1970s, when blowing ceased to be the favored forming method.

10. Harvey Littleton, "A Potter's Experience with Glass," in *Research in the Crafts* (New York: The American Craftsmen's Council, 1983), pp. 42-44.

11. See Bellingham, Washington, Whatcom Museum of History and Art, *Clearly Art: Pilchuck Glass Legacy*, text by Lloyd E. Herman (Seattle: University of Washington Press, 1992).

12. It is important to remember that clay preceded glass in acceptance into college curriculums. See this author's essay "Clay Leads the Studio Crafts into the Art World," in Toledo, Ohio, The Toledo Museum of Art, *Contemporary Crafts and the Saxe Collection* (New York: Hudson Hills Press, Inc., 1993), pp. 90-99.

13. See Frantz (note 1), p. 56.

14. Conversation with Klaus Moje, Wheaton Village, New Jersey, June 10, 1995.

15. It should be noted that Alfred University had offered a laboratory class in glass technology. It was a natural extension of the university's interest in ceramics technology during the same period.

16. For example, *Neues Glas* was published in Germany and *Crafts: The Decorative and Applied Arts Magazine* was published in England.

17. Dr. Sylva Petrová, "Mass and Space: 8 Questions for Stanislav Libenský and Jaroslava Brychtová," *Neues Glas* 2 (1994), p. 16.

18. Stanislav Libenský, "Teaching Activities of Stanislav Libenský," unpub. ms, June 1984, unpag.

19. Yoriko Mizuta, "265 Years of Japanese Glass," *Glass* 51 (Spring 1993), pp. 38-43.

20. See Susanne Frantz, "Not So New in '62," *The Glass Arts Society Journal*, 1988, p. 18.

21. Noris Ioannou, *Australian Studio Glass: the Move-*

ment, Its Makers and Their Art (Roseville East, Australia: Craftsman House, 1995), p. 19.

22. Karen S. Chambers, "Howard Ben Tré: An Artist in Time," *New Work* 15/16 (Summer/Fall 1983), p. 5.

23. Wausau, Wisconsin, Leigh Yawkey Woodson Art Museum, *Americans in Glass* (Wausau, 1978), p. 57.

24. Letter to the author from the artist's wife, Gay Ben Tré, May 4, 1995.

25. Letter to Barry Shifman, Curator of Decorative Arts, Indianapolis Museum of Art, Jan. 29, 1995.

26. Robert G. Loeffler, "Contemporary Hungarian Glass Sculpture," *New Work* 27 (Fall 1986), p. 10.

27. John Perrault, "Jane Bruce: The Search for a Place," *Glass* 64 (Fall 1996), p. 30.

28. Letter to the author, Nov. 21, 1995.

29. Communication with the author, 1996.

30. Letter to the author, Apr. 25, 1995.

31. Artist's statement, 1987.

32. Artist's statement, July 1990.

33. Letter to the author, Jan. 1996.

34. Communication with the author, 1996.

35. Letter to the author, Jan. 21, 1996.

36. Mark S. Talaba, "Profile: Sydney Cash," *Glass* 10, 1 (1982), p. 17.

37. Karen S. Chambers, "Sydney Cash: Moving On," *Neues Glas* 1 (1991), p. 16.

38. New York, Heller Gallery, *Sydney Cash: A Family of Work* (New York, 1995), unpag.

39. See Bellingham, 1992 (note 11).

40. John Krakauer, "Dale Chihuly Has Turned Art Glass into a Red-hot Item," *Smithsonian* 22, 11 (Feb. 1992), p. 93.

41. Ibid.; Scott Sullivan, "The Glass Leprechaun," *Newsweek*, Oct. 16, 1995, p. 52; and Krakauer (note 40), p. 94.

42. Glass artist Richard Meitner and artist Mark Tobey were the other American artists to have solo shows. In Chihuly's case, it was at the Musée des Arts Décoratifs, one of the related museums within the Louvre complex.

43. Geoffrey Wichert, "In the Eye of the Storm," *Neues Glas* 3 (1995), p. 42.

44. Letter to the author [1996?].

45. Ibid.

46. Ibid.

47. Farmington Hills, Michigan, Habatat Galleries, Untitled Exhibition Brochure (Farmington Hills, 1990).

48. Letter to the author, Sept. 13, 1995.

49. Ibid.

50. Wausau, Wisconsin, Leigh Yawkey Woodson Art Museum, *Americans in Glass* (Wausau, 1984), p. 46.

51. The *Spur* group thrived between 1957 and 1972 in Western Europe. They believed that capitalism produces passive consumers who do not actively participate in public life. *Radama* is a group that was aligned with the Movement for an Imaginist Bauhaus, as referred to in the entry.

52. Frantz (note 1), p. 54.

53. Erwin Eisch, "Erwin Eisch: From a talk given at BAG Conference in Stoke-on-Trent," *British Artists in Glass* 6 (May 1992), unpag.

54. Babette Hayes, "Erwin Eisch — a new breath of talent in an established glass family," *Craft Australia* 5 (Nov. 3, 1975), p. 8.

55. Atsushi Takeda, "Interview," in Yokohama Museum of Art, *Expanded Glass: Traditional and Contemporary* (Yokohama, 1995), p. 242.

56. Atsushi Takeda, "Glass and Sensitivity — following a trail of 40 years," in *Kyohei Fujita* (Toyko: Asahi Shimbun, 1991), p. 20.

57. Cage cups (*vasa diatretum*) are a form of ovoid beaker with no foot that are comprised of two or more layers of glass. The exterior layer is carved away in a filigree pattern while still attached to the supporting layer with struts. They are rare and have sparked controversy as to how they were constructed.

58. "Anima" refers to the chance effect that occurs during the processing of art mediums. These random occurrences were believed to express a spirit that was within the object formed.

59. Letter to the author, June 30, 1995.

60. New York, Heller Gallery, *Shadow and Substance: The Glass of Michael Glancy*, text by Lisa Hammel (New York, 1989), p. 1.

61. Ibid.

62. David Huchthausen, Introduction, in Wausau, 1984 (note 50), pp. 7–9.

63. Mark S. Talaba, "Projections and Transformation: Mysteries of the Leitungs Scherben," *Neues Glas* 3 (1983), p. 37.

64. Conversation with the author, Chicago, Nov. 1995.

65. Angela Wibking, "Art Under Glass: Richard Jolley Exhibition Opens," *Nashville Business Journal*, Mar. 21–25, 1994, p. 21.

66. Conversation with the author (note 64).

67. James D. Watts, "Crystal Vision," *Tulsa World*, July 10, 1994, entertainment section, p. 2.

68. Beverly Copeland, "Glass Focus Interviews Kreg Kallenberger," *Glass Focus*, Apr./May 1989, p. 7.

69. Ibid., p. 8.

70. Boris Nelson, "Dominick Labino: A Renaissance Man in the 20th Century," *The Sunday Blade*, Aug. 22, 1982, "Toledo Magazine," p. 8.

71. Daniel E. Hogan, *Dominick Labino: Decade of Glass Craftsmanship 1964–1974* (Toledo: The Toledo Museum of Art, 1974), unpag.

72. Joan Falconer Byrd, "A Conversation with Dominick Labino," in *Dominick Labino: Glass Retrospective* (Cullowhee, North Carolina: Western Carolina University, 1982), p. 9.

73. Ibid., pp. 2–8.

74. Ibid., p. 9.

75. Roger D. Bonham, "Dominick Labino," *Ceramics Monthly* 15, 9 (Nov. 1967), p. 14.

76. Due to language barriers, much of this entry is taken from Susanne Frantz's authoritative exhibition catalogue from The Corning Museum of Glass, *Stanislav Libenský, Jaroslava Brychtová: A 40-year Collaboration in Glass* (Corning, New York, and Munich: Prestel, 1994).

77. Seattle, Elliot Brown Gallery, "A Discussion: Stanislav Libenský and Jaroslava Brychtová with Jiří Šetlík and Katya Kohoutová," in *Stanislav Libenský and Jaroslava Brychtová: Paintings, Drawings and Sculpture* (Seattle, 1995), pp. 4–5. [Essay originally printed in Prague, 1995.]

78. Robert Kehlmann, Review of "Libenský/Brychtová: A Unique Collaboration in Glass," *American Craft* 54, 4 (Aug./Sept. 1994), p. 41.

79. Seattle, 1995 (note 77), p. 7.

80. Ludmila Vachtova, "Unleashed Fire, Frozen Time," in Paris, Clara Scremini Gallery, *Stanislav Libenský and Jaroslava Brychtová* (Paris, 1992), [p. 13].

81. Mike L. Ramirez, "Marvin Lipofsky; An Interview," unpub. ms, College of Arts and Crafts, Oakland, California, no date, unpag.

82. Conversation with the author, Asheville, North Carolina, May 5, 1995.

83. Shawn Waggoner, "Bay Area Glass: Congenitally Worldly, Inherently Irrepressible," *Glass Art*, Nov./Dec., 1990, p. 6.

84. Unpublished notes from a slide lecture delivered by Marvin Lipofsky, 1986.

85. Gianni Toso, a master glassblower and flameworker, is part of the long Murano tradition of Jewish glassmakers who have dominated the field since medieval times.

86. Because his molds are bulky and have only a limited number of usages before they are destroyed, Lipofsky adopted the habit of making molds out of whatever was at hand in each factory, thereby reflecting the personality of each production site.

87. Some of the information included here is drawn from Joan Falconer Byrd's fine essay in Atlanta, The High Museum of Art, *Harvey K. Littleton: A Retrospective Exhibition* (Atlanta, 1984).

88. New York, Heller Gallery, *Harvey K. Littleton: Glass Sculpture*, text by Penelope Hunter-Stiebel (New York, 1982).

89. An exhibition of this material, "Luminous Impressions: Prints from Glass Plates," was organized by The Mint Museum in Charlotte, North Carolina, and curated by Jane Kessler (1987).

90. Susanne Frantz, "Cane and Murrine Decoration in 20th Century Glass," *Glass* 59 (Spring 1995), p. 24.

91. Biographical material is from the artist.

92. Shawn Waggoner, "The work of Klaus Moje: A New Order," *Glass Art* 7 (May/June 1992), p. 4.

93. Rüdiger Joppien, "Klaus Moje's Early Years in Hamburg," in Melbourne, National Gallery of Victoria, *Klaus Moje Glass: A Retrospective Exhibition* (Melbourne, 1995), p. 22.

94. Beverly Copeland, "Glass Focus Interview: Klaus Moje," *Glass Focus*, Dec. 1994/Jan. 1995, p. 11.

95. Conversation with the author, Millville, New Jersey, June 10, 1995.

96. Since 1977 Moje has used rods sawn from bars of suitable glass, instead of the original cross-cut sections. This shift was the result of technical innovation and help from the glass supplier Bullseye.

97. Joppien (note 93), p. 22.

98. Conversation with the author (note 95).

99. Lisa Hammel, "An Apocalyptic Art," *American Craft* 48, 5 (Oct./Nov. 1988), p. 28.

100. Ibid.

101. Ibid.

102. Beverly Copeland, "Glass Focus Interview: Joel Philip Myers," *Glass Focus*, Dec. 1990/Jan. 1991, p. 10.

103. Waggoner (note 92), p. 10.

104. Artist's file, Indianapolis Museum of Art, 1991.

105. Erika Billeter, *Glas heute: Kunst oder Handwerk?* (Zurich: Museum Bellerive, 1972), unpag.

106. Conversation with the author, Asheville, North Carolina, May 10, 1995.

107. This technique, first developed by Emile Gallé, was inspired by wood marquetry. Gallé also carved or engraved the applied sections.

108. Joan Falconer Byrd, "Mark Peiser," *New Work* 37 (Spring 1989), p. 9.

109. Beverly Copeland, "Glass Focus Interview: Mark Peiser," *Glass Focus*, Dec. 1989/Jan. 1990), p. 11.

110. Byrd (note 108).

111. Simon Gate in 1916 improved upon the technique of cased glass used by Emile Gallé and created the cut and etched graal glass. Ariel glass was invented around 1936 by Edvin Öhrström and refers to graal glass that incorporates air bubbles.

112. See Stephen Proctor, "Colin Reid—An Introduction," in Los Angeles, Kurland/Summers Gallery, *Colin Reid* (Los Angeles, 1984).

113. Letter to the author, Sept. 29, 1995.

114. Ibid.

115. Paula Bock, "Mind Over Matter: The Amazing Brain of Ginny Ruffner," *The Seattle Times*, July 16, 1995.

116. Letter to the author, June 6, 1995.

117. Susanne Frantz was the first woman president of the Glass Art Society; Susan Stinsmeuleum-Ahmed was the second.

118. Donald Preziosi, *Rethinking Art History: Meditation on a Coy Science* (New Haven, Connecticut: Yale University Press, 1989), pp. 67–79.

119. Mary Shaffer, "Artist Commentary," *The Value of Glass* [1994], p. 4.

120. Shawn Waggoner, "Your Art Is What You Are," *Glass Art*, Mar./Apr. 1990, p. 64.

121. Karen S. Chambers, "Modern Alchemist: Mary Shaffer," *The World and I*, Feb. 1989, p. 207.

122. Beverly Copeland, "Glass Focus Interview: Paul Stankard," *Glass Focus*, Nov./Dec. 1988, p. 12.

123. Paul Hollister, "Natural Wonders: The Lampwork of Paul J. Stankard," *American Craft* 47, 1 (Feb./Mar. 1987), p. 41.

124. David Brand, "In New Jersey: Capturing Nature in Glass," *Time*, Feb. 8, 1988, p. 12.

125. Ibid., p. 13.

126. William Warmus, "Paul Stankard," *New Work* 37 (Spring 1989), p. 21.

127. An interesting story is recounted by Karen S. Chambers in her unedited article for the April 1994 issue of *Neues Glas*. Statom grew up next door to the painter Kenneth Noland and his family, and their daughter Cady was Statom's closest friend. Noland served as a role model for Statom by proving that one could make a living as an artist. Cady Noland also went on to become an artist and she, as did Statom, came to incorporate everyday fabricated objects in her work.

128. As quoted in Karen S. Chambers, manuscript for "Therman Statom: On the Brink," *Neues Glas* 4 (1994), p. 2.

129. Washington, DC, Renwick Gallery of the National Museum of American Art at the Smithsonian Institution, *Glassworks* (parts I and II), 1990-91. Statom participated in part I.

130. Scott Burton made sculptures that also happened to be thronelike in form; painter David Hockney used chairs as stand-ins for absent people.

131. Lee Fleming, "He Who Builds Glass Houses," *The Washington Post*, Mar. 6, 1993, p. 2B.

132. The other artists were David Bunn, Ries Niemi, Renée Petropoulos, and Ann Preston. This group was funded by the Community Redevelopment Agency.

133. Conversation with the author, Feb. 22, 1996.

134. Much of the early material on Vallien cited here is from Gunnar Lindqvist, *Bertil Vallien*, trans. Angela Adegren (Stockholm: Carlssons, 1990).

135. Ron Glowen, "Metaphorical Cargo," *American Craft* 46, 3 (June/July 1986), p. 39.

136. Lindqvist (note 134), p. 35.

137. Letter to the author, June 1995.

138. Ebeltoft, Denmark, Glasmuseum, *Bertil Vallien's Exhibition*, text by Gunnar Lindqvist (Ebeltoft, 1994), p. 19.

139. William Warmus, "František Vízner," *New Work* 33 (Spring 1988), p. 26.

140. Karen S. Chambers, "Dana Zámečníková: Artist and Magician," *New Work*, Summer/Fall 1985, p. 20.

141. Dr. Kristián Suda, "Zámečníková: A Singular Encounter," *Glass* 45 (Fall 1991), p. 35.

142. Dana Zámečníková, "Personal Mythologies: Notices from Prague," *Glass Art Society Journal*, 1992, p. 79.

143. Dana Zámečníková, "Where Image Meets Form" (Lathrup Village, Michigan: Habatat Galleries, 1993), unpag.

144. Suda (note 141).

145. Yan Zoritchak, excerpt from lecture, *Glass Art Society Journal*, no date, p. 22.

146. Dagmar Sinz, "Yan Zoritchak: The 4th Dimension," *Neues Glas* 1 (1989), p. 18.

147. Letter to Barry Shifman, July 27, 1995.

148. Sinz (note 146), p. 18.

149. Ebeltoft, Denmark, Glasmuseum, *Yan Zoritchak* (Ebeltoft, 1995), p. 18.

150. Mary Blume, "Breaking Point: Free-Form Adventures with Glass," *The International Herald Tribune*, Dec. 3–4, 1994, unpag.

151. Letter to the author, Mar. 21, 1996.

152. Ibid.

153. Shawn Waggoner, "Glass Art People: Toots Zynsky," *Glass Art* 4, 5 (July/Aug. 1989), p. 89.

GLOSSARY

Martha Drexler Lynn

Annealing Oven: An auxiliary oven used for the slow cooling of glass after it has been formed. Without proper cooling the glass will experience stresses and often will shatter when it is completely cooled.

Batch Glass: A mixture of raw materials (typically silica, soda or potash, and lime) that is heated in a pot to form glass.

Battulo: Developed by Venini e C., the term literally means beaten glass and is used as a decorative technique. The surface of the form is satin wheel ground, producing irregular and adjacent markings.

Cased Glass: The application of a thin layer of glass over a contrasting layer of glass.

Cullet: Raw glass, often broken from a cooled melt that is remelted, with fresh ingredients, to form objects. Although it melts faster than fresh glass, cullet can imply an inferior glass.

Dichronic Veiling: A coating that causes glass to reflect colors not usually evident under ordinary lighting conditions.

Ferro: A piece of steel coated with clay that is used as a plate under *murrine* when they are fused.

Filet de verre: A term invented by Toots Zynsky to denote her method of forming vessels out of fused filaments of glass.

Flameworking: Flame- or lampwork uses preformed glass tubes or rods of fusible glass that are heated section by section over a small flame. The heat softens the glass and allows it to be shaped or attached to other glass tubes. Originally the work was done over a fire flame, later a Bunsen burner was employed. The technique was probably invented in the Roman era, and achieved popularity in the seventeenth century for making small figures and glass beads. In the twentieth century it devolved into a carnival staple. Only in its use with paperweights did flameworking keep its connection to art. Most flamework pieces are small as the tubes are small.

Flutex: An industrial product of optically enhanced glass.

Frit or Fritting: A mixture of two or more materials, fused by heating, rapidly cooled, and ground into a powder. Lead is a typical frit added to the glass batch. Fritting is the process of making frit, also called sintering.

Gaffer: The master craftsman in charge of the glassmaking team, traditionally consisting of eight men but today consisting of any number.

Glory Hole: An opening on the side of the glass furnace that is used for reheating glass.

Graal and Ariel Glass: These ornamental glass types were made at Orrefors Glasbruk, Sweden. Graal was developed by Simon Gate in 1916 and involved casing a glass vessel after it had been etched and cut. The reintroduction of the piece to the fire allows the pattern to soften, and receive its final thin flashing of clear glass. Ariel glass, created by Edvin Öhrström in 1936, is a heavier version that features a thick casing over embedded air bubbles to form abstract and figurative patterns.

Kiln-forming: A process for shaping glass by heating it in a mold in the furnace. It is considered a warm-glass technique. Slumping, *pâte de verre*, and fusing are three kiln-forming techniques.

Latticino: A term used to denote glass originally made in Venice and Murano with a clear body to which embedded white threads are applied. The word refers to these white threads.

Lost Wax: A method of glass-forming adopted from metal-forming. The object to be formed is modeled in wax and then cast in plaster. Hot glass is introduced into the form and the wax melts and passes through vents, leaving the glass to conform to the plaster mold. The work is annealed and then released, ready for hand-finishing.

Marver: A flat, smooth forming surface used to roll warm glass, usually while still on the blowpipe.

Metal: Another word for unformed glass.

Murrine: A type of modern mosaic glassware. Mosaic glass is made from molten glass in different colors that are heated together and then pulled to form thin canes. These are then cut into disks and placed side-by-side and fused. The resultant sheet is then formed into the desired object by slumping, blowing, etc. *Murrina* is the singular form, *murrine* the plural.

One-off: Unique.

Pastorale: *Pastorale* is Italian for a shepard's crook; but in glassmaking it refers to the surface that the *ferro* is placed on for transferring to the furnace.

Pâte de verre: From the French for glass paste, it is a material produced from grinding glass into a powder, then adding among other materials a binder and colorants. This mixture is then placed in a mold to fuse the material. Released from the mold, the work produced is often hand-finished. Popular during the nineteenth century, this technology was lost until late twentieth-century studio-glassworkers rediscovered the technology.

Soda Lime: A very malleable type of glass that combines small quantities of sodium carbonate (soda) and calcined limestone (lime) with the glass batch.

Triple-hinge Door: Invented by Dominick Labino, this closing device for the glass-melting furnace allows the opening to be modified in thirds to ease access to the furnace without obstructing the work area and without losing heat from the furnace.

Top-burning Furnace: A furnace in which the heating element is located at the top.

Vitrolite: An opaque mural glass made by Libby Owens Glass Company and Pittsburgh Plate Glass Company before the Second World War. When buildings clad in this material were torn down, some were saved and reused by contemporary glass artists.

CATALOGUE OF THE EXHIBITION

All marks are engraved unless otherwise indicated.

Howard Ben Tré

American, b. 1949

1

Pilaster #8 (from the "Pilaster" series), 1983
Cast white glass with patinated copper inclusions
30½ x 10½ x 5½ inches (77.5 x 26.7 x 14 cm)

PROVENANCE: Habatat Galleries, Pontiac, Michigan

Gift of Marilyn and Eugene Glick
1991.226

2

Second Vase, 1989
Cast glass with gold leaf and bronze
71½ x 23¾ dia. inches (181.6 x 60.3 cm)

PROVENANCE: Charles Cowles Gallery, Inc., New York

Gift of Marilyn and Eugene Glick
1989.113

Zoltán Bohus

Hungarian, b. 1941

3

Parabolic Composition, 1988
Laminated and metalized sheet glass, cut, and acid etched
TWO PARTS
A: 6 x 7 x 12 inches (15.2 x 17.8 x 30.5 cm)
B: 10½ x 7½ x 7 inches (26.7 x 19.1 x 17.8 cm)

MARKS: Bohus 88

PROVENANCE: Habatat Galleries, Pontiac, Michigan

Promised Gift of Marilyn and Eugene Glick

Jane Bruce

English, b. 1947

4

Positive/Negative, 1990
Blown glass with engraving, oil paint, and 23-karat gold leaf
3½ x 28½ dia. inches (8.9 x 72.4 cm)

MARKS: Jane Bruce 1990

PROVENANCE: Kurland/Summers Gallery, Los Angeles

Promised Gift of Marilyn and Eugene Glick

Robert Carlson

American, b. 1952

5

Apis Arcana, 1988
Free and mold-blown glass with painted decoration
30 x 9 x 9 inches (76.2 x 22.9 x 22.9 cm)

MARKS: R. Carlson 1988 c.

PROVENANCE: Dorothy Weiss Gallery, San Francisco

Promised Gift of Marilyn and Eugene Glick

Sydney Cash

American, b. 1941

6

Untitled, 1983
Sandblasted plate glass with wire armature
11½ x 5¼ x 6 inches (29.2 x 13.3 x 15.2 cm)

MARKS: c. SC83

PROVENANCE: Kurland/Summers Gallery, Los Angeles (formerly collection of Samuel Cash)

Promised Gift of Marilyn and Eugene Glick

Dale Chihuly

American, b. 1941

7

Untitled (from the "Macchia" series), 1982
Blown and altered glass
9 x 15½ x 14 inches (22.9 x 39.4 x 35.6 cm)

MARKS: Chihuly 1982

PROVENANCE: Habatat Galleries, Pontiac, Michigan

Promised Gift of Marilyn and Eugene Glick

8

Untitled (from the "Soft Cylinder" series), 1987
Blown glass, shards, with small blanket drawing by Flora Mace
10 x 7 x 7 inches (25.4 x 17.8 x 17.8 cm)

MARKS: Chihuly 1987

PROVENANCE: Holsten Galleries, Palm Beach, Florida

Promised Gift of Marilyn and Eugene Glick

Kéké Cribbs

American, b. 1951

9

Baudino (from the "Scarecrow" series), 1992
Carved and painted wood with canvas and sandblasted plate glass
41 x 24 x 5 inches (104.1 x 61 x 12.7 cm)

MARKS (inscribed): KéKé 1992

PROVENANCE: Helander Gallery, Palm Beach, Florida

Promised Gift of Marilyn and Eugene Glick

Dan Dailey

American, b. 1947

10

Athena (from the "Mythology Head Vase" series), 1989
Blown glass with applied elements
18½ x 11 x 11 inches (47 x 27.9 x 27.9 cm)

MARKS: MH-3-89 Athena Dailey

PROVENANCE: Habatat Galleries, Pontiac, Michigan

Promised Gift of Marilyn and Eugene Glick

11

Study, 1989
Vitrolite with stainless steel and gold-plated brass
26 x 20½ x 5 inches (66 x 52.1 x 12.7 cm)

MARKS (inscribed): Dailey

PROVENANCE: Habatat Galleries, Pontiac, Michigan

Promised Gift of Marilyn and Eugene Glick

Erwin Eisch

German, b. 1927

12

Buddha, 1988
Mold-blown glass with paint and gold leaf
21½ x 7½ x 7 inches (54.6 x 19 x 17.8 cm)

MARKS: Buddha's Zeitzeichen

PROVENANCE: Christie's, New York, April 10, 1989, lot 2

Gift of Marilyn and Eugene Glick
1989.56

Kyohei Fujita

Japanese, b. 1921

13

Red and White Plum Blossoms, 1990
Mold-blown glass, cut, polished, and acid-etched, with platinum and gold foil, and sterling-silver
6 x 5 x 5 inches (15.2 x 12.7 x 12.7 cm)

MARKS: Kyohei Fujita

PROVENANCE: Maurine Littleton Gallery, Washington, DC

Promised Gift of Marilyn and Euguene Glick

Michael Glancy

American, b. 1950

14

Master Gem, 1988
Blown glass, sandblasted, with electroplated copper
5½ x 9 dia. inches (14 x 22.9 cm)

MARKS: Michael M. Glancy 1988 Master Gem [and signature logo]

PROVENANCE: Habatat Galleries, Pontiac, Michigan

Promised Gift of Marilyn and Eugene Glick

15

A Pert de Vue, 1990
Blown glass with electroformed copper
VESSEL: $2^{1}/_{2}$ x 7 x 4 inches
(6.4 x 17.8 x 10.2 cm)
BASE PLATE A: $^{3}/_{4}$ x 8 x 8 inches
(1.9 cm x 20.5 x 20.5 cm)
BASE PLATE B: $^{3}/_{4}$ x 12 x 12 inches
(1.9 x 30.5 x 30.5 cm)
MARKS: A Pert de vue 1990 Michael M. Glancy
[on vessel] [and] A Pert de Vue [on B]
PROVENANCE: Heller Gallery, New York
Promised Gift of Marilyn and Eugene Glick

16

Ur Crustacean, 1990–91
Blown glass with gold foil and
electroformed copper
6 x 9 dia. inches (15.2 x 22.9 cm)
MARKS: Michael Glancy 1990-1991
[and signature logo]
PROVENANCE: Habatat Galleries, Pontiac,
Michigan
Promised Gift of Marilyn and Eugene Glick

David Huchthausen

American, b. 1951

17

Alpine Landscape, 1977
Blown and cased glass with interior decoration
8 x 6 dia. inches (20.3 x 15.2 cm)
MARKS: David R. Huchthausen BADEN bei WIEN
1977 No. 67
PROVENANCE: Marx Gallery, Chicago
Promised Gift of Marilyn and Eugene Glick

18

Leitungs Scherbe (from the "Leitungs Scherben"
series), c. 1987
Glass, fractured, laminated, and optically polished
$10^{1}/_{2}$ x $17^{1}/_{2}$ x $12^{1}/_{2}$ inches (26.7 x 44.5 x 31.8 cm)
MARKS (sandblasted): 872 DRH
PROVENANCE: Christie's, New York, February 13,
1989, lot 152
Gift of Marilyn and Eugene Glick
1989.20

Richard Jolley

American, b. 1952

Assisted by Tommie Pratt

19

Female Bust with Leaves, 1989
Glass with cane drawing, sandblasted
$13^{1}/_{2}$ x 10 x 7 inches (34.3 x 25.4 x 17.8 cm)
MARKS: Richard Jolley 89
PROVENANCE: Kurland/Summers Gallery,
Los Angeles
Promised Gift of Marilyn and Eugene Glick

Kreg Kallenberger

American, b. 1950

20

Period of Mystery (from the "Osage" series), 1989
Cast and polished optical crystal with oil paint
9 x $19^{1}/_{4}$ x 6 inches (22.9 x 48.9 x 15.2 cm)
MARKS: K. Kallen 37289
PROVENANCE: Habatat Galleries, Pontiac,
Michigan
Lent by Marilyn and Eugene Glick

Dominick Labino

American, 1910–1987

21

Untitled, 1968
Blown and manipulated glass
6 x 5 x $6^{1}/_{2}$ inches (15.2 x 12.7 x 16.5 cm)
MARKS: Labino 1968
PROVENANCE: Holsten Galleries, Palm Beach,
Florida
Promised Gift of Marilyn and Eugene Glick

22

Untitled (from the "Emergence" series), 1982
Clear glass with dichroic veiling and cased
crystalline iridescence
$8^{1}/_{2}$ x 4 x 3 inches (21.6 x 10.2 x 7.6 cm)
MARKS: Labino 10-1982
PROVENANCE: Purchased from the artist
Gift of Marilyn and Eugene Glick
1991.219

Stanislav Libenský

Czechoslovakian, b. 1921

Jaroslava Brychtová

Czechoslovakian, b. 1924

23

Head I, c. 1957–58
Mold-formed glass, cut and polished
14 1/2 x 6 5/8 x 4 inches (36.8 x 16 x 10.2 cm)

MARKS: Libenský-Brychtová

PROVENANCE: Sotheby's, New York, February 25, 1994, lot 224

Promised Gift of Marilyn and Eugene Glick

24

Head VI, 1986
Mold-formed glass, cut and polished
21 x 11 1/4 x 8 inches (53.3 x 28.6 x 20.3 cm)
Edition of 5

MARKS: S. Libenský J. Brychtová 86

PROVENANCE: Galerie Rob van den Doel, The Hague

Gift of Marilyn and Eugene Glick
1991.225

Marvin Lipofsky

American, b. 1938

Assisted by Gianni Toso

25

Venini Series—Split Piece, 1975
Blown glass with canes, cut and polished
TWO PARTS
A: 3 1/2 x 10 x 8 1/2 inches (8.9 25.4 x 21.6 cm)
B: 9 x 15 x 10 inches (22.9 x 38.1 x 25.4 cm)

MARKS: Lipofsky 75

PROVENANCE: Christie's, New York, October 4, 1989, lot 228 (formerly collection of Martin and Jean Mensch, New York)

EXHIBITED: New York, Lever House, "Glass America, 1978," October 10–28, 1978 (exh. cat., p. 24)

Promised Gift of Marilyn and Eugene Glick

26

Serie Fratelli Toso—Split Piece, 1977–78
Blown glass, cut and polished
TWO PARTS
A: 7 x 13 x 10 inches (17.8 x 33 x 25.4 cm)
B: 14 x 16 x 18 inches (35.6 x 40.6 x 45.7 cm)

MARKS: Lipofsky 79

PROVENANCE: Christie's East, New York, March 18, 1991, lot 29

Gift of Marilyn and Eugene Glick
1992.147a-b

Marvin Lipofsky

American, b. 1938

27

Flowers/Mountains/Hana/Yama (from the "Otaru" series), 1987–88
Blown glass, cut, sandblasted, and acid-etched
9 1/2 x 12 1/2 x 12 inches (24.1 x 31.8 x 30.5 cm)

MARKS: Lipofsky 87-88 OTARU #10

PROVENANCE: Holsten Galleries, Palm Beach, Florida

Promised Gift of Marilyn and Eugene Glick

Harvey Littleton

American, b. 1922

28

Green Loop (from the "Loop" series), 1978
Pulled and cased glass, with glass base
16 3/4 x 13 1/2 x 5 inches (32.4 x 15.2 x 12.7 cm)

MARKS: Harvey K. Littleton 1978 [and] Harvey K. Littleton © 1978

PROVENANCE: Christie's East, New York, February 24, 1990, lot 763; Heller Gallery, Palm Beach, Florida

EXHIBITED: Charlotte, North Carolina, Mint Museum of Art, "Harvey Littleton," 1979

Promised Gift of Marilyn and Eugene Glick

29

Blue Crown, 1988
Pulled and cased glass
TWELVE PARTS
A: 20 x 10 1/2 x 3 inches (50.8 x 26.7 x 7.6 cm)
B: 15 x 14 x 3 inches (38.1 x 35.6 x 7.6 cm)
C: 14 1/2 x 12 x 3 inches (36.8 x 30.5 x 7.6 cm)
D: 20 x 16 x 3 inches (50.8 x 40.6 x 7.6 cm)
E: 16 x 12 x 3 inches (40.6 x 30.5 x 7.6 cm)
F: 20 x 12 x 13 inches (50.8 x 30.5 x 7.6 cm)
G–L: each 7 x 6 x 3 inches (17.8 x 15.2 x 7.6 cm)

MARKS: ©Harvey K. Littleton/9/1988/3

PROVENANCE: Maurine Littleton Gallery, Washington, DC

Gift of Marilyn and Eugene Glick
1991.221a-l

Richard Marquis

American, b. 1945

30

Murrine Teapot, 1984
Blown glass with *murrine* canes
6 x 6 dia. inches (15.2 x 15.2 cm)

MARKS: c. 1984 Marquis

PROVENANCE: Habatat Galleries, Pontiac, Michigan

Promised Gift of Marilyn and Eugene Glick

31

Wizard Teapot, 1985
Blown glass with *murrine* canes
12 x 6¼ dia. inches (30.5 x 15.9 cm)

MARKS: c. 3.15.85 Marquis

PROVENANCE: Habatat Galleries, Pontiac, Michigan

Promised Gift of Marilyn and Eugene Glick

32

Mirrored Ball Trophy, 1988
Blown glass, mirror squares, and canes
43 x 10 dia. inches (109.2 x 25.4 cm)

MARKS: c. 1988 Marquis

PROVENANCE: Kurland/Summers Gallery, Los Angeles

Promised Gift of Marilyn and Eugene Glick

33

Bubble Boy, 1988
Blown and fabricated glass, *murrine* canes, paint, mirror, and glass shards
30 x 14 dia. inches (76.2 x 35.6 cm)

MARKS: c. 1988 Marquis

PROVENANCE: Sarah Squeri Gallery, Cincinnati, Ohio

Promised Gift of Marilyn and Eugene Glick

34

Marquiscarpa #23, 1992
Glass (*murrine* and *battuto* techniques), blown, fused, slumped, fabricated, and wheel-ground, with gold leaf
5 x 8 x 3½ inches (12.7 x 20.3 x 8.9 cm)

MARKS (inscribed): Marquis 1992 [Marquis *murrina* signature cane fused on piece]

PROVENANCE: Ruth T. Summers, Marina del Rey, California

Promised Gift of Marilyn and Eugene Glick

Klaus Moje

German, b. 1936

35

Untitled ("Songlines"), 1989
Kiln-formed mosaic glass, slumped, with wheel-ground surface
2 x 20 x 20 inches (5.1 x 50.8 x 50.8 cm)

MARKS: Klaus Moje 9-1989#44

PROVENANCE: Habatat Galleries, Pontiac, Michigan

Gift of Marilyn and Eugene Glick
1991.227

36

Untitled, 1989
Fused and slumped glass with wheel-ground surface
2½ x 20½ dia. inches (6.4 x 52.1 cm)

MARKS: Klaus Moje 11-1989#46

PROVENANCE: Habatat Galleries, Pontiac, Michigan

Promised Gift of Marilyn and Eugene Glick

37

Untitled, 1990
Fused and slumped glass with wheel-ground surface
2 x 13½ dia. inches (5.1 x 34.3 cm)

MARKS: Klaus Moje 3-1990#13

PROVENANCE: Kurland/Summers Gallery, Los Angeles

Promised Gift of Marilyn and Eugene Glick

Jay Musler

American, b. 1949

38

Untitled, 1991
Sheet glass elements, sandblasted, with oil paint
4 x 56½ x 10½ inches (10.2 x 143.5 x 26.7 cm)

PROVENANCE: Maurine Littleton Gallery, Washington, DC

Promised Gift of Marilyn and Eugene Glick

Joel Philip Myers

American, b. 1934

39

Dr. Zarkhov's Tower (from the "Dr. Zarkhov" series), 1971
Blown glass with gold luster, glued, and gilded metal base (replacement)
26 1/2 inches (67.3 cm)
BASE: 7 x 11 1/2 dia. inches (17.8 x 29.2 cm)

MARKS: Joel Philip Myers 1971

PROVENANCE: Christie's, New York, October 4, 1989, lot 250 (formerly collection of Martin and Jean Mensch, New York)

Gift of Marilyn and Eugene Glick
1991.223a-b

40

Dr. Zarkhov's Tower (from the "Dr. Zarkhov" series), 1972
Blown glass with platinum luster, glued, and chromed metal base
27 1/2 inches (69.8 cm)
BASE: 7 x 11 1/2 dia. inches (17.8 x 29.2 cm)

MARKS: Joel Philip Myers 1972

PROVENANCE: Christie's, New York, October 4, 1989, lot 250 (formerly collection of Martin and Jean Mensch, New York)

Gift of Marilyn and Eugene Glick
1991.224a-b

41

Knus (Hug), 1975
Blown glass with additions, acid-etched
9 1/2 x 3 1/4 dia. inches (24.1 x 8.3 cm)

MARKS: Joel Philip Myers 1975

PROVENANCE: Purchased from the artist

Promised Gift of Marilyn and Eugene Glick

42

Stoppered Form, 1976
Blown glass with colored shards
8 3/4 x 2 1/4 dia. inches (22.2 x 5.7 cm)

MARKS: Joel Philip Myers 1976 [and] CAG 011-1-77A

PROVENANCE: Christie's, New York, October 4, 1989, lot 246 (formerly collection of Martin and Jean Mensch, New York)

Promised Gift of Marilyn and Eugene Glick

43

Untitled, 1976
Blown white opal glass with additions
10 x 4 1/2 x 4 1/2 inches (25.4 x 11.4 x 11.4 cm)

MARKS: Joel Philip Myers 1976

PROVENANCE: Purchased from the artist

Promised Gift of Marilyn and Eugene Glick

44

White on White II, 1976
Blown white opal glass
10 1/4 x 3 3/4 x 3 3/4 inches (26 x 9.5 x 9.5 cm)

MARKS: Joel Philip Myers 1976

PROVENANCE: Purchased from the artist

Gift of Marilyn and Eugene Glick
1992.54

45

Untitled (from the "Contiguous Fragment" series), 1979
Blown glass, iridized, sandblasted, and acid-etched, with additions
7 3/4 x 5 dia. inches (19.7 x 12.7 cm)

MARKS: Joel Philip Myers 1979

PROVENANCE: Marx Gallery, Chicago

Promised Gift of Marilyn and Eugene Glick

46

Untitled (from the "Contiguous Fragment" series), 1981
Blown glass, iridized, sandblasted, and acid-etched, with additions
10 11/16 x 4 1/8 dia. inches (27.1 x 10.5 cm)

MARKS: Joel Philip Myers 1981

PROVENANCE: Purchased from the artist

Promised Gift of Marilyn and Eugene Glick

47

Untitled (from the "Contiguous Fragment" series), 1981
Blown glass with additions, cane drawing, sandblasted, and acid-etched
12 3/4 x 5 dia. inches (32.4 x 12.7 cm)

MARKS: Joel Philip Myers 1981

PROVENANCE: Purchased from the artist

Promised Gift of Marilyn and Eugene Glick

48

Untitled (from the "Contiguous Fragment" series), 1988
Blown glass, cased, with inclusions
16 1/2 x 22 1/2 x 4 inches (41.9 x 57.2 x 10.2 cm)
MARKS: Joel Philip Myers 1988
PROVENANCE: Purchased from the artist
Promised Gift of Marilyn and Eugene Glick

49

Red Fish III, 1991
Blown glass, cased, with spiral cane drawing and inclusions
9 7/8 x 27 1/8 x 3 1/8 inches (25.1 x 68.9 x 7.9 cm)
MARKS: Joel Philip Myers 1991
PROVENANCE: Purchased from the artist
Promised Gift of Marilyn and Eugene Glick

Tom Patti
American, b. 1943

50

Expanded Echo with Line (from the "Echo" series), 1989
Glass, fused, hand-shaped, ground and polished
3 7/16 x 6 3/8 x 4 9/16 inches (8.7 x 16.2 x 11.6 cm)
MARKS: Patti 1989
PROVENANCE: Holsten Galleries, Palm Beach, Florida
Gift of Marilyn and Eugene Glick
1991.115

51

Solarized Red with Blue and Yellow (from the "Lumina" series), 1992
Glass, fused, hand-shaped, ground and polished
2 1/2 x 6 1/4 x 4 1/2 inches (6.4 x 15.9 x 11.6 cm)
MARKS: Patti 1992
PROVENANCE: Holsten Galleries, Stockbridge, Massachusetts
Promised Gift of Marilyn and Eugene Glick

Mark Peiser
American, b. 1938

52

Lillies of the Valley (from the "Paperweight Vase" series), 1976
Blown glass with flamework
8 1/2 x 5 dia. inches (21.6 x 12.7 cm)

MARKS: Mark Peiser PWV 034 1976
PROVENANCE: Habatat Galleries, Pontiac, Michigan (auction held April 7, 1994, lot 29; formerly collection of Marion Saxon)
Promised Gift of Marilyn and Eugene Glick

53

The Wheat Piece (from the "Paperweight Vase" series), 1978
Blown glass with flamework and gold foil
7 x 7 dia. inches (17.8 x 17.8 cm)
MARKS: Mark Peiser PWV 065 1978
PROVENANCE: Heller Gallery, New York
EXHIBITED: New York, Lever House, "Glass America, 1978," October 10–28, 1978 (exh. cat., p. 28)
Promised Gift of Marilyn and Eugene Glick

54

The Birth of Io (from the "Inner Space" series), 1988
Cast glass, cut and polished
14 1/2 x 9 1/2 x 3 inches (36.8 x 24.1 x 7.6 cm)
MARKS: PEISER IS464 88 c
PROVENANCE: Holsten Galleries, Boca Raton, Florida
Promised Gift of Marilyn and Eugene Glick

Colin Reid
English, b. 1953

55

Double Arches, 1986
Kiln-formed lead glass with oxides
TWO PARTS
A: 11 1/2 x 19 x 1 1/2 inches (29.2 x 48 x 3.8 cm)
B: 11 1/2 x 19 x 1 1/2 inches (29.2 x 48 x 3.8 cm)
A: MARKS: Colin Reid 1986 R173/A
B: MARKS: Colin Reid R173/B 1986
PROVENANCE: Christie's, New York, April 4, 1991, lot 7
Promised Gift of Marilyn and Eugene Glick

Ginny Ruffner
American, b. 1952

56

Stella at the Louvre, 1990
Flameworked glass, sandblasted and painted
17 x 17 x 9 inches (43.2 x 43.2 x 22.9 cm)

MARKS: Ginny Ruffner 90

PROVENANCE: Maurine Littleton Gallery, Washington, DC

Promised Gift of Marilyn and Eugene Glick

Mary Shaffer

American, b. 1947

57

Off Ledge I (from the "Inversion" series), 1994
TWO PARTS
A: Slumped plate glass
32 x 20 x 20 inches (81.3 x 50.8 x 50.8 cm)
B: Cast bronze with furric-nitrate patina
32 x 20 x 20 inches (81.3 x 50.8 x 50.8 cm)

MARKS: Mary Shaffer

PROVENANCE: Purchased from the artist

Promised Gift of Marilyn and Eugene Glick

Paul Stankard

American, b. 1943

58

Cloistered Block with Cactus and Spirit, 1988
Flameworked glass flowers and figures in crystal, cut and polished
4¾ x 2½ x 3 inches (12.1 x 6.4 x 7.6 cm)

MARKS: Paul J. Stankard E36 1988

PROVENANCE: Holsten Galleries, Palm Beach, Florida

Promised Gift of Marilyn and Eugene Glick

59

Morning Glory Bouquet Botanical, 1991
Flameworked glass elements in crystal, cut and polished
5¼ x 3 x 3 inches (13.3 x 7.6 x 7.6 cm)

MARKS: Paul J. Stankard B9 '91

PROVENANCE: Heller Gallery, New York

Promised Gift of Marilyn and Eugene Glick

Therman Statom

American, b. 1953

60

Green Chair with Base, 1991
Sheet glass, blown elements, with painted decoration
45 x 25 x 36 inches (114.3 x 63.5 x 91.4 cm)

PROVENANCE: Habatat Galleries, Pontiac, Michigan

Promised Gift of Marilyn and Eugene Glick

61

Untitled, 1991
Sheet glass and paint, with glass shards by Curtiss Brock, William Morris, Dick Weiss, and others
83½ x 15½ x 2¾ inches (212.1 x 39.4 x 7 cm)

PROVENANCE: Habatat Galleries, Pontiac, Michigan

Promised Gift of Marilyn and Eugene Glick

Karla Trinkley

American, b. 1956

62

Axis, 1985
Pâte de verre
7 x 9 dia. inches (17.8 x 22.9 cm)

PROVENANCE: Sarah Squeri Gallery, Cincinnati, Ohio

Promised Gift of Marilyn and Eugene Glick

Bertil Vallien

Swedish, b. 1938

63

Untitled, 1985
Blown glass
4¼ x 6 x 5 inches (10.8 x 15.2 x 12.7 cm)

MARKS: KOSTA UNIK 5945 B VALLIEN

PROVENANCE: Heller Gallery, Palm Beach, Florida

Promised Gift of Marilyn and Eugene Glick

64

Calendarium, 1990
Sand-cast glass with inclusions and copper-foil elements
5 x 77 x 6 inches (12.7 x 195.6 x 15.2 cm)

MARKS: B. Vallien [and] Kosta Boda unique 1363990174

PROVENANCE: Betsy Rosenfield Gallery, Chicago

Gift of Marilyn and Eugene Glick

1990.64

František Vízner

Czechoslovakian, b. 1936

65

Untitled, c. 1992
Cast glass, cut and polished
3¾ x 11½ dia. inches (9.5 x 29.2 cm)

MARKS: Vízner 92

PROVENANCE: Sanske Galerie, Zurich

Promised Gift of Marilyn and Eugene Glick

66

Untitled, c. 1993
Cast glass, cut and polished
3¾ x 11¼ dia. inches (9.5 x 28.6 cm)

MARKS: Vízner 93

PROVENANCE: Sanske Galerie, Zurich

Promised Gift of Marilyn and Eugene Glick

Dana Záměčníková

Czechoslovakian, b. 1945

67

Pepik/Joe, 1989
Sheet glass, sandblasted, engraved, and painted
8¾ x 8¾ x 4 inches (22.2 x 22.2 x 10.2 cm)

MARKS: Záměčníková 89

PROVENANCE: Maurine Littleton Gallery, Washington, DC

Promised Gift of Marilyn and Eugene Glick

Yan Zoritchak

Czechoslovakian, b. 1944

68

Untitled (from the "Heaven Flowers" series), 1989
Lead glass with additions, cut and polished
23 x 9¾ x 1¾ inches (58.4 x 24.8 x 4.4 cm)

MARKS: Zoritchak Yan 89

PROVENANCE: Verre Biot Galerie, Nice, France

Promised Gift of Marilyn and Eugene Glick

Toots Zynsky

American, b. 1951

69

Untitled (from the "Exotic Bird" series), 1986
Glass threads, fused and kiln-formed
7 x 10 x 9 inches (17.8 x 25.4 x 22.9 cm)

MARKS (formed on underside by glass threads): Z

PROVENANCE: Sarah Squeri Gallery, Cincinnati, Ohio

Gift of Marilyn and Eugene Glick
1991.228

70

Cityscape, 1992
Glass threads, fused and kiln-formed
6½ x 13 x 9 inches (16.5 x 33 x 22.9 cm)

MARKS (formed on underside by glass threads): Z

PROVENANCE: Betsy Rosenfield Gallery, Chicago

Promised Gift of Marilyn and Eugene Glick

Design

Elizabeth Finger, Belmont, California

Editing

Terry Ann R. Neff, t.a. neff associates, inc., Tucson, Arizona

Photography

Hadley Fruits, under the guidance of John A. Geiser, Indianapolis Museum of Art; all other photographs supplied by owner unless otherwise indicated.

Printing

Dai Nippon Printing, Hong Kong